More Hot Links

More Hot Links

Linking Literature with the Middle School Curriculum

Cora M. Wright

2002
Libraries Unlimited
Teacher Ideas Press
A Division of Greenwood Publishing Group, Inc.
Greenwood Village, Colorado

I'd like to thank my husband, Tom, and our two sons, Adam and Jonathan, for sharing my love of literature. Our family's passion for discovering and discussing good books is exciting, rewarding, and just plain fun. This book wouldn't exist without your support, encouragement, and love. Thanks, guys.

LIBRARIES UNLIMITED
Teacher Ideas Press
A Division of Greenwood Publishing Group, Inc.
7730 East Belleview Avenue, Suite A200
Greenwood Village, CO 80111
1-800-225-5800
www.lu.com

ISBN 1-56308-942-4

Contents

Acknowledgments vii

Introduction ix

Chapter 1: Biographies 1

Chapter 2: English—Classics 13

Chapter 3: English—Use of Language 17

Chapter 4: Fine Arts 25

Chapter 5: Greatest of the Latest..37

Chapter 6: Humor 51

Chapter 7: Mathematics...57

Chapter 8: Multicultural 65

Chapter 9: Myths, Folktales, and Legends..77

Chapter 10: Picture Books for All Ages..87

Chapter 11: Poetry 95

Chapter 12: Read Alouds..107

Chapter 13: Science 113

Chapter 14: Series..129

Chapter 15: Social Studies—Ancient and Early Cultures 147

Chapter 16: Social Studies—United States History...............................163

Chapter 17: Sports and Games..177

Chapter 18: Unique Presentations 183

Literature Links 189

Index 203

Acknowledgments

Many thanks to the staff members of El Dorado Middle School, Concord, California, who are always willing to do trial runs with newly discovered books to see if they work with their curriculum and their students. Thanks also to the students who enthusiastically read the new fiction books I try out on them. The materials that receive good reviews end up in *Hot Links*.

Special thanks go to my library partners, Lorraine Taylor and Sue Edmonds, for their invaluable assistance with the books and technology. This volume wouldn't exist without their expertise.

Introduction

The world of children's literature is an exciting place with outstanding works published in the past and thousands of marvelous new books produced every year. The quality of writing and illustrating continues to change and improve, making the creation of children's literature a true art form. With so many high-quality books from which to choose, book selection by librarians, teachers, parents, and students can be difficult. The goal of this book is to guide the user in book selection to choose top-quality literature for recreational reading and in connection with all curriculum areas. The books in this volume are aimed primarily at middle school, encompassing grades four through ten. The books were chosen on the basis of quality writing, effective illustration, high student interest, current availability, and strong curriculum connection.

If you used the previous Hot Links: Literature Links for the Middle School Curriculum, you'll notice that all new titles are cited in this edition. I have added sections on humor, series, and picture books for all ages. You'll meet up with many familiar authors and illustrators, as well as new, exciting ones. Many of the books included are multifaceted, allowing them to fit into more than one category or curriculum. The main annotation is included in the section considered most appropriate for each book, but if it fits into another category, a brief summary is included in that category as well. A table at the back of the book, arranged alphabetically by title, indicates the curriculum connections for each book.

If you'd like to discuss children's literature with me or if you have a great book you'd like to share, please e-mail me at tandcwright@hotmail.com.

Happy Reading!

Chapter 1

Biographies

Wonderfully written, attractive, and informative biographies are plentiful in the children's literature world, and students love to read the "real" stories behind well-known people. The books in this section were selected because of their close connection with other curricula, making them useful in conjunction with specific topics or enjoyable as recreational reading to help readers discover inspiring, interesting people.

Aliki. **William Shakespeare & the Globe.** New York: HarperCollins, 1999. 48p. $16.00. ISBN 0-06-027821-8, 0-06-443722-1pa.

The story of William Shakespeare's life is told in five acts. Each scene within the act is told in a few lines, accompanied by watercolor drawings depicting life at that time with written descriptions. Every two-page spread has a quote from one of his plays, which ties to the text. Aliki uses art, drama, quotations, maps, and sketches in addition to text to tell the story of the life of the playwright she has admired since grade school. A list of Shakespeare's works, a chronology of his life, words and expressions used during that time, and a list of sites that celebrate Shakespeare in and around London and Stratford-upon-Avon make this a thorough and useful work.

Anderson, Matthew T. **Handel, Who Knew What He Liked.** Illus. Kevin Hawkes. Cambridge, Mass: Candlewick Press, 2001. 40p. $17.00. ISBN 0-7636-1046-1.

> Energetic text and the clever illustrations work together to give a picture of George Frideric Handel's life. From a very early age, young Handel knew what he wanted and wouldn't take no for an answer. His father said he couldn't study music, so he smuggled a clavichord into the attic. With the help of a duke, he continued studying in Germany and later traveled to Italy, where he fell in love with opera. He took this passion to England and convinced the British to love opera, also. He was successful for a time, but he became despondent when a rival company performed plays that made fun of his operas. In deep despair, Handel wrote what he thought would be his swan song, *The Messiah,* which was first performed in Dublin, Ireland, in 1742. The story is well researched and told with humor, conveying the spirit of Handel's music. The illustrations are filled with humorous touches, adding to the flavor of the text. Decorative panels throughout the book explain technical terms, adding to the book's usefulness. A chronology of Handel's life, a discography, and a bibliography are included.

Andronik, Catherine M. **Hatshepsut, His Majesty, Herself.** Illus. Joseph Daniel Fiedler. New York, Atheneum Books for Young Readers, 2001. 40p. $17.00. ISBN 0-689-82562-5.

> Hatshepsut, the only female Egyptian pharaoh, often had to pose as a man to gain the respect of her advisors and people. This and many other facts and anecdotes are well presented in this book on the life and times of Hatshepsut, a most unusual woman who came to power at age fifteen. The rulers that followed her did their best to obliterate her from history, so her story is one that is still unraveling. Each chapter begins with an inscription from ancient records, adding interest to the text. Pronunciation guides used liberally throughout the text; formal, Egyptian-style illustrations; the bibliography of books for more information; and a paragraph on places to look for more information on Hatshepsut work together to make this an outstanding book for browsing as well as research. Don't be fooled by the cover, a single large picture that, at first glance, appears to be King Tut. After reading the text, it becomes apparent whom the cover depicts and why Hatshepsut dressed the way she did, including donning a fake gold beard.

Burleigh, Robert. **Home Run: The Story of Babe Ruth.**

The importance of the legendary Babe Ruth is told with a few well-placed words, a bubble gum baseball card on each page that provides facts and statistics, and lifelike, full-page illustrations. This effective picture book captures the amazing abilities of Babe and the magic of baseball in a poetic manner and evokes the emotion and excitement of hitting a home run. *See* SPORTS AND GAMES.

Christensen, Bonnie. **Woody Guthrie: Poet of the People.** New York: Alfred A. Knopf, 2001. 32p. $17.00. ISBN 0-375-91113-8.

The artwork, text, and layout of this book work together beautifully to celebrate Woody Guthrie's life, his dedication to his cause, and the legacy he left us. His life's story is told with all its trials and tribulations, illustrating how difficulties gave him empathy for the downtrodden and mistreated. His talent to write and sing folk songs about what he saw, made him one of America's most influential folksingers. A portion of his most famous song, "This Land Is Your Land," is printed on each page in large, bold letters, along with mixed-media paintings that look like woodcuts. All seven verses of "This Land Is Your Land" are printed in the back, along with a chronology of important events in Guthrie's life. This book is useful when studying folk songs, singers' biographies, and life in the United States during the first half of the twentieth century.

Dash, Joan. **The Longitude Prize.**

In the eighteenth century, John Harrison, an uneducated village carpenter, sets out to win the prize of 20,000 pounds, offered by the British government, for devising an instrument that would determine longitude at sea. By so doing, he would save ships from wreckage when the crew didn't know exactly where they were. After years of hard work, he succeeds in inventing the chronometer but is denied the prize because of his lack of status and education. He finally receives due recognition—and the 20,000 pounds—only after fifty years of struggle. This book stresses the importance of math and science in his work and to the shipping industry. *See* MATHEMATICS.

Demi. **Gandhi.** New York: M. K. McElderry Books, 2001. 32p. $20.00. ISBN 0-689-84149-3.

Gandhi, who came from a wealthy background, grew up shy and frightened. After attending law school in London, he set up a practice in South Africa. He often experienced prejudice and hatred in his own life, but as time went on, he developed an inner peace and the philosophy that peaceful love triumphs over violent hatred. He spent his adult life using this philosophy and his law background to achieve civil rights for all people. The story of his life and work is told in a simple, straightforward manner, presenting Gandhi's social and political goals with reverence. Demi's signature artwork, using gold borders and accents of brilliant color, accompany the text well. The author's notes provide additional information, along with her "great hope that we will all try to live our lives in Gandhi's honor—in truth, peace, and love."

Fritz, Jean. **Leonardo's Horse.**

Leonardo da Vinci's dream of building a twenty-four-foot-tall bronze horse finally came true in 1999, thanks to another dreamer, Charles Dent, who read about da Vinci's unfulfilled dream and began building it. Dent died before the horse was finished, but a foundation he had formed hired New York sculptor Nina Akamu to finish the job. The huge horse now stands in Milan, Italy, as a tribute to two dreamers, Leonardo da Vinci and Charles Dent. *See* FINE ARTS.

Glass, Andrew. **Mountain Men: True Grit and Tall Tales.**
Biographies of seven legendary mountain men—John Colter, Jedediah Smith, Hugh Glass, Jim Bridger, Mike Fink, Kit Carson, and Jim Beckwourth— are told using facts as well as tall tales. The adventures of these men inspired pioneers to brave the difficult trails and head west, making them an important part of United States history. *See* SOCIAL STUDIES—UNITED STATES HISTORY.

Greenberg, Jan, and Sandra Jordan. **Frank O. Gehry: Outside In.** New York: DK Ink, 2000. 47p. $20.00. ISBN 0-7894-2677-3, lib. bdg. 0-8109-5829-5.
No one since Frank Lloyd Wright has had as profound an effect on architecture as has California architect Frank O. Gehry. This book follows his life from his formative early years as the son of Polish immigrants, through his early, sometimes shocking, and not always well-received efforts, to his current status as one of the most renowned and sought-after architects of our time. This is the story of an individual whose work reflects his belief that "life is chaotic and buildings should reflect it." The incredible transformation of Bilbao, Spain, from a failing, postindustrial city to an international destination is due almost solely to the construction of Gehry's Guggenheim Museum, now widely regarded as one the most influential buildings of the past century. This biographical picture essay reflects Gehry's unconventional approach with strikingly unique graphics, sidebars, ghost images, and colorful fonts. This is an inspiring story of what creativity, perseverance, and courage can achieve.

Hamanaka, Sheila, and Ayano Ohmi. **In Search of the Spirit: The Living National Treasures of Japan.**
In the 1950s, Japan began a Living National Treasures program in an effort to preserve ancient crafts, techniques, and art forms. Six of those National Treasures are described using text, color photographs, and a step-by-step description of how these works of art are created. Kimono painting, bamboo weaving, basket weaving, puppet making, sword making, Noh theater, and pottery making are included. *See* FINE ARTS.

Herbert, Janis. **Leonardo da Vinci for Kids: His Life and Ideas: 21 Activities.** Chicago: Chicago Review Press, 1998. 90p. $17.00. ISBN 1-55652-298-3, 1-55652-298-3 pa.
This remarkable, attractive book packs in a biography of Leonardo da Vinci, art lessons, recipes, Italian language instruction, science information, gardening tips, a history of art and artists, world history, and excellent

reproductions of some of da Vinci's most famous works. His life is told by incorporating directions for many student activities, such as how to set up a studio. The directions are simple and easy to follow, yet thorough. Filled with information on da Vinci's myriad interests, plus illustrations, maps, and activities, this book still manages not to become too crowded or busy. The paperback format allows students to lay it flat when following directions. A time line, a glossary, biographies of Renaissance artists and historical figures, a list of where to see da Vinci's works, Web sites, and a bibliography help to make this a must purchase.

Hoose, Phillip M. **We Were There, Too!: Young People in U.S. History.**
Biographies of sixty-seven young people, aged ten and up, who contributed to history-making events are collected in this remarkable book. Some of the names are well known adults, but the contributions don't focus on what these individuals are known for today; instead, they describe events that took place when they were young. Most of the selections are about unknown heroes, however. Entries finish with a paragraph about what happened to the subjects when they grew up. This outstanding collection makes history come alive. *See* SOCIAL STUDIES—UNITED STATES HISTORY.

Jiménez, Francisco. **Breaking Through.**
This sequel to **The Circuit** begins with the Jiménez family being deported by *la migra* because the parents don't have proper visas. This humiliating experience prompts Francisco to work even harder to succeed at school, to work to help support the family, to maintain his Hispanic culture, and to "fit in" to the American social scene. He set his sights very high, but thanks to encouragement and guidance from teachers and counselors, he succeeded. Today he is the head of the Modern Languages and Literatures department and the director of the ethnic studies program at Santa Clara University in California. *See* MULTICULTURAL.

Jiménez, Francisco. **The Circuit: Stories from the Life of a Migrant Child.**
Twelve short stories chronicle the author's early life as a child in a migrant worker's family in California. The family experiences poverty, illness, constant mobility, prejudice, and never-ending hard work, but they also have a sense of hope and a belief that through honesty and diligence, their lives will improve. This inspiring story should be shared with all children, but especially children in English as a Second Language classes, who may be struggling to find their place in a new world. *See* MULTICULTURAL.

Krull, Kathleen. **Lives of Extraordinary Women: Rulers, Rebels (and What the Neighbors Thought).** Illus. Kathryn Hewitt. San Diego, Calif.: Harcourt, 2000. 95p. $20.00. ISBN 0-7398-3074-0, 0-15-200807-1.
Lively stories of twenty historically significant women are told with Krull's usual humor and knack for including little-known, interesting facts.

Well-known women such as Cleopatra, Eleanor of Aquitaine, Joan of Arc, Isabella I, Elizabeth I, Catherine the Great, Marie Antoinette, Harriet Tubman, Eleanor Roosevelt, Golda Meir, Indira Gandhi, and Eva Perón are included. Lesser known women include Nzingha, Tz'u-his, Wilma Mankiller, Aung San Suu Kyi, and Rogoberta Menchú. Hewitt's caricature drawings can be found after every three- to four-page entry, plus an "Ever After" section that gives interesting tidbits of information about the woman. A bibliography is included.

Krull, Kathleen. **Lives of the Presidents: Fame, Shame, and What the Neighbors Thought.** Illus. Kathryn Hewitt. San Diego, Calif.: Harcourt, 1998. 96p. $20.00. ISBN 0-8172-4049-7, 0-15-2000808-X.

Every president of the United States, except our most recent, President George W. Bush, is included in chronological order in this volume. Krull manages to find fun anecdotes about each president and details that won't be found in most biographies or encyclopedias. In her introduction Krull states that she wants us to know our "presidents as fathers, husbands, pet owners and neighbors." She tells "stories about hairstyles, attitudes, diets, bad habits, ailments, fears, money, sleep patterns, and underwear." Hewitt's signature watercolors present a caricature of the president with an enlarged head and a small body, with his favorite things surrounding him and a small insert of his wife. What a fun way to get to know our presidents!

Krull, Kathleen. **They Saw the Future: Oracles, Psychics, Scientists, Great Thinkers and Pretty Good Guessers.** Illus. Kyrsten Brooker. New York: Atheneum Children's Books, 1999. 108p. $20.00. ISBN 0-689-81295-7.

A mix of twelve interesting people, each possessing the ability to see the world differently from their peers, are arranged in chronological order. Krull points out that we'll never know for sure what sets each of these people apart. Perhaps it was just luck, but there are some similarities among all twelve people, which are discussed in the introduction. It's easy to understand why Krull included some of the entries, such as the Oracle at Delphi, the Sibyls, Nostrdamus, Leonardo da Vinci, Jules Verne, H.G. Wells, Edgar Cayce, and Jeane Dixon, but others, such as the Maya, Hildegard of Bingen, Nicholas Black Elk, and Marshall McLuhan, require a little extra thought. After reading each entry, however, the thread of seeing into the future—in one way or another—becomes clear. A full-page, color illustration of each prophet is included, along with a further reading section and an index.

Lasky, Kathryn. **A Brilliant Streak: The Making of Mark Twain.** Illus. Barry Moser. San Diego, Calif.: Harcourt Brace & Co., 1998. 41p. $18.00. ISBN 0-15-252110-0.

Using anecdotes, quotes and a lively text, Lasky captures the life of America's best-known and most celebrated storyteller, Samuel Clemens.

Clemens was born November 30, 1835, the night Halley's comet streaked across the sky. He died seventy-five years later, on April 20, 1920, when Halley's comet appeared again. He had a mischievous childhood, which set the stage for his adventurous, devil-may-care life. Lasky is correct when she says, "It would only be stretching the truth a little to say that Samuel Clemens had one of the longest childhoods in history." He was always up for an adventure, and he recorded them with great insight and humor. This book captures his overactive imagination, his penchant for stretching the truth, and his life's experiences. Students will better understand his works after reading this account of his life.

Lester, Julius. **The Blues Singers: Ten Who Rocked the World.**
Ten of the world's top blues and blues-related singers are included in this outstanding collective biography. Both the text and the illustrations convey the importance of Bessie Smith, Robert Johnson, Mahalia Jackson, Muddy Waters, Billie Holiday, B.B. King, Ray Charles, Little Richard, James Brown, and Aretha Franklin. Lester writes as if he were telling the stories to his granddaughter, so the text is folksy and conversational in tone. *See* FINE ARTS.

Lewis, Patrick J. **Freedom Like Sunlight: Praisesongs for Black Americans.**
Thirteen noteworthy African Americans are presented through the use of poetry in this remarkable collaboration of art and poetry. Biographical sketches, poems, and portraits of Arthur Ashe, Harriet Tubman, Sojourner Truth, Louis Armstrong, Martin Luther King, Jr., Satchel Paige, Rosa Parks, Langston Hughes, Jesse Owens, Marian Anderson, Malcom X, Wilma Rudolph, and Billie Holiday are included in this important work. *See* POETRY.

Marcus, Leonard S., compiled and edited by. **Author Talk: Conversations with Judy Blume . . . et al.** New York: Simon & Schuster, 2000. 103p. $22.00. ISBN 0-689-81383-X.
It's always fun to learn personal information about authors, and this book gives us this pleasure. Fifteen favorite authors, including Judy Blume, Bruce Brooks, Karen Cushman, Russell Freedman, Lee Bennett Hopkins, James Howe, Johanna Hurwitz, E.L. Konigsburg, Lois Lowry, Ann M. Martin, Nicholasa Mohr, Gary Paulsen, Jon Scieszka, Seymour Simon, and Laurence Yep, are interviewed in this collective biography. Each chapter begins with an informative biographical sketch of the author, followed by a question-and-answer session. Similar questions are asked of each person, but some vary depending on the author. Each author was asked what advice he or she had for young people who want to write, and nearly every one answers that they should read profusely and practice writing again and again without becoming discouraged. Each author's section has photographs, often from their childhood, and many authors include an example of an edited manuscript. A listing of books follows each interview by the author,

but it's not always a complete listing for some of the authors. The interviews show that imagination and hard work are necessary to be a writer, and they also provide encouragement to those who want to write.

Meltzer, Milton. **Ten Queens: Portraits of Women of Power.** Illus. Bethanne Andersen. New York: Dutton Children's Books, 1998. 134p. $25.00. ISBN 0-525-45643-0.

The ten queens that Meltzer writes about in this collective biography were chosen because they didn't come to power merely by marrying a king, but because they "held power in their hands and used it." Covering a two-thousand-year time span, Meltzer showcases Esther, Cleopatra, Boudicca, Zenobia, Eleanor of Aquitaine, Isabella of Spain, Elizabeth I, Christine of Sweden, Maria Theresa, and Catherine the Great. Each biographical sketch begins with a full-length, color portrait, along with flowing text. Basic information is given about each person, but Meltzer also adds interesting, little-known facts that make the reading fun as well as informative. Maps, information boxes, illustrations, notes on sources used, a bibliography, and an index work together to make this an excellent research tool, as well as an entertaining book for browsing.

Myers, Walter Dean. **Bad Boy: A Memoir.** New York: HarperCollins, 2001. 214p. $16.00. ISBN 0-06-029523-6.

Walter Dean Myers's early years in Harlem in the 1940s and 1950s included love and caring from his adoptive parents. But money was scarce, street life was filled with pitfalls and temptations, he was often left unattended, his illiterate father didn't understand his behavior, and his peers were rough and tough. He excelled at sports and was fiercely competitive, but he also loved reading and writing—not a popular activity with his peers. School should have been easy for him, but he didn't soar because of his volatile behavior and a speech impediment. He led a dual life, playing sports with his street friends but hiding books and sneaking off to read when his friends weren't watching. This duplicity caused him great difficulty, and he eventually dropped out of high school to join the military. Through his rocky coming of age, reading was Myers's mainstay, giving his life purpose. In this frank autobiography, he tells the story of his early life, which is the backdrop for much of his writing. His ability to endure hardships, yet maintain his love for learning and reading, is an inspiring story to share with readers of all ages.

Myers, Walter Dean. **Malcolm X: A Fire Burning Brightly.** Illus. Leonard Jenkins. New York: HarperCollins, 2000. 34p. $17.00. ISBN 0-06-027708-4.

Malcolm Little grew up listening to his outspoken father preaching about black pride—a radical thing to do in the 1920s—and it planted the seed that directed his life. After his father's death, Little's early life was turbulent, and he ended up in prison, where he did a great deal of reading, writing, and studying. After prison, he joined the Nation of Islam, changed his name to Malcolm X, and became a fiery speaker, encouraging black people to revolt and demand equal rights. His message became so violent that the Nation of Islam eventually rejected him. He went on a pilgrimage to Mecca, where he began to understand the need to unite all races, rather than speaking only for blacks. Still, many did not agree with his newfound beliefs, and he was assassinated at age thirty-nine in 1965. Myers captures the dedication and daring of this man who gave his life for the eradication of racism. Important quotations by Malcolm X are given throughout the text and again in the chronology in the back of the book. The illustrations, done in acrylic, pastel, and spray paint vividly portray the text. This moving, powerful picture book is a must for every biography section.

Nelson, Marilyn. **Carver: A Life in Poems.**
Nelson tells the story of George Washington Carver's life through a series of fifty-nine poems, each depicting a particular time in his life, an incident he witnessed, or an event in which he was involved. This unique collection of poetry aptly tells the story of an unusual and inspiring man. *See* POETRY.

Paulsen, Gary. **Caught by the Sea: A Life in Boats.** New York: Delacorte Press, 2001. 103p. $16.00. ISBN 0-385-326645-9, 0-385-90025-2 lib. bdg.
In this brief autobiographical work, Gary Paulsen describes his love of the sea and boats, a love affair that began when he was seven years old. In a light-hearted, humorous manner, he relates his sailing adventures with various boats, sharing his lifelong passion for the sea and the creatures that inhabit it. Sailboat lovers will relish this volume, but landlubbers, too, can appreciate Paulsen's adventures and humor. In his typical matter-of-fact manner, he describes "the number one law of the sea: If given a chance a container of oatmeal will open, mix with an open container of coffee grounds, further combine itself with eight or ten gallons of seawater and then find its way into your sleeping bag." A map in the front of the book shows Paulsen's travels; a map in the back shows his plans for future voyages.

Paulsen, Gary. **Guts: The True Stories Behind Hatchet and the Brian Books.** New York: Delacorte Press, 2001. 148p. $17.00. ISBN 0-385-32650-5.
Gary Paulsen displays his extensive knowledge of nature in this autobiographical work describing real-life incidents that shaped Brian's adventures in **Hatchet** (1987) and the other Brian books. The six chapter headings give a good sketch of the topics covered in this fascinating work: (1) Heart Attacks, Plane Crashes and Flying, (2) Moose Attacks, (3) Things That Hurt, (4) Killing to Live: Hunting and Fishing with Primitive Weapons, (5) Eating Eyeballs and Guts or Starving: The Fine Art of Wilderness Nutrition, and (6) The Joy of Cooking. The reader needs to be ready

for some graphic descriptions and some "blood and guts." Told with humor and vividly descriptive language, this book is a true winner.

Pinkney, Andrea Davis. **Let It Shine: Stories of Black Women Freedom Fighters.** Illus. Stephen Alcorn. San Diego, Calif.: Harcourt, 2000. 107p. $20.00. ISBN 0-15-201005-X.

This inspiring book showcases the biographies of ten black women who were influential in abolition, women's rights, and civil rights. Pinkney writes in a storytelling manner, giving the text an easygoing feeling. For example, the opening statement for Sojourner Truth's biography reads, "When the good Lord was handing out the gift of conviction, he gave a hefty dose to Sojourner Truth." Biddy Mason's description says, "As a slave she was forbidden to read. So Biddy gathered her smarts by *doing*. And, oh, did Biddy *do*." The biographies are in chronological order, beginning with Sojourner Truth and continuing with Biddy Mason, Harriet Tubman, Ida B. Wells-Barnett, Mary McLeod Bethune, Ella Josephine Baker, Dorothy Irene Height, Rosa Parks, Fannie Lou Hamer, and ending with Shirley Chisholm. Pinkney describes the importance and bravery of the women, pointing out that their courage and strong convictions paved the way for the betterment of all people. Stephen Alcorn's full-page, stylized portraits open each chapter, along with smaller illustrations sprinkled throughout the text. Symbolic, allegorical details in the artwork depict the subjects' significant work. Alcorn portrays Harriet Tubman, for example, as a bridge over a railroad track, her arms outstretched, with black slaves crossing from one hand to the other. This outstanding collection is highly recommended for personal and library use.

Rosen, Michael. **Shakespeare: His Work & His World.** Illus. Robert Ingpen. Cambridge, Mass.: Candlewick, 2001. 96p. $20.00. ISBN 0-7636-1568-4.

This vivid account of Shakespeare's life is presented in large type on oversized pages, with quotations in bold print and watercolor illustrations that range from two-page spreads to paintings that run in and through the text. This account is much more than a biography; it explains life during Shakespeare's time, which was filled with difficulty and danger and strongly influenced his writing and theater productions. Rosen describes the role of the theater at that time, and sketches of the Globe Theatre give a sense of where it was located and how it worked. Quotations from Shakespeare's plays, citing the work, act, and line, are featured throughout the book. Rosen also includes summaries of *Macbeth, King Lear, The Tempest,* and *Romeo and Juliet.* Readers will find the index and the extensive, detailed time line of Shakespeare's life and works especially useful. The layout and the artwork make this an inviting book for browsing, pleasure reading, and research.

Ryan, Pam Muñoz. **Riding Freedom.** Illus. Brian Selznick. New York: Scholastic, 1998. 138p. $16.00. ISBN 0-590-95766-X, 0-439-08796-1 pa.

During the 1800s, there wasn't much a girl could do for a living except household jobs. Charlotte Parkhurst, an orphan, wanted to work with horses, so she disguised herself as a boy and set out to fulfill her dreams. After working in several famous stables, she became so well known, she was hired as a stagecoach driver. As she matured, she moved to California, where she continued to drive stagecoaches, but she also bought and worked a ranch, always disguised as a man. She voted in the 1868 presidential election as a man, and so technically was the first woman in America to vote. Through this fictionalized biography, Ryan has captured the spunk and skills of this early Californian, emphasizing the need for personal freedom to follow one's dreams. The author's notes give additional information about Charlotte Parkhurst, also known as One-Eyed Charley, Cockeyed Charley, and Six-Horse Charley, but never as Charlotte.

Stanley, Diane. **Joan of Arc.** New York: Morrow Junior Books, 1998. 44p. $16.00. ISBN 0-688-14329-6, 0-688-14330-X lib. bdg., 0-06-443748-5 pa.

Stanley retells the remarkable story of Joan of Arc with detailed text and intricate gilded artwork. The introduction tells the saga of the Hundred Years War in the fourteenth and fifteenth centuries, setting the stage for Joan's work. Joan came from humble beginnings, but early in her life she heard voices that told her what to do to help the French win the war. She followed those voices, which led her from one treacherous battle to the next. Thanks to her, the dauphin was crowned king, but his poor leadership later led to many losses. She was sold to the English as a prize and burned at the stake for her loyalty to her church and country. Joan of Arc's story is complicated, but Stanley moves it along, making it easy to follow and understand. The illustrations are meticulous and detailed, capturing the content perfectly and portraying life during the Middle Ages, as well as telling Joan's story. The afterword tells what happened after Joan's death and is followed with a bibliography. This outstanding work should be a part of every middle school library.

Stanley, Diane. **Michelangelo.**

Stanley uses the extended-text picture-book format to tell Michelangelo's intriguing story. Computer-manipulated drawings of his actual work and Stanley's original watercolors work together to make this an outstanding piece of art, as well as a thorough, easy-to-understand story. *See* FINE ARTS.

Chapter 2

English—Classics

The original **Hot Links** (1998) listed modern classics—books published within the last 40 years that have stood the test of time and continue to delight readers. This edition concentrates on books written some time ago that are considered true classics. The selections included here are reprints and retellings with updated illustrations and special touches that make them appealing to the young reader.

Barrie, J. M. **Peter Pan.** Illus. compiled by Cooper Edens. San Francisco: Chronicle Books, 2000. 173p. $20.00. ISBN 0-8118-2297-4.

This unabridged version of the classic story of the boy who doesn't want to grow up is unique because of the illustrations. More than one hundred pictures by more than sixteen artists from the early 1900s have been compiled to illustrate this book, making it an art collection as well as a reprint of the classic tale. Works by the original illustrator, F. D. Bedford, are included, along with works by other well-known artists such as Arthur Rackham, Roy Best, and Alice Woodward. Artwork from playbills and posters from 1904 through 1934 are also included. A list of acknowledgments serves as an index to the illustrations. This unique collection of art gives this work historical significance.

Carroll, Lewis. **Alice in Wonderland.** Illus. Lisbeth Zwerger. New York: North-South Books, 1999. 103p. $20.00. ISBN 0-7358-1166-0.

In this version of Lewis Carroll's classic, Zwerger uses an oversized format with twelve full-page illustrations, one per chapter, along with a variety of smaller drawings dotted throughout the text. Alice fans will have fun noticing the new twists on favorite scenes. Zwerger illustrates Alice's unusual size after she has drunk the liquid by showing only her legs, which fill up the entire room. In several of the full-page illustrations, the action is depicted, but Alice is missing. The high-quality paper and the large size make the book feel good in the reader's hands.

Coville, Bruce. **William Shakespeare's Romeo and Juliet.** Illus. Dennis Nolan. New York: Dial Books, 1999. 38p. $17.00. ISBN 0-8037-2462-4.

Students love the tale of Romeo and Juliet, but reading the original can be difficult. Retellings in story form such as this one are always welcome. Coville is faithful to the story, and the muted watercolor illustrations instill a feeling of romance. The balcony scene unfolds vertically to show the action more completely. This is a great addition to a Shakespeare collection.

London, Jack. **White Fang.** The Whole Story series. Illus. Philippe Munch. New York: Viking, 1999. 237p. $24.00. ISBN 0-670-88479-0.

London's legendary story of White Fang, half dog and half wolf, is retold, unabridged, using outstanding illustrations, detailed and illustrated notes in the margins, and high-quality paper. Every book in this series is worth purchasing.

McCarty, Nick. **The Iliad.** Illus. Victor Ambrus. New York: Kingfisher, 2000. 95p. $23.00. ISBN 0-7534-5330-4, 0-7534-5321-5 pa.

The colorful descriptive language used in this retelling of the age-old tale makes this an excellent choice for students. Action-packed illustrations and large print, along with the fast-paced text, take away the tedium that can be a problem in retellings of classic tales. McCarty includes a glossary of the main characters, divided into a list of "The Greeks and their allies," "The Trojans and their allies," and "The gods and their fates," which helps readers to keep the cast of characters straight. This version is a very effective read aloud to middle school students.

Pinkney, Jerry. **Aesop's Fables.** New York: SeaStar Books, 2000. 87p. $20.00. ISBN 1-5817-000-0.

Aesop's age-old morals are retold, accompanied by Pinkney's brilliant and vivid illustrations. As the introduction notes, we never outgrow our need for Aesop's fables, and this collection of more than 60 of his best and most familiar stories fills that need beautifully. The intricately detailed watercolor illustrations draw the reader into the story, helping to explain the moral written in italics at the end of each story. This outstanding collection should be part of every reader's collection, both for its stories and its artwork.

Poe, Edgar Allen. **The Pit and the Pendulum and Other Stories.** The Whole Story series. Illus. Jame's Prunier. New York: Viking, 1999. 153p. $26.00. ISBN 0-670-88706-4, 0-670-88725-0pa.

   Viking Press is in the process of reproducing some of the best-loved classic stories. Each book is complete and unabridged, uses superior quality paper, and is filled with a generous amount of informative annotations and illustrations. This contribution contains seven of Poe's most popular stories: "The Gold-Bug," The Oval Portrait," "The Pit and the Pendulum," The Cask of Amontillado," "Some Words with a Mummy," "The Tell-Tale Heart," and "The Murders in the Rue Morgue."

Sewell, Anna. **Black Beauty.** The Whole Story series. Illus. William Geldart. New York: Viking, 2001. 206p. $22.00. ISBN 0-670-89496-6, 0-670-89497-4pa.

   This is a retelling of the classic story of the life of a horse, Black Beauty, in nineteenth-century England. The story has been reissued many times, but the high-quality paper, remarkable illustrations, and detailed illustrated margin notes make this an outstanding choice. Special quotations from the text highlighted in the margins are an additional feature.

Wells, Rosemary. **Rachel Field's 1930 Newbery Award–Winning Story Hitty, Her First Hundred Years.** Illus. Susan Jeffers. New York: Simon & Schuster, 1999. 102p. $22.00. ISBN 0-689-81716-9.

   It's a daring act to redo and spruce up a classic like **Hitty,** but Wells and Jeffers, as a team, decided the wonderful book was rarely read anymore, and it was time to "dust off Hitty and give her a new lease on life." In 1829, an Irish peddler carves Hitty from a piece of mountain ash and gives her to a little girl, Preble, a sea captain's daughter. The next one hundred years are spent traveling around the world, going from one little girl to the next, until she ends up in a pawn shop after "the crash." She witnesses her first airplane while waiting in the shop's window. Wells edited, shortened, and trimmed; omitted African American dialect; and changed South Sea "Injuns" to "Islanders," but the story basically stays the same until the Civil War. At that point, Hitty is mailed to a little girl in the South, where she gets a completely different perspective on history. Jeffer's colorful paintings have the nostalgic feeling of early-twentieth-century illustrations. The full-page paintings, along with smaller detailed illustrations interspersed on the pages of the text, help to make this work a masterpiece. A map at the end details Hitty's travels. The refurbished Hitty is alive and well, ready to go for another hundred years.

Chapter 3

English—Use of Language

It's fun to play with words and language usage, and the books in this section do just that. They can be used to teach a particular concept or skill, or they can simply be enjoyed for their humorous presentations.

Agee, Jon. **Elvis Lives!: And Other Anagrams.** New York: Farrar, Straus & Giroux, 2000. 80p. $13.00. ISBN 0-374-32127-2.

Anagrams state a word or phrase and then rearrange the letters to make a new word or phrase. Agee has done an outstanding job of tracking down sixty anagrams and illustrating them with his trademark line drawings, cleverly showing the humor and fun in playing with words. For instance, "a decimal point" becomes "I'm a dot in place." The word "astronomer" can be "moonstarer," and "eleven plus two" translates to "twelve plus one." Agee gives credit to the creators of many of the anagrams at the back of the book and includes a bibliography. Students can have fun creating their own anagrams after experiencing this collection.

Agee, Jon. **Sit on a Potato Pan, Otis!: More Palindromes.** New York: Farrar, Straus & Giroux, 1999. 80p. $15.00. ISBN 0-374-31808-5.

Jon Agee is back with another palindrome book, after **Go Hang a Salami! I'm a Lasagna Hog!** (1992) and **So Many Dynamos!** (1994). A palindrome is a word or phrase that reads the same forward and backward, such as "Dracula valu-card" or "we lost a fatso, Lew." Agee includes a humorous pen-and-ink drawing with each phrase, helping to explain some of the nonsensical phrases. For example, "desserts stress Ed" has a cartoon of Ed approaching an ice cream sundae with great anxiety. Agee's work encourages us to play with words. Students will have fun deciphering these palindromes and then attempting to create their own.

Agee, Jon. **Who Ordered the Jumbo Shrimp?: And Other Oxymorons.** New York: HarperCollins, 1998. 80p. $13.00. ISBN 0-06-205159-8.

      Jon Agee is a master at using simple line drawings to show meanings of words. In this work, he plays with oxymorons. He provides an oxymoron, accompanied by a silly, humorous illustration of it. For example, a "minor catastrophe" shows a beach with people unconcerned that there has just been an earthquake of .00021 on the Richter scale. A "sun shower" shows a man who has pulled off to the side of a road in the desert to take a shower. A "cold sweat" shows sweat pouring from a man's forehead in the form of ice cubes. This book is a useful tool to help students understand this use of words and to help them think of other oxymorons.

Brook, Donna. **The Journey of English.** Illus. Jean Day Zallinger. New York: Clarion Books, 1998. 38p. $17.00. ISBN 0-395-71211-4.

      More people use English than any other language in the world; it can be heard around the globe and is used regularly in more than eighty countries. How it began and how it evolved into the present-day language is explored in this expanded picture book. Anyone curious about languages will find this an interesting journey. The main emphasis is on the history of English, tracing it from the invaders who brought words with them to England, through present-day use of the language around the world, but the influence of other tribes and languages also enters into the mix to help tell the story. Maps, color illustrations, a section on dictionaries, an entomology section, and a bibliography help to make our language come alive.

Butterfield, Helen. **The Secret Life of Fishes: From Angels to Zebras on the Coral Reef.**

      A remarkable array of fish swim by in this alphabetically arranged book of fish found in coral reefs. This book can provide an excellent example when students have an assignment to make an alphabet book of their own on a specific subject. The outstanding watercolors and the detailed text and drawings can illustrate to students that ABC books aren't just for little kids. *See* SCIENCE.

Cleary, Brian P. **Hairy, Scary, Ordinary: What Is an Adjective?** Words Are Categorical series. Illus. Jenya Prosmitsky, Minneapolis, Minn.: Carolrhoda Books, 1999. 32p. $15.00. ISBN 1-5705-401-9.

A fat cat points to a sign with the definition of an adjective, then rhyming text and a host of crazy cats proceed to illustrate what an adjective actually is. Cleary presents and clarifies adjectives in a fast-paced, humorous manner, highlighting adjectives in bright colors. For example, "They tell us things are orange or green, / Hot or cold or in-between, / Leaky, squeaky, ancient, new, / Easy, breezy, broken, blue." This book makes learning a part of speech clear, easy, and fun.

Cleary, Brian P. **A Mink, a Fink, a Skating Rink: What Is a Noun?** Words Are Categorical series. Illus. Jenya Prosmitsky, Minneapolis, Minn.: Carolrhoda Books, 2000. 32p. $15.00. ISBN 1-5705-402-7.

Each page presents a particular noun, illustrated with the help of comical cats. This book isn't quite as fast-paced as the other two in the series, but the rhyming text does touch on proper nouns, as well as illustrating that nouns name a person, animal, place, or thing. This is a terrific book to use when introducing or reviewing nouns.

Cleary, Brian P. **To Root, to Toot, to Parachute: What Is a Verb?** Words Are Categorical series. Illus. Jenya Prosmitsky, Minneapolis, Minn.: Carolrhoda Books, 2001. 32p. $15.00. ISBN 1-57505-403-5.

A sign opposite the title page gives a definition of a verb: "A word that shows action or being." The text immediately gives meaning to that definition with a host of slapstick cats cavorting all over the pages to explain verbs. "Verbs are words like sing and dance,/ pray or practice,/ preach or prance,/ toss and tumble,/ jump and jam,/ whine and whisper,/ sleep and slam." To help illustrate a concept, the cats sing, play piano, preach, ride a stick horse, throw a mouse, cram a basketball into a hoop, and finally sleep. Every page is action filled and lively, giving a simple overview of verbs, getting the point across in a humorous manner.

Conover, Sarah. **Kindness: A Treasury of Buddhist Wisdom for Children and Parents.** The Little Light of Mine series. Spokane, Wash.: Eastern Washington University Press, 2001. 163p. $20.00. ISBN 0-910055-67-X.

Thirty-one stories and thirty-four quotations and sayings are presented in a calm, soft, and lyrical voice with the purpose of introducing young readers to Buddhist beliefs and traditions. *Jataka* tales—stories of the Buddha in past incarnations—are included, along with parables and stories widely read and retold to Buddhist children throughout the world. The introduction and preface help the reader to understand the philosophies and ideas of Buddhism and give an explanation of how these stories and sayings can provide solace and encouragement in our daily lives. The author includes detailed source notes for the quotes, sayings, and stories. A bibliography of books for further reading is included. This is an excellent resource for "jumping-off" ideas in a creative writing class or to use when studying religions of the world.

Foltz, Charlotte. **Eat Your Words: A Fascinating Look at the Language of Food.** Illus. John O'Brien. New York: Delacorte Press, 1999. 87p. $17.00. ISBN 0-385-32575-4, 0-385-32578-9pa.

Cultures are closely entwined with food, and this book sets out to show the origins of many common foods and how they got their names. For instance, Caesar salad has nothing to do with the Roman emperor. It was started in 1924 by a chef in Tijuana, Mexico, who ran out of his usual menu items, so he put whatever food he had left together in a salad. Customers loved it, so he continued to serve it and named it after his brother, Caesar. This book is filled with information about the history of foods, the origin of food phrases such as "spill the beans," laws concerning food (did you know it is illegal to have rotten eggs in your possession in Iowa?), foods named after geographic places (baked Alaska), festivals based on foods, foods named after animals (hush puppies), the origins of fun foods such as lollipops, and common words that originated with food (the word "salary" comes from the Latin word for salt, *sal*). The line drawings add to the fun and help emphasize the explanations. A bibliography and an index are included.

Gardner, Sally. **The Fairy Tale Catalog: Everything You Need to Make a Fairy Tale**. San Francisco: Chronicle Books, 2001. 34p. $16.00. ISBN 0-8118-3320-8.

This is a made-to-order book when teaching the parts of fairy tales. Done in an overstated, humorous manner, the characters and objects needed to produce a fairy tale of your choice are spelled out in catalog form. The shopper is encouraged to go through each section, make choices, and end up with the perfect tale. The sections include dresses, wands, and other fairy things, as well as beauty products, a prince charming, a family, a love story, a wedding, friends, a living situation, food, carriages, garden items, houses, books, and spells. The reader needs to be familiar with famous fairy tales to understand the humor and the illustrations.

Harley, Avis. **Fly with Poetry: An ABC of Poetry**. Honesdale, Penn.: Wordsong, Boyds Mills Press, 2000. 48p. $14.00. ISBN 1-56397-798-2pa.

This clever collection of twenty-seven poems, one for each letter of the alphabet, uses examples of poems to show types of poetry. For example, the letter A has poems that show abecedarian and two types of acrostic forms. The abecedarian-form poem, "Forgotten Giants," arranges the letters A to Z to form the first letters of every line. "Ancient / Bogs / Contain / Dinosaur / Eggs, / Forgotten / Giants / Hidden / Inside / Jurassic / Kingdoms. / Like / Memories / Never / Opened, / Prehistoric / Quagmires / Retain / Secrets. / This / Unknown, / Vanished / World, / X-tinct: / Yesterday's

/ Zoo." The author continues with "B" is for blank verse, "C" is cinquain, and "D" is doublet, moving all the way through the alphabet. A concise explanation of the poetic device is given at the bottom of each page. Brightly colored illustrations accompany each poem, giving additional explanation to the entry. The author gives encouragement and information in the introduction, and a list of additional poetic forms is given at the end. This book is essential for teaching poetry forms to children of all ages. Each poem is an excellent example of the poetic device presented, and the explanation at the bottom of each page adds to the usefulness.

Hepworth, Cathi. **Bug Off!: A Swarm on Insect Words.** New York: G. P. Putnam's Sons, 1998. 28p. $16.00. ISBN 0-399-22640-0.

Hepworth uses insects such as moths, mites, and bees to show us how fun it is to play with words. Each page presents a word that has a type of insect as a part of the spelling, such as, app**roach,** f**rant**ic and si**gnat**ures. The accompanying color illustrations cleverly and humorously describe the work. For example, si**gnat**ures is a drawing of the Declaration of Independence with tiny John Hancocks in the form of gnats pushing a quill pen for the name signing. The first section, "A Real Fly-by-Night Operation" stars bees, moths, and gnats. "Don't Let the Bedbugs Bite" features mites, ticks, and lice, and the final section, "The Unwelcome Houseguests," has words that include roaches and ants. This clever use of words can be used as a springboard for lessons across the curriculum involving a specific set of words. Her previous book, **Antics!** (1992), an alphabet book , cleverly uses the same idea of looking for words inside words.

Janeczko, Paul B., selected by. **A Poke in the I: A Collection of Concrete Poems.**

Letters arranged in various patterns and vivid illustrations go hand in hand to create thirty lively, attractive, and action-packed concrete poems. A variety of clever shapes and sizes are used to describe the topic of each poem. This is an excellent book to use when teaching concrete poems. *See* POETRY.

Katz, Bobbi. **A Rumpus of Rhymes: A Book of Noisy Poems.** Illus. Susan Estelle Kwas. New York: Dutton Children's Books, 2001. 32p. $16.00. ISBN 0-525-46718-1.

This "noisy" book is filled with twenty-eight original poems that describe ordinary situations in onomatopoeic form. The lively sounds of spring are captured in "Spring Conversations": "'Whisk!' / whirls the jump rope, / twirling / around. 'Thud!' / say the sneakers, / bouncing off the ground. 'Smack!' / says the ball to the catcher's mitt. / 'Whack!' / says the bat when it makes a hit." In some poems, made-up words describe the sounds made, as in "Washing Machine." The sounds of the machine are described as "Glubita glubita / glubita / glubita glubita / glubita . . . / glub.

Swizzle-dee-swash / Swizzle-dee-swash." Some poems use describing words to portray the idea of the sound, as in "Sea Speak." Katz describes the sea as "thundering / whacking / smacking splashing / lashing / slapping / lapping / licking / tickling / gurgling / spurting / spritzing / pounding." The "sound" words are in a variety of type styles, shapes, and colors, emphasizing their noisiness. The poems in this book can be used to help teach onomatopoeia and can encourage students to write their own noisy poems.

Lewis, C. S. **The Wisdom of Narnia.** Illus. Pauline Baynes. New York: HarperCollins, 2001. 64p. $10.00. ISBN 0-06-623851-X.

This brief book consists of a collection of quotations from all seven Chronicles of Narnia books. Each Narnian quotation, selected by the illustrator Pauline Baynes, is intended to be used as a basis for understanding our real world. Some are true words of wisdom and can be used in many situations, including discussions, story starters, and thoughts for the day. Some are a bit weak, but Narnia fans will enjoy the entire work.

Lewis, J. Patrick. **Doodle Dandies: Poems That Take Shape.**

When teachers need examples of concrete poems, this collection of inventive poems is the perfect teaching tool. Each of the nineteen poems cleverly blends with the rich illustrations to become part of the artwork. *See* POETRY.

Rosen, Michael. **Shakespeare: His Work & His World.**

If the study of Shakespeare is a part of your curriculum, this book begs to be used to help explain the playwright's life, the dangers and difficulties of life in his time, his works, and the importance of theater. It also includes summaries of some of his works, as well as a detailed, five-page time line of his life and works. The outstanding watercolor paintings and lively text make this an excellent book for browsing as well as research. *See* BIOGRAPHIES.

Senn, J. A., compiled and edited by. **Quotations for Kids.** Illus. Steve Pica. Brookfield, Conn.: Millbrook Press, 1999. 256p. $30.00. ISBN 0-7613-0267-0.

Over two thousand quotations appropriate for use by students are arranged alphabetically by a wide range of subjects. The extensive "how to use this book" section at the beginning makes a search easy and successful. The book can be used in three ways: quotations can be browsed just for fun, they can be located by subject, or they can be accessed by a particular author using the People Index. The extensive subject index lists all the subjects, topics, and fictional characters included in the book. A bibliography is also included. The compiler used kid-friendly sources, from Dr. Seuss to famous athletes to historical figures. This well-researched work is a must in every library's reference section.

Tobias, Tobi. **A World of Words: An ABC of Quotations.** Illus. Peter Malone. New York: Lothrop, Lee & Shepard, 1998. 48p. $18.00. ISBN 0-688-12130-6.

Simple, common words are used in alphabetical order, such as "animal," "book," and "circus." Each word is accompanied by one or more quotations from a famous or influential person, making this a wonderful playground of words. For instance, the word "dream" includes the quote, "Why ever did I wake up!" he cried. "I was having such beautiful dreams," by J. R. R. Tolkien. "Ice Cream" has the famous quote by Wallace Stevens, "The only emperor is the emperor of ice-cream." The humorous, dreamlike, surreal illustrations create a visual world that matches the text. This book is a fun example of the power of words to conjure up images.

Chapter 4

Fine Arts

The books cited in this section include various aspects of art, architecture, crafts, music, and theater. Biographies of important people who have contributed to the arts are also included. These are all important topics in their own right, but they are also valuable resources that connect with other curricular areas such as math, science, and social studies.

Aliki. **William Shakespeare & the Globe.**
The story of Shakespeare's life is told in five acts, with each act divided into scenes. Aliki's drawings with captions depict life at that time. Maps, sketches, drawings, quotations, a list of all Shakespeare's works, a chronology of his life, a list of words and expressions he used, and a list of sites to visit make this an outstanding work. *See* BIOGRAPHIES.

Anderson, Matthew T. **Handel, Who Knew What He Liked.**
The humorous and energetic text and Kevin Hawkes's entertaining and detailed drawings work together to tell the story of George Frideric Handel's life. Handel was a headstrong man who knew what he wanted and how to achieve it. He had many successes, but at a low point in his life, he produced *The Messiah* as a last resort, thinking his career was over. *See* BIOGRAPHIES.

Batt, Tanya Robyn. **The Fabrics of Fairytale: Stories Spun from Far and Wide.**
Artwork from around the world is presented in this unique collection of stories told through the use of woven fabrics. The story and the artwork go hand in hand to describe the culture presented. The border patterns on each page, as well as the full-page spreads, help to illustrate each countries' artwork. *See* MULTICULTURAL.

Brenner, Barbara, selected by. **Voices: Poetry and Art from Around the World.**
More than 350 poems and art pieces from six continents are collected in this outstanding combination of poetry, art, and geography. A representative work of art matches at least one of the poems on each page. The artwork includes paintings, sculpture, ceremonial objects, textiles, and photographs, making this a multicultural masterpiece. *See* POETRY.

Carter, David A., and James Diaz. **The Elements of Pop-up: A Pop-up Book for Aspiring Paper Engineers.** Illus. and assistant designer, Leisa Bentley. photographs by Keith Sutter. New York: Little, Simon, 1999. 16p. $30.00. ISBN 0-689-82224-3.
This stunning book of more than fifty working pop-up models is the ultimate guide and instruction manual telling how to make pop-up pages. It begins with an introduction and a glossary set amid a spectacular, stark white pop-up design that is sure to catch the reader's eye. It goes on to give descriptions and examples of eighteen types of parallel folds, twelve angle folds, four wheels, and eight pull-tabs. The endpapers explain how a pop-up is made, including a list of tools and materials needed and step-by-step instructions for a heart-shaped greeting card with flowers popping out of the middle. The authors include the URL for their Web site so that young artists can download die drawings for the pop-ups presented in the book. This is not only an instruction manual, but a work of art in itself.

Castillo, Ana. **My Daughter, My Son, the Eagle, the Dove: An Aztec Chant.**
Ancient Aztec chants originally recorded in pictures are interpreted into a tribute to sons and daughters as they go off into the world. The illustrations are glyphs depicting ancient Aztec figures, which help to blend poetry and art in this moving work. *See* MULTICULTURAL.

Christensen, Bonnie. **Woody Guthrie: Poet of the People.**
Woodcut-like paintings and simple yet thorough text tell the story of folksinger Woody Guthrie. Lines from "This Land Is Your Land" splash across every page, and the lyrics for all seven verses are printed at the end of the book, along with a chronology of Guthrie's life. *See* BIOGRAPHIES.

Demi. **Kites: Magic Wishes That Fly Up to the Sky.** New York: Crown, 1999. 31p. $15.00. 0-517-80049-7.

Kites have historically been an important part of Chinese life. Demi incorporates vividly colored illustrations with legends to tell about the importance of kites and how they evolved, devoting several two-page spreads to various types of kites and what they represent. The last four pages explain how to construct a kite, giving a list of supplies and step-by-step directions. This multifaceted book fits well with the middle school curriculum when studying ancient cultures.

Fritz, Jean. **Leonardo's Horse.** Illus. Hudson Talbott. New York: G. P. Putnam's Sons, 2001. 48p. $17.00. ISBN 0-399-23576-0.

Leonardo da Vinci was a dreamer, and out of his many dreams came great works. One dream, however, was never fulfilled—his dream to build a twenty-four-foot horse. The duke of Milan had agreed to sponsor the project, and da Vinci constructed a clay model. Unfortunately, the 58,000 pounds of tin and copper needed to make the bronze had to be used to make weapons to fight Napoleon, and da Vinci was forced to put his project on hold. For the remainder of Leonardo's life, he mourned for the horse that was never built. In 1977, another dreamer, Charles Dent, read about the unfulfilled quest and decided to complete da Vinci's work. Work was begun on the horse, but in 1994 Charlie died of Lou Gehrig's disease. A trust was set up to complete the project and New York sculptor Nina Akamu completed it in 1999. The horse was unveiled in Milan on September 10, 1999, exactly five hundred years to the day that the French invaded Milan. The story is intriguing, and the pictures showing the process—from clay to plaster to bronze—of how the horse was constructed, shipped, and reconstructed are amazing. The author's notes give additional information about Charlie's project. The book is a rectangle topped by a semicircle, which becomes a dome on the inside. Fritz's informal writing style, the shape of the book, and the seldom-told story make this a fascinating work.

Greenberg, Jan. **Heart to Heart: New Poems Inspired by Twentieth-Century American Art.**

This anthology of original poems was written in response to pieces of art chosen by the poets. Forty-three contemporary poets chose their favorite piece of American artwork, which includes paintings done in a variety of media, photographs, sculptures, and prints. Artists represented include Alexander Calder, Christo, Chuck Close, Grandma Moses, Georgia O'Keeffe, and thirty-five others. This outstanding work that combines art and poetry should be a part of every art teacher's professional collection. *See* POETRY.

Greenberg, Jan, and Sandra Jordan. **Frank O. Gehry: Outside In.**
This stunning biography of the avant-garde California architect Frank O. Gehry is told through text, photographs, sketches, ghost images, sidebars, and drawings. A glossary, bibliography, and list of building locations are included. *See* BIOGRAPHIES.

Guthrie, Woody. **This Land Is Your Land.** Illus. Kathy Jakobsen. Boston: Little, Brown, 1998. 34p. $16.00. ISBN 0-316-39215-4.
America's favorite folk song is presented in all its glory with Jakobsen's magnificent paintings to bring us a one-of-a kind book. The vibrant, detailed paintings that accompany the song depict American scenes, showing the nation's varied terrain and landscapes and its variety of people. Readers can spend hours studying the detail on each page. Guthrie originally wrote this song to bring attention to the plight of the needy in the 1920s and 1930s, but the topics are just as appropriate now. The song finishes with a three-page foldout showing the United States from the west to the east. The back of the foldout has a touching tribute to Woody Guthrie written by Pete Seeger. It includes Guthrie's biography, accompanied by photographs, along with the score and complete lyrics to the song.

Hamanaka, Sheila, and Ayano Ohmi. **In Search of the Spirit: The Living National Treasures of Japan.** Calligraphy by Ayano Ohmi. New York: Morrow Junior Books, 1999. 48p. $18.00. ISBN 0-688-14608-2.
During World War II, much of Japan's artwork and crafts were lost, and in postwar times, machines began to replace the work of artisans. In an effort to preserve ancient traditions, the Japanese government set up a Living National Treasures program in the 1950s to honor those artisans who were still practicing the old ways of doing things by offering grants so these people could continue their work. Six individuals are profiled in this book, including a kimono artist, a bamboo weaver, a puppet master, a sword maker, a Noh actor, and a potter. Each of the six segments includes a biography of the artist, his work, and a step-by-step description in words and sketches of how the work is done. Color photographs of the artisan and his work, calligraphy, and drawings, help to make this a unique work that honors Japanese history and culture.

Herbert, Janis. **Leonardo da Vinci for Kids: His Life and Ideas: 21 Activities.**
High-quality reproductions of da Vinci's work accompany his biography, along with information on art history and techniques, world history, philosophy, science, and how-to projects. *See* BIOGRAPHIES.

Herbert, Janis. **Lewis and Clark for Kids: Their Journey of Discovery with 21 Activities.**

This informational book about the Lewis and Clark journey is accompanied by twenty-one fun activities that tie in with the text. Most are art activities and include things such as making a teepee, a dance rattle, a buffalo mask, moccasins, a basket, and a drum. *See* SOCIAL STUDIES—UNITED STATES HISTORY.

Jones, Lynda. **Kids Around the World Celebrate!: The Best Feasts and Festivals from Many Lands.**

Festivals from around the world are used to illustrate the customs and cultures of various countries. Each of the sixteen festivals presented include art and food projects with easy-to-follow instructions and black-and-white line drawings. *See* MULTICULTURAL.

Katz, Alan. **Take Me out of the Bathtub and Other Silly Dilly Songs.**

Fourteen well-known tunes such at "Home on the Range," "Take Me Out to the Ballgame," and "I've Been Working on the Railroad" have new lyrics, thanks to Alan Katz, who has created a hilarious collection of ludicrous songs done to the tunes of familiar ditties. The full-page color illustrations with action-packed, odd-looking creatures add to the craziness. This is the perfect book to use to spice up chorus classes, to use as camp songs, or just for fun when a little humor is needed. *See* HUMOR.

Knight, Margaret. **Fashion Through the Ages: From Overcoats to Petticoats.**

Need a good pattern for what people wore during a particular time? This lift-the-flap book describes and shows garments of men, women, girls, and boys from ancient Rome through the 1960s. Each part of the garment lifts to reveal the next layer, all the way down to the underwear. A description of the garment is given on the back of the each piece. The margins around the large picture are filled with drawings of hairstyles, shoes, and other accessories. *See* UNIQUE PRESENTATIONS.

Koscielniak, Bruce. **The Story of the Incredible Orchestra: An Introduction to Musical Instruments and the Symphony Orchestra.** Boston: Houghton Mifflin, 2000. 32p. $15.00. ISBN 0-395-96052-5.

Before the 1600s, there was no such thing as an orchestra, just small ensembles. Then, in 1597, Giovanni Gabrieli wrote a piece of music requiring larger groups of instruments, setting the stage for the baroque period, 1600–1750; the classical period, 1750–1820; the romantic period, 1820–1910; and the new sound era from the early 1900s until now. Koscielniak discusses each of these periods in musical history and takes a brief look at the future of music and instruments. Whimsical watercolor illustrations show groups playing music, as well as detailed drawings of individual instruments. The front endpaper features pen-and-watercolor sketches of early instruments, and the back endpaper shows modern-day instruments. The author describes the history of orchestras, the music written for them, and the development of instruments in this upbeat, jam-packed book that serves as an excellent introduction to music appreciation.

Lester, Julius. **The Blues Singers: Ten Who Rocked the World.** Illus. Lisa Cohen. New York: Jump at the Sun/Hyperion Books for Children, 2001. 47p. $16.00. ISBN 0-7868-0463-7.

Lester writes as if he is telling the stories of ten top blues singers to his granddaughter, a style that gives the text a folksy, conversational, storytelling tone. He obviously loves music and wants to impress on his granddaughter the impact these African American singers have had on our world. He includes biographies of Bessie Smith, Robert Johnson, Mahalia Jackson, Muddy Waters, Billie Holiday, B. B. King, Ray Charles, Little Richard, James Brown, and Aretha Franklin. Each entry includes a full-sized portrait in a bold, chunky style that captures the prominent features of the singer. Lester speaks frankly about each person's background and includes their difficulties in life as well as their triumphs. Quotations by other musicians and influential people are sprinkled in each entry, using a variety of type styles and designs. A bibliography and "recommended listening" list are included. This is one of Lester's finest works and can be shared with people of all ages.

Lester, Julius. **From Slave Ship to Freedom Road.** Illus. Rod Brown. New York: Dial, 1998. 40p. $18.00. ISBN 0-8037-1893-4.

These twenty-two dramatic and emotional paintings by Rod Brown, depicting slaves and slavery in America, were first shown in gallery exhibits around the United States. Lester later added the narrative, and the combination creates a powerful and important work. The paintings show the history of slavery, beginning with the horrible conditions of the slave ships, which carried the captive Africans across the Atlantic in dank, dark quarters, packed tightly together, side by side. They brilliantly portray slave markets, backbreaking labor, punishment, and hangings; they tell of slaves who attempted escape, of the Underground Railroad, and finally of the Civil War. Lester's text provides information about slavery and also includes thought-provoking "Imagination Exercises," some for black people, some for white people, and some for everyone. In each exercise, he sets a scene and asks us to think about and react to it. This outstanding work should be shared with people of all ages.

Lithgow, John. **The Remarkable Farkle McBride.** Illus. C. F. Payne. New York: Simon & Schuster Books for Young Readers, 2000. 40p. $16.00. ISBN 0-689-83340-7.

Farkle McBride is a child prodigy who masters the violin at age three, the flute at age five, the trombone when he's seven and the entire percussion section at age nine. At age ten, just when he's about to lose all interest in music, the conductor becomes ill and Farkle is called upon to take his place. The scene is a dramatic four-page panoramic fold-out showing the entire orchestra with Farkle, now the conductor, taking a bow, with a smile that spreads from ear to ear. Farkle's story is written in verse, with musical sounds in onomatopoeic form. The cartoon-like illustrations add to the fun and merriment.

Lomas Garza, Carmen. **Magic Windows: Cut-Paper Art and Stories.**

This delightful dual-language book looks at the world of the author's Mexican-American family life in the Southwest. Each page has a short story written in English and repeated in Spanish. The illustrations are colorful cut-paper images that are fun to make according to the directions given in the companion book, **Making Magic Windows** (1999). *See* MULTICULTURAL.

Lomas Garza, Carmen. **Making Magic Windows: Creating Papel Picado, Cut-Paper Art.** San Francisco, Children's Book Press, 1999. 61p. $10.00. ISBN 0-89239-159-6 pa.

This paperback workbook is a companion to **Magic Windows: Cut-Paper Art and Stories** (1999). It teaches how to create the festive colorful banners called *banderitas*. Lomas Garza stresses scissors safety and includes directions on how to use a craft knife safely. Step-by-step instructions tell how to hold, fold, and cut the paper to create eight *papel picado* designs, which depict Mexican American daily life and the natural world. The technique gives the young artist experience with positive and negative spaces.

Markel, Michelle. **Cornhusk, Silk, and Wishbones: A Book of Dolls from Around the World.**

This book combines the hobby of doll collecting with history and geography from around the world, arranged in alphabetical order. This idea could spark splendid multicultural art projects, with students inventing their own dolls or replicating dolls from the part of the world from where they or their ancestors came. *See* MULITICULRURAL.

Merrill, Yvonne Y. **Hands-on Asia: Art Activities for All Ages.** Salt Lake City, Utah: Kits Publishing, 1999. 87p. $20.00. ISBN 0-9643177-5-3.

More than fifty art activities based on Asian cultures are presented with easy-to-follow directions, sketches to help during construction, and large color photographs of the finished product. Folk-art projects are given from Japan, China, Tibet, Mongolia, Korea, and Southeast Asia. Most projects can be done in the classroom using easy-to-find materials. Information is included that gives an understanding of the cultures portrayed. One section explains Buddhism, Confucianism, Hinduism, and Shintoism. The book also includes a map of Asia, a points-of-interest page, an index, and a bibliography, as well as patterns for a snow leopard mask, a shadow puppet, a yakko kite, and paper chains. Cultural patterns symbolic of the Japanese, Chinese, Indonesian, and Hmong civilizations are given. This book is an excellent tie-in with the middle school social studies curriculum.

Myers, Christopher A. **Black Cat.**
A confident cat winds its way through Harlem, giving a picture of city life in rhythmic poetry. Photographs serve as a background for the illustrations, with paint layered on top, to give an ominous, yet exciting feeling. Art students will enjoy examining the artwork in this visually exciting book. *See* POETRY.

Nordine, Ken. **Colors.**
Twelve free-wheeling poems depicting unusual shades of several hues (green, yellow, azure, black, lavender, orange, chartreuse, burgundy, flesh, purple, olive, and magenta) come alive with jazzy, colorful pages filled with intriguing detail. This is a true feast for the eyes. *See* POETRY.

Rochelle, Belinda. **Words with Wings: A Treasury of African-American Poetry and Art.**
Twenty poems are paired with art, all of which were created by African Americans. The result is a stunning and emotional anthology. Artists include Jacob Lawrence, Lev T. Mills, Charles Dawson, Robert Scott Duncanson, William H. Johnson, Henry Ossawa Tanner, Hughie Lee-Smith, Romare Bearden, Charles Searles, Elizabeth Catlett, Beauford Delaney, Allan Rohan Crite, Horace Pippin, Augusta Savage, Aaron Douglas, and Emilio Cruz. *See* POETRY.

Rosen, Michael. **Shakespeare: His Work & His World.**
This biography of Shakespeare includes what life was like during his time, the role of the theater, an explanation and sketches of the Globe Theater, summaries of some of his plays, and an extensive time line of his life and work, with ample quotations from his works interspersed throughout the book. The watercolor paintings range from two-page spreads to paintings that run in and through the text. This spectacular work should be explored when performing Shakespeare. *See* BIOGRAPHIES.

Stanley, Diane. **Michelangelo.** New York: HarperCollins, 2000. 48p. $16.00. ISBN 0-688-15086-1, 0-688-15085-3 pa.
Stanley uses the chronology of Michelangelo's life to explain the style, technique and meaning of his sculptures, architecture, and paintings.

Michelangelo had the good fortune to learn sculpting from the stonecutter who had helped to raise him. While working as an artist's apprentice, he was invited to work in the Florence palace of Lorenzo de' Medici, which was a great honor. After Lorenzo's death, Michelangelo worked in Rome. At each stage in his life, he learned new skills, but he was always at the mercy of his sponsor. He really didn't want to do the Sistine Chapel, one of his most famous works, but Pope Julius II insisted. It cost him four long, lonely years. The following years were spent working for leaders of the Catholic church and other patrons, who seldom allowed him to do the work to which he truly aspired. Only in the last years of his life was he able to live without such constraints, and he spent this period with two dear friends, Vittoria Colonna and Tommaso de' Cavalieri, who offered him companionship and true friendship. Stanley depicts each stage of Michelangelo's life with computer-manipulated images of his work, making this an outstanding art piece as well as an informative biography

To Every Thing There Is a Season: Verses from Ecclesiastes. Illus. Leo and Diane Dillon.

Sixteen full- and double-page paintings are used to present the words from Ecclesiastes I: 4 and III: 1–8, adapted from the King James Version of the Bible. Each painting represents a different culture, often from an ancient time, and is done in an art style that best illustrates the culture. Studying this book is like a stroll through an art gallery; a true feast for the eyes and the soul. *See* PICTURE BOOKS FOR ALL AGES.

Temko, Florence. **Traditional Crafts from Africa.** Culture Crafts series. Illus. Randall Gooch, photographs by Robert L. Wolfe and Diane Wolfe. Minneapolis, Minn.: Lerner, 1996. 64p. $18.00. ISBN 0-8225-2936-X.

Eight traditional crafts representing various cultures from Africa are presented with well-organized, easy-to-follow directions. An overview of the importance of crafts from Africa, a simple map, and a list of materials and supplies needed for the projects preface the instructions. Included are directions for Senufo mud paintings, Asante Adinkra stamping, Fon story pictures, Ndbele bead bracelets, Tutsi baskets, the Kigogo game, an Islamic art box, and Guro animal masks. The directions include sketches, diagrams and color photographs, giving them additional clarity. A metric conversion chart, a glossary, a list of further readings, and an index are included.

Temko, Florence. **Traditional Crafts from the Caribbean.** Culture Crafts series. Illus. Randall Gooch. Minneapolis, Minn.: Lerner, 2001. 64p. $18.00. ISBN 0-8225-2937-8.

Temko offers background information on the significance of crafts, a simple map of the Caribbean, a list of materials and supplies, drawings, photographs, and diagrams. A metric conversion chart, a glossary, patterns, a list of further readings, and an index all work together with the step-by-step directions to make this an excellent how-to craft resource. The crafts from the Caribbean include Jamaican woven fish, Puerto Rican *vejigante* mask, tap-tap trucks, yarn dolls, and metal cutouts.

Temko, Florence. **Traditional Crafts from China.** Culture Crafts series. Illus. Randall Gooch. Minneapolis, Minn.: Lerner, 2001. 64p. $18.00. ISBN 0-8225-2939-4.

Temko offers easy-to-follow directions for eight crafts from ancient China in this volume, which also includes information on the importance of crafts in the Chinese culture, a simple map, a list of materials needed for the projects, a metric conversion chart, a list of further readings, a glossary, and an index. The crafts include paper cutouts, dough clay figures, kites, string puppets, needlework purses, wheat straw pictures, and picture scrolls. A section on patterns includes patterns for tangrams, figures used in several of the projects, and Chinese writing characters. The diagrams, sketches, and color photographs help to make the construction of the intricate crafts easy yet involving.

Temko, Florence. **Traditional Crafts from Japan.** Culture Crafts series. Illus. Randall Gooch. Minneapolis, Minn.: Lerner, 2001. 64p. $18.00. ISBN 0-8225-2938-6.

Handicrafts and art projects are a natural extension when studying Japanese culture. The eight projects that Temko describes with step-by-step instructions in this book help students understand and appreciate this culture. A discussion of why crafts are important in Japanese life, a list of materials and supplies, a simple map of Japan, a metric conversion chart, a glossary, a list of further readings and an index add to the usefulness of this book. The projects that Temko describes are *daruma* dolls, *ka-mon* (family crests), *koi nobori* (fish-shaped wind socks), *maneki neko* (welcoming cat figurines), origami cranes, stenciled fabrics, and *tanabata* festival paper decorations. Color photographs, diagrams, and sketches help in the construction of the handicrafts.

Temko, Florence. **Traditional Crafts from Mexico and Central America.** Culture Craft series. Illus. Randall Gooch, photographs by Robert L. Wolfe and Diane Wolfe. Minneapolis: Lerner, 1996. 64p. $18.00. ISBN 0-8225-2935-1.

This multicultural experience gives an explanation of what crafts are and their importance to Mexico and Central America. A list of materials and supplies, a pattern section, a metric conversion chart, a glossary, a bibliography of fiction and nonfiction books pertaining to the crafts, an index, and a map help to make this an effective book. Temko describes how to make tin ornaments, *papel picado* (tissue paper banners, place mats, and tablecloths), Guatemalan weaving, Otomi paper figures, Day of the Dead skeletons, the tree of life (made from clay), Guatemalan worry dolls, and *Cuna molas* (a cloth rectangle stitched with pictures).

Temko, Florence. **Traditional Crafts from Native North America.** Culture Craft series. Illus. Randall Gooch, photographs by Robert L. Wolfe and Diane Wolfe. Minneapolis, Minn.: Lerner, 1997. 64p. $18.00. ISBN 0-8225-2934-3.

This volume is helpful for classes making crafts representative of various Native American tribes. Tribal members still make and use the items described, and the color photographs show modern-day American Indians with these articles. A general section on crafts, followed by a list of materials and supplies, the importance of crafts to Native American tribes, a map of tribal locations, a metric conversion chart, a glossary, a list for further reading, and an index are included. The handicrafts described are Lakota dreamcatchers, Blackfoot beadwork, Iroquois cornhusk dolls, Seminole patchwork, Pueblo storyteller dolls, and Southwestern *cascarones*.

Chapter 5

Greatest of the Latest

Keeping up with the latest in children's literature is exciting yet challenging because of the many new books marketed daily. The fiction titles included in this section are some of the very best published recently. Some of the selections are by our favorite authors, and others showcase new authors, creating a mix of high-quality literature.

Almond, David. **Heaven Eyes.** New York: Delacorte Press, 2001. 233p. $16.00. ISBN 0-385-32770-6.

Erin Law and two fellow orphans, January and Mouse, run away from Whitegates Orphanage, riding down a murky river in England, on a raft made from three old doors loosely tied together. Their raft becomes stranded on a muddy bank, dubbed the Black Middens. They are rescued by an unusual girl, Heaven Eyes, and a man she calls Grampa. The orphans are taken to an abandoned printing house guarded by Grampa. Heaven Eyes speaks in a mystical manner ("I memory little. There is nothing but a deep deep dark."), has webbed fingers and toes, and it's difficult to tell if she's merely a mysterious child, a dream, or a ghost. The time spent at the warehouse is shrouded in mysticism with many surreal encounters with Grampa and Heaven Eyes. The children eventually decide to return to Whitegates, their only "real" home, and Heaven Eyes goes with them. This third work by Almond is dreamlike and surrealistic, but filled with life's lessons concerning life and death, self-discovery, and self-knowledge. This is for older readers ready to handle fantasy, mysticism, and imagery.

Avi. **Don't You Know There's a War On?** New York: HarperCollins, 2001. 200p. $16.00. ISBN 0-380-97863-6, 0-06-029214-8 pa.
   In 1943, Howie's life has changed dramatically because his father is in the merchant marine and his mother works long hours at the navy yard. The war affects most of his classmates and friends, leaving all of them feeling unsettled and powerless. When he overhears a conversation about the firing of his beloved teacher, Miss Gossim, he feels he must find a way to reverse that decision. He has no power to make his father return or his mother to work fewer hours, but perhaps he can have some control over the situation at school. In this humorous yet sad story, Avi gives readers a glimpse of how the children in the United States were affected by World War II. Howie is sixteen years old, looking back on his experiences of five years earlier.

Avi. **Midnight Magic.**
   Ghosts, murder, dark and secret passageways, deceit, and magic all work together in fifteenth century Italy to create a great mystery. Magnus the magician doesn't believe in magic, but reason. However, when he and his young servant, Fabrizio, are summoned to solve a mystery at the king's castle, he pulls out all the stops and uses whatever means he can to unravel a series of strange events. *See* SOCIAL STUDIES—ANCIENT AND EARLY CULTURES.

Bauer, Joan. **Hope Was Here.**
   Hope and her Aunt Addie relocate often because Addie, a cook, moves regularly from job to job. This time, they move from New York to rural Wisconsin, and Hope is sure she'll wilt from culture shock. Instead, she becomes involved with local politics, Addie marries the owner of the restaurant, and everyone learns a great deal about life, love, and politics. Hope's story is told in a delightful, humorous manner. *See* HUMOR.

Blackwood, Gary L. **Shakespeare's Scribe.**
   In this sequel to **The Shakespeare Stealer** (1998) Widge is no longer stealing plays, but acting as Shakespeare's scribe, transcribing what Shakespeare dictates. Widge is also a part of the troupe, learning the ropes of the theater. Blackwood does an excellent job describing life in Elizabethan England, making the reader feel a part of the scene. *See* SOCIAL STUDIES—ANCIENT AND EARLY CULTURES.

Blackwood, Gary L. **The Shakespeare Stealer.**

Fourteen-year-old Widge, an orphan, is hired by a mysterious traveler to use his knowledge of shorthand to copy Shakespeare's new play, *Hamlet.* In Blackwood's book, readers can learn about London during Shakespeare's time, particularly about the Globe Theater. Mystery, intrigue, swashbuckling, and adventure make this terrific historical fiction. *See* SOCIAL STUDIES—ANCIENT AND EARLY CULTURES.

Cooper, Susan. **King of Shadows.**

Nat Field, a member of a summer Shakespeare drama troupe, is transported back in time to become one of Shakespeare's actors. This entertaining adventure provides a great deal of information about Shakespeare and his time. *See* SOCIAL STUDIES—ANCIENT AND EARLY CULTURES.

Creech, Sharon. **Ruby Holler.** New York: Joanna Cotler Books, 2002. 310p. $17.00. ISBN 0-06-027733-5.

Thirteen-year-old twins Dallas and Florida have grown up in an orphanage run by mean-spirited Mr. and Mrs. Trepid. The twins are convinced they're clumsy, stupid, and unlovable. They were placed in various foster homes, each one with disastrous results. They fantasize about running away on the night train, but this fantasy doesn't materialize because they have no money and no place to go. An elderly, loving and affectionate couple, Sairy and Tiller, who live in Ruby Holler, take them as temporary companions to accompany them on separate adventures. Time, patience, home-cooked food, and love prove to the twins that Sairy and Tiller really care for them and that leaving on the night train won't be necessary. The book is filled with humor, adventure, mischief, mystery, and good will, making this an entertaining read. It gives the reader a satisfied, calm, and fulfilled feeling.

Curtis, Christopher Paul. **Bud, Not Buddy.** New York: Delacorte Press, 1999. 245p. $16.00. ISBN 0-385-32306-9, 0-440-41328-1 pa.

Bud Caldwell's mother died when he was six, leaving him with a suitcase filled with secret things: a list of "Bud Caldwell's Rules and Things for Having a Funner Life and Making a Better Liar out of Yourself" and a poster of Herman E. Calloway's jazz band. After enduring four miserable years of foster families and orphanages, he decides he needs to be on his own and locate the man on the poster, who he thinks is his father. The ten-year-old's journey from Flint, Michigan, to Grand Rapids, Michigan, is filled with pitfalls, but he never gives up because he has his rules to live by. He does find the band, but Mr. Calloway is not pleased to have him around until he makes the connection about who Bud's mother was. The story portrays a spunky boy who insists on being called Bud, rather than Buddy, because his mother had emphasized that he was too important to have a nickname. This spunk and determination, combined with a dose of naivete and innocence, set during the Depression era, make this an engrossing and memorable story. Curtis has talent for exaggerating characters and situations, yet keeping the story believable. The afterword tells that some of the characters are based on real people, including his grandfathers, which helps to give the story its rich blend of danger, humor, sadness, and eventual happiness. This work is the winner of the Newbery Award (2000) and the Coretta Scott King Award (2000).

Cushman, Karen. **Matilda Bone.**

Matilda, an orphan, is sent to serve the town's local bonesetter, Red Peg. Matilda has no interest in or knowledge of medical practices during the fourteenth century and prefers to call on the saints for answers. The author does an excellent job describing medical knowledge of the Middle Ages. *See* SOCIAL STUDIES—ANCIENT AND EARLY CULTURES.

DiCamillo, Kate. **Because of Winn-Dixie.** Cambridge, Mass.: Candlewick, 2000. 182p. $16.00. ISBN 0-7636-0776-2, 0-7636-1605-2 pa.

Ten-year old India Opal's father is a minister, recently transferred to Naomi, Florida. Opal befriends a scruffy dirty dog at the Winn-Dixie grocery store and takes him home, against her father's wishes. Opal calls the dog Winn-Dixie. With the help of this unusual dog and his crazy antics, Opal meets a variety of unique people, and her loneliness begins to fade. Still, she has a desire to know about her mother, who left when she was very young. Her father has never recovered from this loss and tells Opal little about her mother. When Winn-Dixie disappears during a storm, Opal and her father search frantically for him, but her father gives up. This gives Opal the opportunity to give her father a pep talk about giving up and loss and causes him to open up and share more about her mother. This small novel is upbeat, funny and filled with well-developed characters. It won the Newbery Honor Award in 2001.

DiCamillo, Kate. **The Tiger Rising.** Cambridge, Mass.: Candlewick, 2001. 116p. $13.00. ISBN 0-7636-0911-0.

After Rob's mother dies, both he and his father bottle up their grief, move to Florida, and live in the Kentucky Star Motel, existing on boxed macaroni and cheese. "Rob had a way of not-thinking about things." He imagines he has stuffed all his feelings into a suitcase and has "locked it shut." He is mercilessly bullied at school and is as unhappy as an angry new girl who starts school, Sistine (named for the chapel). She also lives in Florida against her will and is sure her father will arrive soon to take her away. When Rob discovers a caged tiger hidden in the woods, he shares his secret with Sistine and Willie May, the motel's housekeeper, because they all can understand being trapped in situations against their will. The tiger becomes a symbol of Rob's caged emotions and feelings. With the help of his new friends and by freeing the tiger, Rob begins to have a new feeling, one he remembers as happiness. Words are used sparingly in this brief novel, but it is packed with emotion and feeling.

Fleischman, Paul. **Mind's Eye.** New York: Henry Holt, 1999. 108p. $16.00. ISBN 0-8050-6314-5, 0-440-22901-4pa.

At age sixteen, Courtney is paralyzed after an accident. She is confined in a nursing home, feeling intense anger and helplessness. Her roommates are May, an aging Alzheimer's patient, and Elva, a retired teacher with failing eyesight. Elva devises an imaginary trip to Italy using a 1910 guidebook. Courtney becomes Elva's eyes, and using fantasy and art, Elva becomes Courtney's escape . The power of imagination begins to give new meaning to Courtney's life. Several quotes stress the power and pleasure of reading. This small, powerful book is inspiring and uplifting, a true treasure. Told entirely in dialogue, it can be used as reader's theater or to stage a dramatic production.

Haddix, Margaret Peterson. **Among the Impostors.** New York: Simon & Schuster , 2001. 172p. $15.00. ISBN 0-689-83904-9.

In this sequel to **Among the Hidden** (1998, discussed in Chapter 12), Luke, a third child in a future world that permits families to have no more than two, has assumed a new identity and enters the Hendricks School for Boys. He is hazed and harassed by the other students, and the teachers make his life miserable, but he is determined to understand the mysterious workings at this school. He discovers that other "hidden children" attend this school, and they are just as frightened and bewildered as he is. Fans of **Among the Hidden** will want to continue with Luke (now Lee) on his quest for freedom.

Haddix, Margaret Peterson. **Turnabout.**

Melly and Anny Beth are one hundred years old, living in a nursing home when they are given the opportunity take a serum that will reverse aging. Going backward in age gives them the opportunity to right some mistakes they made the first time around, but as they become teenagers in 2085, they begin to worry about who will be their caretaker as they become younger. This fast-paced science fiction novel brings out the moral dilemmas involved with cloning, genetics, scientific experimentation, aging, and immortality. *See* SCIENCE.

Hesse, Karen. **Witness: A Novel.**

This unusual novel, written as a five-act play, in free verse, about the Ku Klux Klan's infiltration in a small town in Vermont in 1924, will best be understood by students if it is read aloud to them or presented as reader's theater. *See* UNIQUE PRESENTATIONS.

Hobbs, Will. **Down the Yukon**.

Sixteen-year-old Jason Hawthorn and his girlfriend, Jamie, participate in the Great Race across Alaska in an attempt to win the $20,000 prize money. Excitement and adventure await them around every bend of the Yukon River. *See* SCIENCE.

Hobbs, Will. **Jason's Gold.**

Jason Hawthorne and his brothers, Abe and Ethan, join the Alaskan gold rush frenzy in 1897. Jason misses them in Seattle and has to make his way to Dawson City by himself. With the help of his trusty dog, King, he encounters and triumphs over numerous difficulties while hiking the Dead Horse Trail and the Chilkoot Pass. *See* SCIENCE.

Hobbs, Will. **The Maze**.

A teenager in trouble with the justice system runs away and ends up in Canyonlands National Park (Utah) in an area called the Maze. Rick meets a biologist who is raising condor chicks and preparing them for release into the wild. Two thieves intent on killing Lon, the biologist, bring mystery and suspense to this action-packed page-turner. Hobbs gives us a good dose of adventure as well as a look at hang gliding and condors. *See* SCIENCE.

Holt, Kimberly Willis. **Dancing in Cadillac Light.** New York: G.P. Putnam's Sons, 2001. 167p. $16.00. ISBN 0-399-23402-0.

Eleven-year-old Jaynell's grandfather moves in with her family after grandma dies and Grandpap seems confused and senile. It's Jaynell's job to keep an eye on him as he wanders all over the area, visiting grandma's grave and various neighbors and stores. The setting is Moon, Texas, in 1968, the year man first walked on the moon. Written in southern dialect, Holt presents the social structure of a small southern town, as well as the foods, the way of life, the values, and the struggles of the time. Many offbeat characters are introduced into the story, which makes Grandpap's confusion seem almost normal. Jaynell is fiercely loyal to Grandpap, even when he buys an emerald green Cadillac and gives his home to a "white trash" family, throwing his own family into a frenzy. The story is unusual and gives readers a peek into that time and place.

Holt, Kimberly Willis. **My Louisiana Sky.** New York: Henry Holt, 1998. 200p. $16.00. ISBN 0-8050-5251-8, 0-440-41570-5pa.

Tiger Ann has always known her parents are a little "different," but the summer before seventh grade, her comfortable life in the 1950s Louisiana countryside changes dramatically. The girls in her school don't want anything to do with her because of her retarded parents, her best buddy, Jesse Wade, changes their friendship by kissing her, and her strong and loving Granny, who has always managed the household, suddenly dies. Tiger is faced with being her parent's keeper, either taking Granny's place or moving to Baton Rouge to live with her successful Aunt Dorrie. The author presents a sticky dilemma, but Tiger sorts things out and comes to the decision that is right for her. This lovely coming-of-age story moves gracefully, much like the dialogue of the people.

Holt, Kimberly Willis. **When Zachary Beaver Came to Town.** New York: Henry Holt, 1999. 227p. $16.00. ISBN 0-8050-6116-9, 0-440-22904-9pa.

   Antler, Texas, is the most boring place on earth according to thirteen-year-old Toby Wilson, until a trailer pulls into town carrying Zachary Beaver, "the fattest boy in the world." At first, Zachary is a novelty, and Toby joins the crowd, willing to pay $2.00 to get a peek at the 643-pound boy. After Zachary's guardian abandons him, however, Toby and his friend Cal begin to take care of him. Zachary is no longer a novelty, but they get to know him as a sad, lonely boy in need of friends. The story deals with topics of friendship, prejudice, self-acceptance, and compassion, plus a sprinkling of light-heartedness and humor.

Jiménez, Francisco. **Breaking Through.**

   This sequel to **The Circuit** (1999) begins with the Jiménez family being deported by *la migra* because the parents don't have proper visas. This humiliating experience prompts Francisco to work even harder to succeed at school, to work to help support the family, to maintain his Hispanic culture, and to "fit in" to the American social scene. He set his sights very high, but thanks to the encouragement and guidance from teachers and counselors, he succeeds. *See* MULTICULTURAL.

Jiménez, Francisco. **The Circuit: Stories from the Life of a Migrant Child.**

   Twelve short stories chronicle the author's early life as a child in a migrant worker's family in California. The family experiences poverty, illness, constant mobility, prejudice, and never-ending hard work, but they also have a sense of hope and a belief that through honesty and diligence, their lives will improve. This inspiring story needs to be shared with all children, but especially children in English as a second language classes who are struggling to succeed. *See* MULTICULTURAL

Konigsburg, E. L. **Silent to the Bone.** New York: Atheneum Children's Books, 2000. 261p. $16.00. ISBN 0-689-83601-5, 0-689-83602-3pa.

   Branwell's baby sister, Nikki, has been dropped and is in a coma. The babysitter indicates Branwell did it, and he's jailed. This trauma causes Branwell to become mute, and he's unable to defend himself. His loyal friend, Connor, visits Bran daily in the detention center and is convinced of Bran's innocence. Connor plays detective to try to discover who was really responsible. After patiently trying every possible means of getting Bran to speak, Connor realizes that because of their strong friendship, they don't need to speak to communicate. Connor devises a system of flash cards and blinking, and communication begins. The deep friendship between the boys, the family dynamics, and the mystery all combine to make this one of Konigsburg's best.

Lawrence, Iain. **Lord of the Nutcracker Men.** New York: Delacorte Press, 2001. 212p. $16.00. ISBN 0-385-90024-4.

Ten-year-old Johnny's father is a toy maker who often whittles toy military men for his son. These are great fun until World War I breaks out and Johnny's father goes to serve in the British army in France. Johnny is sent to live with Auntie Ivy, his father's sister, in a small town away from the bombing in London. He hates his new situation and plays endlessly with his military men. His father sends letters on a regular basis and always includes a new toy soldier. The first letters and soldiers are easygoing and jovial, but as the war progresses, the letters are more and more depressing, and the toys reflect the horrors of the war. Johnny is convinced that what happens with his men during his play will actually happen on the battlefield. He blames himself when his friend Sara's father is killed in battle. The battles become too real, and he finally packs the men into a box and hides them under his bed for four years until his father comes home. Two other subplots, one involving his teacher, Mr. Tuttle, and the other a deserter named Murdoch, are integrated into the story. Both stories further point out the horrors of war. The story is based on Lawrence's grandfather and three great-uncles who served in the Great War "that killed millions, and crippled millions more." This well-researched tale, told in the first person, is intense and filled with emotion, but it teaches a great deal about World War I.

Lawrence, Iain. **The Buccaneers.** High Seas Trilogy, Book 3. New York: Random House, 2001. 244p. $16.00. ISBN 0-385-90008-2.

In this sequel to **The Smugglers** (1999), Sixteen-year-old John Spencer sails *The Dragon*, to the Caribbean to bring back sugar and other valuable cargo. Early in the voyage, the crew saves a strange man floating aimlessly in the sea. The man seldom talks about his past, but little by little his story unfolds to reveal a cruel story of pirates. Spencer's voyage encounters fierce storms, illness, and buccaneers, making this a high-seas adventure filled with mystery and intrigue.

Lawrence, Iain. **The Smugglers.** High Seas Trilogy, Book 2. New York: Delacorte, 1999. 183p. $16.00. ISBN 0-385-32663-7, 0-440-41596-9pa.

John Spencer has been selected to be the representative of his father's shipping firm on a voyage to bring wool from Kent to London on the newly purchased schooner, *The Dragon*. John and his crew are told that mystery surrounds the schooner—it had been used for smuggling. It seems what they heard is true, for even before they set sail, John's father is shot, but survives, and the captain is murdered. A Captain Crowe is hired, but they're not far into the voyage before John discovers that many of the crew, including the captain, are scalawags, not to be trusted. After many adventures, John accomplishes his journey, only to agree to set sail in a month for the Indies. As in **The Wreckers** (1998), Lawrence creates a fast-paced adventure filled with well-developed characters. The work is based on well-researched historical facts as noted in the author's notes section.

Lawrence, Iain, **The Wreckers.** High Seas Trilogy, Book 1. New York: Delacorte Press, 1998. 196p. $16.00. ISBN 0-385-32535-5, 0-440-41545-4pa.

One of the most exciting adventure series to come along in the last few years is Lawrence's High Seas Trilogy. In this first book, fourteen-year-old John Spencer of London sets sail on his father's merchant ship, the *Isle of Skye*. They encounter a ferocious storm near Cornwall and head for what looks like a safe shore. Unfortunately, the ship wrecks on the shoals. John manages to get ashore, but what he discovers—to his horror—is that the townspeople shine lights on the dangerous shore, making the crew think it's safe. The ships are wrecked, and the townspeople make their living looting the cargo of lost ships. When John witnesses a surviving shipmate murdered by the townspeople, he understands his life is in danger and thus begins a fast-paced chase. Various people befriend him, but John never knows whom he can trust. John uses his wits to outsmart the villains and in the process discovers his father is alive and being held prisoner. There are few dull moments in this fast-moving mystery, adventure, and survival story. Lawrence bases this work on historical fact, which he describes in the author's notes at the back of the book.

Levine, Gail Carson. **Dave at Night.** New York: HarperCollins, 1999. 281p. $16.00. ISBN 0-06-28154-5, 0-06-440747-0pa.

When Dave's father dies in 1926, Dave is sent to the Hebrew Home for Boys. He despises the place because of the cruelty and lack of caring of those who work there. He vows to escape as soon as he recovers an intricate carving made by his father that the headmaster has stolen from him. He discovers a way to climb the wall at night and meets a host of artists, authors, and musicians—all involved in the Harlem Renaissance. They want him to stay with them, but he returns every night because he still does not have his carving and because he's formed a close bond with the other boys. His new adult friends help to change the orphanage, thus giving Dave the best of both worlds. Readers will become familiar with New York City during the 1920s and come to appreciate the artistic energy of the time.

Lisle, Janet Taylor. **The Art of Keeping Cool.**

After Robert's father is sent to fight in Europe during World War II, his family moves to Rhode Island to live with his father's parents. As this multifaceted story unfolds, Robert begins to understand the family dynamics and his friendship with a German painter and hermit shows him the horrors of prejudice. The story is powerful and important. *See* SOCIAL STUDIES—UNITED STATES HISTORY.

Lowry, Lois. **Gathering Blue.** Boston: Houghton Mifflin, 2000. 215p. $15.00. ISBN 0-618-05581-9.

Kira's world of the future is almost medieval, filled with violence, bleakness, anger, and hostility. Kira has a deformed leg, which usually results in abandonment by the community. After her mother's death, however, the Council of Guardians votes to allow her to live because of her unusual skill at embroidery. She is sent to live at the Council Edifice and given the honorable job of Threader; her task is to repair and embellish the robe worn once a year by the Singer, the person who recounts the history of the community. While she and another resident of the Edifice, Thomas, a carver, live in luxury, they are actually prisoners and can only do the bidding of the Council. She knows her work would be even better if she had blue thread, so she enlists her friend Matt to go out into the world to look for it. To her surprise, he brings back her father, who she thought was dead. Her father helps her to understand more fully how evil the community is. She has the opportunity to go back with her father to the safe healing community he has discovered, but she decides it is her duty to use her gifts to bring about change so the two communities can become one. This powerful story is bleak, overwhelmingly so at times, but it also portrays hope, change, and enlightenment.

Myers, Walter Dean. **Monster.** Illus. Christopher Myers. New York: HarperCollins, 1999. 281p. $15.00. ISBN 0-06-028077-8, 0-06-028070-6, 0-06-028078-6, 0-06440731-4pa.

While awaiting trial for a murder he claims he didn't commit, teenager Steve Harmon tells the story of his arrest and his life as an inner-city black male. Steve uses handwritten journal entries to depict life in prison and his own troubled past. He is ultimately acquitted of murder, but moral issues abound, making this book more appropriate for seventh grade and older. Written as a movie screenplay, it includes directions and dialogue. This powerful book won the Newbery Honor Award and the Coretta Scott King Award and was a finalist for the National Book Award in 2000.

Paulsen, Gary. **Alida's Song.** New York: Delacorte Press, 1999. 88p. $16.00. ISBN 0-385-32586-X, 0-440-4147-1pa.

In this semibiographical novella, Paulsen revisits the grandmother in **The Cookcamp** (1991). The boy, now fourteen, needs to be rescued from his abusive parents, so grandma requests that he come to work on the Minnesota farm where she cooks for two Norwegian bachelor brothers. Through hard work, money paid to him by Olaf and Gunnar, and grandma's warmth, love, and understanding, the boy is able to pull his life together. He writes this story as an adult, revisiting the memories of the best summer of his life. After grandma's death, he discovers a letter in a cigar box telling that "each Saturday his grandmother had handed Olaf eighteen dollars to give to the boy so that her grandson would think he was working for pay." Paulsen's love for the outdoors and his deep appreciation to those who helped him during his difficult childhood are brought together in this stirring book.

Paulsen, Gary. **Brian's Return.**

Brian, from **Hatchet** (1987), **The River** (1991), and **Brian's Winter** (1996), is having a difficult time adjusting to normal high school life. With the help of a counselor, he decides to gather supplies and gear and return to the wild. This is not an adventure book, but one of self-discovery. *See* SCIENCE.

Paulsen, Gary. **Soldier's Heart: A Novel of the Civil War.**

Fifteen-year-old Charley Goddard volunteers to fight for the North, convinced he can make a difference. He soon experiences the stark realities of war. Charley tells his own story in simple, matter-of-fact language, allowing the story to flow. After severe injuries suffered at Gettysburg, Charley goes home, never to fully recover—either physically or mentally. The author's note tells about the actual Charley and the outcome of his life. This is a must for all students studying the Civil War. *See* SOCIAL STUDIES—UNITED STATES HISTORY.

Peck, Richard. **A Long Way from Chicago: A Novel in Stories.** New York: Dial Books for Young Readers, 1998. 148p. $16.00. ISBN 0-8037-2290-7, 0-14-130352-2pa.

As an adult, Joe is able to look back on the seven summers, from 1929 to 1935, when he and his younger sister, Mary Alice, leave Chicago and go by train to live with their Grandma Dowdel. As children, Joey and Mary Alice didn't always understand their Grandma, but as he ages, he appreciates her outrageous behavior. Grandma wants to keep to herself, which is difficult to do in a small town, but when she really needs something or sees an injustice being committed, she uses every means possible to make things right. Each of the seven chapters, one for each summer, tells a story of Grandma using her wit, even if it calls for cheating, trespassing, and conniving to solve a problem. The first story has her playing a trick on a reporter and her worst enemy, Effie Wilcox, by bringing a corpse into her house and making it look as though the body is moving. In "A One-Woman Crime Wave, 1931," the Great Depression is well depicted, with Grandma feeding the drifters even though the town fathers forbid it. The irreverence and the humor, along with easygoing language, make this an excellent book to read aloud. It won the Newbery Honor Award in 1999.

Peck, Richard. **A Year Down Yonder.** New York: Dial Books for Young Readers, 2000. 130p. $17.00. ISBN 0-8037-2518-3.

    In this sequel to **A Long Way from Chicago** (1998), fifteen-year-old Mary Alice is sent to live with Grandma Dowdel for an entire year because her parents are struggling with the 1937 recession. At this age, Mary Alice is appalled and embarrassed at her grandmother's eccentric ways, and having to attend the small-town high school is almost more than she can bear. As each story unfolds, however, Mary begins to join in the high jinks and appreciates Grandma despite her gruffness and shameless tactics. Several of the stories center around holidays. Grandma doesn't have any pumpkins or pecans in her garden, but that doesn't keep them from making a midnight raid and gleaning what they need from the neighbors to make delicious pies. Grandma makes the most of a Veteran's Day celebration by overcharging for the drinks she sells, then gives all the proceeds to Mrs. Abernathy, whose son was severely injured in World War I. At Christmastime Grandma manages to have a tree and greenery, thanks to another midnight raid. Washington's birthday is celebrated with Grandma playing a trick on the venerable ladies from the Daughters of the Revolution by serving spiked punch along with the cherry tarts. Each vignette has hardhearted Grandma demonstrating hidden kindness. This marvelous collection of stories won the Newbery Award in 2001.

Rees, Celia. **Witch Child.**

    Mary Newbury's life in the New World is told through her journal entries from 1659 to 1660. She has special powers that she hides to prevent being branded a witch and suffering persecution. Excellent information about witchcraft is given, along with a picture of life in Massachusetts in the 1650s. *See* SOCIAL STUDIES—UNITED STATES HISTORY.

Salisbury, Graham. **Lord of the Deep.** New York: Delacorte Press, 2001. 182p. $16.00. ISBN 0-385-72918-9, 0-385-90013-9 lib. bdg.

    At age thirteen, Mikey is now able to work as a deckhand on his stepfather's charter fishing boat, the *Crystal-C,* in Hawaii. Money is always tight because Mikey's little brother has extensive health problems that create enormous medical bills, so Mikey is happy to work for no pay. Also, he loves and respects his stepfather, Bill, and wants to please him. All is well until two obnoxious men, Cal and Ernie, hire Bill and his boat for three days to catch marlin. On the first day a marlin is snagged but manages to escape because Mikey handles the boat incorrectly. The second day a prize-winning one is caught, but technically Cal and Ernie can't claim the prize because they didn't do all the work to reel it in. They bribe Bill to say they did it all, and Mikey is included in this moral dilemma. The story is fast-paced, and the waters around Hawaii are described so well that the reader feels like a passenger on the boat.

Taylor, Mildred D. **The Land.** New York: P. Fogelman, 2001. 375p. $18.00. ISBN 0-8037-1950-7.

   This prequel to **Roll of Thunder, Hear My Cry** (1976) takes us back to the Civil War and the Reconstruction. Paul Edward Logan, the grandfather of Cassie from **Roll of Thunder,** is the son of a wealthy landowner and his slave and companion, who is part Indian and part black. Paul was raised with his siblings from the white family, and his father taught him to read and write. Even so, he was never totally a part of white society, but he didn't fit in with black people because of his education and light color. His bitter enemy is Mitchell Thomas, a black neighbor. After many battles, the boys come to a truce and eventually become best friends. After a heartbreaking incident that further underscores the difficulty of being neither black nor white, he breaks with the white family and heads out to fulfill his dream— to own land. He and Mitchell have many adventures working for whoever will hire them. He finally settles in Mississippi to work as a furniture maker and horse trainer to save money for his land. He finds the exact piece of land he wants and strikes a deal with the landowner to clear the land as partial payment. He and Mitchell work nearly day and night to meet the deadline, but in the end, the landowner refuses to honor the contract because of Paul's race. After a series of difficulties, he does obtain a perfect piece of land. This outstanding work is historically correct, based on the true saga of Mildred Taylor's great-grandfather, which she discusses in the author's note at the end of the book. Paul's story of fierce determination to succeed despite his constant experiences with racial hatred and bigotry makes this a powerful work. It is the winner of the 2002 Coretta Scott King Award.

Taylor, Theodore. **A Sailor Returns.** New York: Blue Sky Press, 160p. $17.00. ISBN 0-439-24879-5, 0439-24880-9pa.

   Evan's father pays little attention to him, and his mother is expecting a new baby. So when word comes that his grandfather—who hasn't been heard from in thirty years—is coming to visit, Evan is elated. He and his seventy-year-old grandfather, Tom, begin to bond immediately when they go fishing, then build a boat, and, best of all, when Tom tells stories about his seafaring days. Evan has a club foot and grandfather limps because of an old sailing accident, which adds to their closeness. Evan's father is furious that Tom would reappear after deserting his wife when she was a young child, but Evan's mother is overjoyed to regain the father she never knew. Family tension abounds, especially when grandfather is accused of murder. The murder is solved, father comes out looking good, and Tom leaves, knowing he has been forgiven and has gained a very special bond with his grandson.

Werlin, Nancy. **Black Mirror.** New York: Dial Books for Young Readers, 2001. 250p. $17.00. ISBN 0-8037-2605-8.

Frances has draped her dormitory mirror with a black scarf because her brother, Daniel, committed suicide, and she partly blames herself for not realizing he had been in such deep despair. In his memory, she joins the Unity Service, a charitable group in which Daniel had been an active member. Through a series of mysteries and adventures at the private boarding school, Pettengill, she discovers that Unity is really a front for a widespread drug ring, and that Daniel was gathering information for the FBI. The head of the operation, Patrick Leyden, a wealthy philanthropist, discovered Daniel's plans and had him killed. The path to Frances's discoveries is filled with heart-stopping twists and turns—just the thing that mystery lovers will devour.

Whelan, Gloria. **Homeless Bird.**

Thirteen-year-old Koly is left a "homeless bird" after the death of her sixteen-year-old husband. She cannot return to her family and is not welcome at her in-law's home. She is abandoned in a holy city, where she meets a widow who recognizes her embroidery talents, and Koly makes a new life for herself. Set in modern-day India, the author offers insight into Hindu customs and daily life. *See* MULTICULTURAL.

Zindel, Paul. **The Gadget.**

Stephen leaves London to escape the bombings in 1944 and goes to Los Alamos, New Mexico, to live with his father who is doing research on "the gadget." Security is very tight, and his father is mysteriously quiet about his work. Stephen and another boy living in the compound do some research and discover that the scientists are working on the atomic bomb. Readers will find the chronology of important events of World War II and the making of the atomic bomb sections helpful in understanding the topic. Mini-biographies of some of the people associated with the bomb are included at the back of the book, as is a bibliography. *See* SOCIAL STUDIES—UNITED STATES HISTORY.

Chapter 6

Humor

We all need a little humor in our lives, which is exactly what the books in this section provide. Students often ask for a "funny" book, and this isn't always easy to find. This section collects some old favorites along with new works to make us chuckle and smile.

Bauer, Joan. **Hope Was Here.** New York: G. P. Putnam's Sons, 2000. 186p. $17.00. ISBN 0-399-23142-0.

Every time sixteen-year old Hope and her aunt Addie leave a city to move to a new part of the country, she writes "Hope Was Here" somewhere, to make the statement that she'd been there. Aunt Addie, a cook, adopted her when she was little, and her life has been a succession of moves from restaurant to restaurant, city to city. Their latest adventure takes them to southern Wisconsin, where they put down some roots by becoming involved with the local town politics. The restaurant's owner, G. T. Stoop, enters the mayoral race, even though he suffers from leukemia, because he wants to stop local corruption and restore honesty to the town. Aunt Addie and G. T. fall in love and get married; Hope learns a great deal about life, love, work, and politics—all in a humorous manner. Joan Bauer is a master at dealing with a serious topic with humor and fun, making her work a true delight. It's easy to see why this won the Newbery Honor in 2001.

Katz, Alan. **Take Me out of the Bathtub and Other Silly Dilly Songs.** Illus. David Catrow. New York: M. K. McElderry Books, 2001. 29p. $15.00. ISBN 0-689-82903-5.

    Outlandish, hilarious words have been set to fourteen well-known tunes, creating a ludicrous and "silly dilly" collection. The title song, "Take Me out of the Bathtub!" is a new rendition of "Take Me out to the Ballgame." "I've Been Cleaning up my Bedroom" is done to the tune of "I've Been Working on the Railroad." Laughter and giggles are inescapable with "Stinky, Stinky Diaper Change" done to the tune of "Twinkle, Twinkle, Little Star." Parents will get the last laugh with "Go, Go, Go to Bed," a reworking of "Row, Row, Row Your Boat." "Rock-a-bye Baby," now known as "Sock in the Gravy," begins "Sock in the gravy / Glove in the soup / Tie in the meat loaf / And here's a scoop . . . / If you don't like clothes in your baked beans / Don't cook your food in washing machines!" The illustrations are as wacky as the lyrics, with full-page, action-packed, odd-looking characters acting out the crazy songs. These will make perfect camp songs or liven up the classroom when humor is needed.

Marshall, James. **Swine Lake.** Illus. Maurice Sendak. New York: HarperCollins, 1999. 40p. $16.00. ISBN 0-06-205172-5.

    Combine Marshall's writing and Sendak's illustrations in a spoof involving pigs and a wolf, and you have a winner. The wolf sees an ad for the Boarshoi Ballet doing Swine Lake at the Hamsterdam Theater. He's determined to get into the performance, where he plans to jump onto the stage and have a large tasty lunch. He breaks open his piggy bank, buys a ticket, goes into the theater disguised in a cloak and becomes so enthralled with the pigs' performance, he completely forgets about lunch and spontaneously jumps onto the stage to join the troupe in the grand finale. The newspaper reviews rave about the special guest appearance stealing the show, which causes the wolf to "execute a couple of flashy dance steps." The text is hysterical, and the illustrations perfectly express the craziness. This is in picture-book format, but the humor is better suited to older kids.

Park, Barbara. **Almost Starring Skinnybones.** New York: Random House, 1999. 108p. $10.00. ISBN 0-394-82591-8pa.

    If you enjoyed meeting and laughing with Alex Frankovitch in **Skinnybones** (1997), this sequel will find a welcome audience. Alex is back, with the same wit and humor that helped him deal with life's problems in the previous book. This time, he is convinced he'll become a television star because he's won a cat food contest, giving him the opportunity to make a commercial. In typical Alex style, he goofs everything up, and his fan club attracts only two members. This book was first published in 1988, but it has the same lasting qualities as its predecessor, making it a favorite of students in grades four through six.

Park, Barbara. **Skinnybones.** New York: Random House, 1997. 111p. $10.00. ISBN 0-679-88792-Xpa.

Twelve-year-old Alex Frankovitch's biggest dream is to be a great baseball player. Unfortunately, he's lousy at the game and ends up winning the Most Improved award each year, which shows him just how bad he really is. His sense of humor in dealing with his lack of athletic talents helps him to cope with everything in his life, including the school bully. The short, fast-paced chapters will have the reader laughing out loud as Alex relates his everyday life in a hilarious fashion. This was first published in 1982 but has lasting qualities because students can relate to and sympathize with Alex and his predicaments.

Paulsen, Gary. **Guts: The True Stories Behind Hatchet and the Brian Books.**

Gary Paulsen displays his extensive knowledge of nature in this autobiographical work describing the real-life incidents that shaped Brian's adventures in **Hatchet** (1987) and the other Brian books. Paulsen's descriptions are told with great humor, often taking a serious and dangerous situation and looking at it in a light vein. One of the funniest scenes is in chapter 1, when Paulsen and his dogs are being rescued in a small airplane that's having problems taking off because of the weight. His description of repeatedly throwing the dogs to the front of the plane is not to be missed. *See* BIOGRAPHIES.

Paulsen, Gary. **Harris and Me: A Summer Remembered.** San Diego, Calif.: Harcourt Brace, 1993. 157p. $15.00. ISBN 0-15-292877-4, 0-440-40994-2pa.

If you're looking for humor for secondary students, this is the funniest book in the library. In this autobiographical tale, Paulsen relates his experiences from the summer he lived with his aunt and uncle and their two children, Glennis and Harris. Nine-year-old Harris is rude and crude—a natural troublemaker filled with wild and crazy ideas. He and Paulsen team up to perform one hilarious antic after another. The ample supply of "hells" and "damns," references to French postcards, and serious injury to Harris's "business" makes this a book for older students. It was first printed in 1993 but is timeless and will never be outdated.

Peck, Richard. **A Long Way from Chicago: A Novel in Stories.**

The antics of an eccentric grandmother are told by the grandson, Joe, now an adult. For seven summers he and his sister, Mary Alice, lived with Grandma Dowdel, the zaniest grandmother imaginable. The entertaining and often irreverent stories are told in an easygoing, humorous manner. *See* GREATEST OF THE LATEST.

Peck, Richard. **A Year Down Yonder.**

At age fifteen, Mary Alice's parents send her to stay with nonconforming Grandma Dowdel for an entire year. What she thought was a fate worse than death turns out to be an opportunity to learn that Grandma is an eccentric treasure, who teaches life's lessons in unique ways. Wit, humor, and vivid descriptions make this a fun read. *See* GREATEST OF THE LATEST.

Prelutsky, Jack. **Awful Ogre's Awful Day.**
Eighteen ghoulish, macabre, hysterically funny poems follow Awful the Ogre through his day, from the time he gets up to his bedtime when he has the nightmare that everything is peaceful, beautiful, and calm. *See* POETRY.

Prelutsky, Jack. **The Gargoyle on the Roof: Poems.**
Every scary creature imaginable can be found in this collection of seventeen poems. Trolls, gremlins, griffins, goblins, gargoyles, vampires, werewolves, and bugaboos all show up to create scary, humorous fun. *See* POETRY.

San Souci, Robert D. **Cinderella Skeleton.**
Many versions of Cinderella are on the market now, but this one, written in rhyme, takes place in a graveyard. Cinderella and the entire cast of characters, including the prince, are skeletons. It's macabre, gruesome, and very funny. Middle-schoolers love it! *See* MYTHS, FOLKTALES, AND LEGENDS.

Snicket, Lemony. **The Bad Beginning, The Reptile Room, The Wide Window, The Miserable Mill, The Austere Academy, The Ersatz Elevator, The Vile Village, The Hostile Hospital.**
Each title is an episode in the Series of Unfortunate Events series, which features the three Baudelaire children who are orphaned after the tragic and sudden death of their parents. Count Olaf, a distant cousin is after their money, so each episode involves the desire on the part of the children to find a home, yet escape the clutches of the evil Olaf. The stories are told in a tongue-in-cheek manner, in a Roald Dahl vein. *See* SERIES.

Van Draanen, Wendelin. **Flipped.** New York: Alfred A. Knopf, 2001. 212p. $15.00. ISBN 0-375-91174-X.
Bryce Loski and Juli Baker first met when Bryce moved into Juli's neighborhood when they were second graders. Juli thinks he's wonderful, and Bryce despises her. They carry on this love–hate relationship until eighth grade, when, through a series of incidents, they see each other differently. Juli begins to see Bryce's faults and shortcomings, and Bryce sees Juli's worthy strong points. They take a fresh look at each other, begin an entirely new relationship, and end up falling for each other. Each episode is first told from Bryce's point of view and then Juli's, so it's fun to see each person's perspective on the same event. There are some serious episodes involving family relationships that help them rediscover each other, but most of the episodes are very funny, making this a sure winner that teenagers can relate to.

Wiesner, David. **The Three Pigs.**

In this hilarious fractured fairy tale, the three pigs escape the wolf with the help of nursery rhyme and fairy-tale characters. The reader needs to know the original stories and nursery rhymes to understand the humor, making this appropriate for the secondary level. *See* MYTHS, FOLKTALES, AND LEGENDS.

Chapter 7

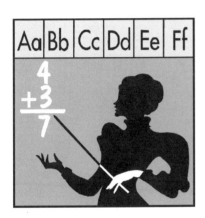

Mathematics

The true meaning of mathematics is best realized in real-life situations rather than through worksheets filled with computational problems. Each book in this section presents mathematics using practical applications, often to explore a specific concept. Some entries show the importance and uses of mathematics throughout time. The following books, often done with humor, will help teach concepts and add spark and excitement when exploring mathematics.

Adler, David A. **How Tall, How Short, How Faraway.** Illus. Nancy Tobin. New York: Holiday House, 1999. 32p. $16.00. ISBN 0-8234-1375-6.

  Measuring makes sense when presented in this colorful and delightful book. The first portion of the book gives the history of measurement and tells how our present-day measurements evolved from the ancient Egyptians and the Romans. Hands-on activities are included, encouraging readers to use the information described. The second half explains the customary and metric systems of measurement, how they evolved, and how they're used today. Again, readers are encouraged to use the information presented to do the suggested hands-on activities. The pages are filled with cartoon-like drawings that help to explain the text. Students of all ages will have fun exploring the information and activities presented in this valuable book.

Dash, Joan. **The Longitude Prize.** Illus. Dušan Petricic. New York: Farrar, Straus & Giroux, 2000. 200p. $16.00. ISBN 0-374-34636-4.

    During the glory days of trade and exploration in the sixteenth and seventeenth centuries, thousands of sailors lost their lives to shipwrecks because it was impossible to know their exact position. Latitude was easy to determine, but no reliable method had been devised to accurately determine longitude. European governments offered monetary prizes to anyone who could invent such a method. John Harrison, an uneducated village carpenter from Yorkshire, England, set out in the early 1700s to build an instrument that would show longitude, hoping to win the 20,000-pound prize (roughly equal to $12 million today) offered by the British Parliament. Dash enthusiastically tells the story of his struggles and determination in this well-researched biography. His use of math and science is astounding, considering his lack of education. He eventually wins the prize, but only after fifty years of hard work; he also had to overcome prejudice against him because he was a commoner who lacked a formal education. Today it is said that Britain owed their naval superiority to Harrison because of his invention of the chronometer. The afterword provides additional information about navigational positioning and also explains what happened to Harrison's models. A glossary and index are included, along with a time line of math developments to determine placement, beginning with Pythagoras in the sixth century B.C. Math teachers could use passages from this book to point out the importance of math.

Duffy, Trent. **The Clock.**

    Duffy traces the history of timekeeping devices from early humans through today and discusses future developments. The development of clocks relied strongly on math, as can be seen in the section about John Harrison's invention of the chronometric clock, used to help plot the position of ships. This is an excellent use of math and science together. *See* SCIENCE.

Maestro, Betsy. **The Story of Clocks and Calendars: Marking a Millennium.** Illus. Giulio Maestro. New York: Lothrop, Lee and Shepard, 1999. 48p. $17.00. ISBN 0-688-14549-3.

    This multifaceted book provides a thorough discussion of timekeeping devices of all types, including calendars, sundials, hourglasses, clocks, and watches. It is well organized and equally well illustrated. Maestro traces the history of these devices, using artifacts and early writings. This inclusive work covers many topics but manages to make complicated facts understandable. Illustrations accompany the text, adding information with captioned diagrams, sketches, and paintings. The additional information in the back includes important dates found on a variety of calendars (such as the Julian, Gregorian, Jewish, Muslim, and Chinese calendars), an explanation of expressions and facts having to do with timekeeping, divisions of time, a glossary, days of the week in other languages, a paragraph about computers, and an index. This valuable work should be in every library and math classroom.

Neuschwander, Cindy. **Sir Cumference and the Dragon of Pi: A Math Adventure.** Illus. Wayne Geehan. Watertown, Mass.: Charlesbridge, 1999. 32p. $12.00. ISBN 1-57091-164-9, 0-439-18031-7pa.

    The king, Sir Cumference, turns into a dragon after taking a dose of "Fire Belly" medicine from the doctor's workroom. The people of the kingdom, not realizing who the dragon is, organize an army and intend to kill it the next morning. Meanwhile, the king's son, Radius, returns to the workroom to find an antidote to "Fire Belly." He locates it, but the amount of the dosage is written in riddle form. "Measure the middle and circle around, / Divide so a number can be found. / Every circle, great and small— / The number is the same for all. / It's also the dose, so be clever, / Or a dragon he will stay . . . / forever." By measuring around pies his sister is baking, wagon wheels being made (by the carpenter Geo of Metry and his brother Sym), and articles in the kitchen, Radius draws diagrams and discovers the answer to the riddle is 3 1/7. He quickly administers 3 1/7 teaspoons of the medicine to his father, and the king returns to his original state. To celebrate, they eat the pies made by his sister, and they name the mathematical answer Pi declaring "pie with an e will be for eating. Pi without an e will be the name of the number for all things round." It's a corny, but fun story that can be used to teach the idea of pi.

Neuschwander, Cindy. **Sir Cumference and the First Round Table: A Math Adventure.** Illus. Wayne Geehan. Watertown, Mass.: Charlesbridge, 1997. 32p. $15.00. ISBN 1-57091-160-6, 1-57091-152-5pa.

    King Arthur is having a problem fitting all twelve knights around his rectangular table. With the help of his wife, Di of Ameter, his son, Radius, and his carpenter, Geo of Metry, they come up with a square table, a parallelogram, an oval shape, and an octagon, but none of the shapes is satisfactory. While on a ride through the countryside, they spot the trunk of a fallen tree and get the idea for a round table. They saw off a cross-section and take it back to make a satisfactory tabletop. At the end of the book Di, Radius, and Geo demonstrate the terms diameter, radius, and circumference. The story is cleverly contrived to illustrate mathematical terms, but it's done in a humorous way that older students can understand.

Neuschwander, Cindy. **Sir Cumference and the Great Knight of Angleland: A Math Adventure.** Illus. Wayne Geehan. Watertown, Mass.: Charlesbridge, 2001. 32p. $17.00. ISBN 1-57091-170-3, 1-57091-169-Xpa.

    Prince Radius is on a quest to earn his knighthood. To do this, he must rescue King Lell, who has disappeared. His father, Sir Cumference, and his mother, Lady Di of Ameter, give him a circular medallion (a protractor) to help him on his way. As he enters the courtyard of a suspicious-looking castle, he finds a parchment that reads, "Warning, stranger, friend or foe, / Dangers wait as forth you go. / You must make a Knightly Right, / Finding next Big, Straight, and Slight. / One wrong turn means lost to all, / In a writhing, screaming fall. / Find the Right to reach the king, / Or you will feel the dragon's sting! / The Brothers Zig and Zag." He uses the clues and his medallion to measure every angle and is triumphant in finding the king through the use of geometry. The story is trumped up but fun and makes the useful point that geometry is important.

Packard, Edward. **Big Numbers: And Pictures That Show Just How Big They Are!** Illus. Salvatore Murdocca. Brookfield, Conn.: Millbrook Press, 2000. 32p. $18.00. ISBN 0-7613-1570-5.

Beginning with one pea, the number of peas on each page increases exponentially, up to a trillion and then infinity. The pile of peas grows on each page until it takes up the table top, the kitchen, the entire house, the yard, the town, and eventually creates a mountain of a quadrillion peas. This large, comical book presents the concept of expressing large numbers in exponential form in a zany, humorous way, with dialogue balloons and insets giving additional information. The large size of the book, 9-by-13 inches, helps to illustrate the "bigness" expressed in the text.

Pilegard, Virginia Walton. **The Warlord's Puzzle.** Illus. Nicolas Debon. Gretna, La.: Pelican, 2000. 32p. $13.00. ISBN 1-56554-495-1.

An artist proudly presents a powerful Chinese warlord with a one-of-a-kind blue tile. It slips from the artist's hands and breaks into seven pieces. The warlord is furious and demands that the tile be mended. People from throughout the kingdom arrive to attempt to put the pieces together to form the former square, but none are able to complete the task. Finally, a poor fisherman's young son solves the puzzle, which earns the family a place in the palace. The puzzle is a tangram, which, according to an explanation at the end of the story, originated in China during the Tang dynasty. A black line drawing of a tangram is drawn in the back of the book, which can be copied and used by the reader. The story is simply told and is augmented by brightly colored, somewhat exaggerated illustrations. This is a fun story that clearly explains tangrams.

Schmandt-Besserat, Denise. **The History of Counting.** Illus. Michael Hays. New York: Morrow Junior Books, 1999. 45p. $18.00. ISBN 0-688-14119-6.

The idea of counting is so familiar to us, we tend to take it for granted. This book gives a historical overview of our system of counting, showing how it has evolved over time and is a collection of ideas from various parts of the world. Schmandt-Besserat carefully researched and wrote this book to include all necessary aspects of our counting system. The large acrylic illustrations, done on linen, help to interpret the concepts explained in the text. The book is presented in picture-book format, but the expanded text is aimed at older students. A glossary and index are included.

Schwartz, David M. **G Is for Googol: A Math Alphabet Book.** Illus. Marissa Moss. Berkeley, Calif.: Tricycle Press, 1998. 57p. $16.00. ISBN 1-883672-58-9.

This entertaining alphabet book is probably one of the best math concept books available. Each letter of the alphabet represents a math concept, followed by a sizeable explanation. In addition, other math terms that begin with the same letter are written in the margin, providing a useful list of math terms. The humorous cartoon illustrations add fun and explanation to the text. Schwartz and Moss manage to make math fun, giving it meaning and relevance. Their characters repeatedly wonder why we have to study this stuff. Schwartz's lighthearted approach is evident in the letter "W," which is for "When are we ever gonna use this stuff, anyway?", a complaint that is no doubt familiar to many math teachers. The author includes an extensive glossary of math terms. Whether used as a resource or for browsing, this book should be available in every math teacher's classroom.

Schwartz, David M. **If You Hopped Like a Frog.** Illus. James Warhola. New York: Scholastic, 1999. 29p. $16.00. ISBN 0-590-09857-8.

The ideas of ratio and proportion are clearly illustrated in this dramatic book. Each example compares what an animal can do compared with a human being. For instance, "If you swallowed like a snake, you could gulp a hot dog thicker than a telephone pole." "If you high-jumped like a flea, you could land on Lady Liberty's torch." Each entry is accompanied by large, colorful illustrations that dramatize the ideas. The last four pages list each entry and detail how ratio was used to calculate it. This is a fun way to present ratio and proportion.

Schwartz, David M. **On Beyond a Million: An Amazing Math Journey.** Illus. Paul Meisel. New York: Random House, 1999. 32p. $16.00. ISBN 0-385-32217-8, 0-440-41177-7pa.

Professor X and his dog Y help kids count their out-of-control popcorn kernels by teaching them about the powers of 10. They then move outdoors to count bats and bees, then on to the seashore to count thousands of animals at low and high tide and back in time to count how many years ago the dinosaurs appeared and then on to the North Pole. The pages are jammed with many people, animals, and objects and with cartoon dialogue balloons that help explain large numbers. The "Did You Know" sidebars tell about large numbers found in everyday life. The reader needs to think big when browsing through this book. This is an excellent tool for teaching exponents and the decimal system.

Skurzynski, Gloria. **On Time: From Seasons to Split Seconds.** Washington, D.C.: National Geographic Society, 2000. 41p. $18.00. ISBN 0-7922-7503-9.

Brightly colored photographs, paintings, sketches, diagrams, and maps are all used along with a lively text to present the many facets of time. The information moves from nature's timekeepers, the seasons, to artificial divisions of time—such as hours, weeks, months, and years. Timekeeping devices are presented as is the importance of time in navigation. The latter portion of the book deals with periods of time little known to us: split seconds that include the millisecond, microsecond, nanosecond, picosecond, and femtosecond. Especially interesting is the discussion of space-time and looking backward into deep time. Anecdotes are given to help explain specific concepts. The information in this book could spark some great discussions.

Tang, Greg. **The Grapes of Math: Mind-Stretching Math Riddles.** Illus. Harry Briggs. New York: Scholastic, 2001. 40p. $17.00. ISBN 0-439-21033-X.

Sixteen math riddles, written in rhyming couplets, encourage the reader to solve math questions by using visual clues. Each double-page spread presents a math problem that can be solved by carefully studying the brightly colored drawings and devising a strategy. The title poem, "The Grapes of Math," shows a vine with bunches of green and purple grapes. The poem asks the reader to discover how many grapes are on the vine without counting each one individually. An answer section is given in the back with a small copy of the original color page, the answer to the problem, and an explanation of how the author arrived at that answer. This is a multifaceted book incorporating art, math, and poetry.

Thompson, Lauren. **One Riddle, One Answer.** Illus. Linda S. Wingerter. New York: Scholastic, 2001. 32p. $16.00. ISBN 0-590-31335-5.

A wealthy Persian sultan's daughter, Aziza, is ready to marry, but no suitor pleases her. She loves math and riddles, so she devises a math riddle and vows to marry whoever answers the riddle correctly. The riddle is as follows: "Placed above, it makes greater things small. Placed beside, it makes small things greater. In matters that count, it always comes first. Where others increase, it keeps all things the same. What is it?" The sultan's men travel throughout the countryside, but each contestant fails. Finally, a young farmer, Ahmed, gives the answer, which is the number one. He wins the sultana's hand; the sultan makes Ahmed his chief advisor of farming and Aziza his chief advisor in numbers. An extensive explanation of the riddle is given in the back of the book. The story line gives us a strong, educated woman, and the colorful acrylic paintings beautifully depict the Persian setting, making this a book that can be used for many purposes.

Wells, Robert E. **Can You Count to a Googol?** Morton Grove, Ill.: Albert Whitman, 2000. 32p. $16.00. ISBN 0-8075-1060-2.

Clever illustrations using commonly found objects such as bananas and ice cream cones show the progression from the number one to very large numbers, ending with a googol and beyond. The simple accurate text shows how numbers increase tenfold when a zero is added to a number. The final page tells how the googol was named. It also gives uses for very large numbers, such as calculating the numbers of atoms in the universe, the distance in miles from our sun to Proximas Centauri, and dating things such as dinosaurs and stars. The book is written on an elementary level, but the information is also applicable to the middle school curriculum.

Woods, Michael, and Mary B. Woods. **Ancient Computing: From Counting to Calendars.**

The concepts of counting, problem solving, number systems, measurement, and gathering and recording information date back to prehistoric times. This book includes the use of computing numbers and using data in the Stone Age, ancient Middle East, Egypt, India, China, Greece, Rome, and the early Americas. It serves as a great tie-in with mathematics when examining the history of math systems. *See* SERIES.

Chapter 8

Multicultural

Countries and cultures from around the world are presented through the use of beautiful literature and artwork to help readers celebrate diversity. This is a time in our history when we need to think globally, learn about other cultures, and come to realize how much alike we are, rather than concentrate on our differences. The works in this section are dedicated to people from all walks of life in all corners of the world.

Alarcón, Francisco X. **Iguanas in the Snow and Other Winter Poems/ Iguanas en la Nieve y Otros Poemas de Invierno.**

This collection of seventeen poems written in English and Spanish touch on life, particularly in winter, in San Francisco and Northern California. The children's stories, written in free verse, are told from an Hispanic point of view, making these excellent sources to use with Spanish-speaking children. The brightly colored full-page illustrations are upbeat and add to the fun. *See* POETRY.

Aliki. **Marianthe's Story, One, Painted Words, Marianthe's Story, Two, Spoken Memories.** New York: Greenwillow Books, 1998. 34p. and 30p. $16.00. ISBN 0-688-15661-4, 0-688-15662 lib. bdg.

Looking for a better life, Marianthe's family leaves their homeland and moves to the United States. The setting is Greece, but given the subject matter, it could be anywhere in the world. The first book sets the stage, vividly describing life in the land where Marianthe was born. Her father leaves first, works very hard, and eventually sends for the family. It's difficult to leave, but Marianthe's drawings help to relieve the pain. Turn the book over, and the second episode depicts the mysteries of the family's new home, and particularly of Marianthe's new school. Mari, as she is known in her new school, describes her thoughts and feelings with her drawings, helping her teacher and the other students to understand her, even before she has the words to express herself in English. This Life Story, as Aliki calls it, actually tells Aliki's story, who was uprooted and moved to a strange environment as a child. Anyone who has ever had this experience can empathize with Mari. This book can help children of all ages who are in transition to know that they are not alone and that other people have gone through similar situations.

Batt, Tanya Robyn. **The Fabrics of Fairytales: Stories Spun from Far and Wide.** Illus. Rachel Griffin. New York: Barefoot Books, 2000. 80p. $20.00. ISBN 1-84148-061-4.

Folktales from seven cultures are told using fabrics as a storytelling vehicle. In "Clever Anaeet," an Armenian tale, the king weaves a secret message into a rug, which saves his life. "The Cloth of the Serpent Pembe Mirui," a Swahili tale, shows how the African use of raffia cloth began, and "The Silk Brocade" explains the history of Chinese silk. Also included are "The Feather Cloak" from Hawaii, "The Three Fayes" from Sweden, "The Patchwork Coat" a Jewish tale, and "The Crocodile's Blessing" from Indonesia. The colorful, full-page appliqué artwork vividly illustrates each story. The border patterns are especially interesting with their use of sewing materials to illustrate ideas. Students should be encouraged to study the details of the illustrations carefully to discover the characters and ideas presented in the stories.

Bierhorst, John. **The People with Five Fingers: A Native Californian Creation Tale.**

In the beginning, Coyote and all the animals are busily preparing California for people. Lizard insists on giving humans five fingers for basket weaving. After the arrival of people, there is so much laughing and talking—all in different languages—that the animals go to the waters, the sky, and the air and never speak again. This beautiful myth is told in a simple manner, accompanied by outstanding watercolor illustrations. *See* MYTHS, FOLKTALES, AND LEGENDS.

Brenner, Barbara, selected by. **Voices: Poetry and Art from Around the World.**
More than 350 poems and art pieces from six continents are collected in this outstanding combination of poetry, art, and geography. A representative work of art matches at least one of the poems on each page. The artwork includes paintings, sculpture, ceremonial objects, textiles, and photographs, making this a multicultural masterpiece. *See* POETRY.

Casanova, Mary. **The Hunter: A Chinese Folktale.**
A young hunter befriends a small snake and is rewarded by the snake's father, The Dragon King. The hunter now has the gift to communicate with animals, which helps him to bring more food to the ancient Chinese village. One day the animals warn him that a dangerous storm is coming that will destroy the village. The people refuse to leave until he reveals his secret, which causes him to turn to stone. Because of his sacrifice, the villagers are saved. The story is beautiful and the Ed Young illustrations are outstanding. Chinese characters appear on each two-page spread and the translation is given on page one. *See* MYTHS, FOLKTALES, AND LEGENDS.

Castillo, Ana. **My Daughter, My Son, the Eagle, the Dove: An Aztec Chant.**
Illus. S. Guevara. New York: Dutton Children's Books, 2000. 50p. $13.00. ISBN 0-525-45856-5.
This unusual book presents ancient Aztec chants given by parents and elders to their children as a rite of passage as they move from one phase of their lives to another. The chant to "My daughter, the Dove" is section one; the second section is for "My Son, the Eagle, the Tiger." The words of admonition and love begin with "My daughter, / precious / as a golden necklace, / precious / as a quetzal plume, / you are my blood, / my image— / Now you have awoken: / you are of the age of reason. / Listen! / So that you may understand / the ways of this world. Listen! / It is important / that you know well / how to live, / how to walk your path." The final words of wisdom to the son include "May the gods / who are near and far / and know all secrets, / see all things, / watch over you always. / May you be blessed with peace. / With this my duty is done. / My greatest treasure, / my son, my beloved one." Castillo reworks the Nahuatl chants, which were originally written in hieroglyphs, and gives them lasting meaning. The illustrations use decorative glyphs in traditional Aztec art to make this a remarkable work. The book is also available in Spanish under the title **Mi Hija, Mi Hijo, El Aguila, La Paloma: Un Canto Azteca.**

Chen, Kerstin. **Lord of the Cranes.**
The Lord of the Cranes, Tien, goes to the city to test the people for their generosity. He meets Wang, an innkeeper who gives him all he needs. As a reward, Tien draws cranes on the wall that come alive and dance, which draws

large crowds of patrons and makes Wang wealthy. In return, Wang promises to teach others to share with those less fortunate. This beautiful story, based on a recurring figure from Buddhist stories, works well with a unit on ancient China. The artwork depicts life from the Qing dynasty at the end of the nineteenth century. *See* MYTHS, FOLKTALES, AND LEGENDS.

Clinton, Catherine, selected by. **I, Too, Sing America: Three Centuries of African American Poetry.**
Twenty-five African American poets and their works are included in this outstanding anthology, arranged in chronological order. Clinton presents a biographical sketch of each poet, followed by a poem or two, and an abstract illustration to accompany the poetry. This is a marvelous way to present the history, talent, and richness of the African American experience. *See* POETRY.

Coburn, Jewell Reinhart. **Angkat: The Cambodian Cinderella.**
This Cambodian version of Cinderella takes some unusual twists and turns, but the basic story is familiar. Dr. Coburn discovered this story among some eighteenth-century French essays while researching Khmer culture and folklore. The people and the landscape described in the illustrations depict this culture. *See* MYTHS, FOLKTALES, AND LEGENDS.

Compestine, Ying Chang. **The Runaway Rice Cake.**
The Chang family wants to celebrate Chinese New Year, but they only have enough rice to make one cake, which they decide to share. But the rice cake comes alive and runs through the town. It is finally devoured by a starving old woman, and the family is rewarded by the neighbors, who bring a sumptuous feast to them. This is a combination of "The Gingerbread Man" and a retelling of the traditional folktale of the bottomless rice jar, and it provides information about the Chinese New Year. *See* MYTHS, FOLKTALES, AND LEGENDS.

Demi. **The Emperor's New Clothes: A Tale Set in China.**
This version of the classic Hans Christian Anderson tale about the vain emperor is set in ancient China. Demi uses Chinese symbols in the illustrations. The author's note explains these symbols, their meanings, and where to look for them. *See* MYTHS, FOLKTALES, AND LEGENDS.

English, Karen. **Nadia's Hands.** Illus. Jonathan Weiner. Honesdale, Penn.: Caroline House/Boyds Mills Press, 1999. 32p. $16.00. ISBN 1-56397-667-6.
Pakistani customs are beautifully displayed when Nadia is chosen to be a flower girl in her aunt's wedding. Her aunt painstakingly uses henna paste (*mehndi*) to paint and decorate her hands with the traditional intricate patterns. The close-up oil pastel paintings show the fine details of the paintings of orange flowers and stars. She loves the paintings but is worried that the children at school will make fun of her. This is a beautiful story of a

child learning to combine the richness of her family's culture with that of her home, the United States. The note section at the beginning of the book helps the reader understand the text by listing several Pakistani words and their meanings and pronunciations. This can be used successfully when studying Middle Eastern cultures.

Gregorowski, Christopher. **Fly, Eagle, Fly!: An African Tale.**
A farmer discovers an eagle chick, which he takes home and raises as a chicken. The eagle becomes so accustomed to behaving like a lowly chicken, it doesn't learn how to soar. Finally, two friends carry it to a mountaintop and teach it to strive for greater heights. This beautiful tribute to learning how to reach our top potential is prefaced by an inspirational message by Desmond Tutu. *See* MYTHS, FOLKTALES, AND LEGENDS.

Jackson, Ellen B. **Here Come the Brides.** Illus. Carol Heyer. New York: Walker, 1998. 32p. $16.00. ISBN 0-8027-8469-0.
A wedding is a time of celebration, a common custom found through-out the world and across time. This fascinating book shows the gowns, hair-styles, makeup, jewelry and adornments, symbols, and special customs that are typical in cultures from around the world. Readers will especially enjoy the "oddities" section that points out unusual practices of some cultures. For instance, after a Greek wedding, the "bride throws a ripe pomegranate at a door smeared with honey. If seeds stick to the door, people believe that the marriage will be happy and blessed with many children." In medieval times, the bride's bouquet "included garlic, bay leaves, chives and other herbs to scare off evil spirits." The illustrations are vibrant and colorful, beautifully depicting the styles and customs.

Jiménez, Francisco. **Breaking Through.** Boston: Houghton Mifflin, 2001. 195p. $15.00. ISBN 0-618-01173-0.
This sequel to **The Circuit** (1999) begins with the family being humil-iated as they are deported to Mexico because not everyone in the family has proper visas. Jiménez tells his story as an adolescent growing up as a mi-grant worker in California. The family manages to stay in one location long enough for him to finish high school, but he must also spend long hours be-fore and after school cleaning office buildings; his weekends are spent working in the strawberry fields. All this is necessary to earn money to sus-tain the family. The father can no longer work because of his bad back, due to the long hours of field labor. In spite of it all, Francisco is determined to live like an American, doing the things other kids do, like studying, going to dances, wearing the right clothes, meeting girls, and becoming a student leader. The struggle between maintaining his Hispanic culture and becom-ing a part of the American culture is depicted beautifully. Both powerful and moving books were written as a tribute to the author's teachers, who

recognized his abilities and gave him encouragement. Jiménez also wrote them in appreciation of the American Dream that all people can succeed. This book should be at the top of secondary students' must-read lists.

Jiménez, Francisco. **The Circuit: Stories from the Life of a Migrant Child**. Boston: Houghton Mifflin, 1999. 116p. $15.00. ISBN 0-395-97902-1, 0-8263- 1797-9pa.

Jiménez relates his childhood as the child of migrant workers in California. He uses twelve chronological stories to tell about his family's life of backbreaking work in the fields, moving every few months, with little opportunity for school. He describes digging through garbage dumps to find clothing and furnishings for their meager dwellings and the prejudice experienced because the family couldn't speak English. He was in the fifth grade before he ever entered a real house; his family had always lived in tents, garages, shacks, or whatever shelter was available. He repeated first grade because of his poor English skills and the family's constant mobility. It's a story of strong family ties and loyalty. This is not a tale of woe, but of triumph. Jiménez is now the chairman of the Modern Languages and Literatures Department at Santa Clara University in California. This is a story to share with all children again and again.

Jones, Lynda. **Kids Around the World Celebrate!: The Best Feasts and Festivals from Many Lands.** Illus. Michele Nidenoff. New York: John Wiley, 2000. 124p. $13.00. ISBN 0-471-34527-Xpa.

Four main headings—"Welcoming the New Year!", "Celebrating Before and After Fasts," "Giving Thanks," and "Renewing the Spirit"—include festivals and holidays from various countries that fall within these topics. Jones describes each celebration and details related hands-on projects. For example, when describing Carnevale in Venice, Italy, Jones includes an explanation of the festival and its history, followed by a section on mask making that includes step-by-step directions. She also includes information on foods; for Carnevale, she includes a recipe for *tramezzini* sandwiches, a typical food of Venice. An index is included. This is an outstanding book to use when studying cultures from around the world and when exploring holidays.

Lankford, Mary D. **Dominoes Around the World.**

People of the world have many more similarities than differences, which can be seen in the games we play. In two previous books, Lankford explored jacks and hopscotch around the world; this time she tells the history and rules of dominoes from eight countries. *See* SPORTS AND GAMES.

Lewis, Patrick J. **Freedom Like Sunlight: Praisesongs for Black Americans.**

Thirteen noteworthy African Americans are presented through poetry in this collaboration of art and poetry. Biographical sketches, poems, and portraits of Arthur Ashe, Harriet Tubman, Sojourner Truth, Louis Armstrong, Martin

Luther King, Jr., Satchel Paige, Rosa Parks, Langston Hughes, Jesse Owens, Marian Anderson, Malcolm X, Wilma Rudolph, and Billie Holiday are included in this important work. *See* POETRY.

Lomas Garza, Carmen. **Magic Windows: Cut-Paper Art and Stories.** Told to Harriet Rohmer, translated by Francisco X. Alarcón. San Francisco: Children's Book Press, 1999. 32p. $16.00. ISBN 0-89239-157-X.

Stories from Lomas Garza's life are written in both English and Spanish, illustrated with *papel picado,* cut-paper art. Heavy outlines on brightly colored paper make the designs look like stained-glass windows. Each page has a short story from the author's life as a Mexican American growing up in the Southwest. The artwork is fun to make and is further described in the companion workbook, **Making Magic Windows** (1999). Both culturally authentic works can be used effectively in classrooms for students learning English, in art classes, and in Spanish classes.

Lomas Garza, Carmen. **Making Magic Windows: Creating Papel Picado, Cut-Paper Art.**

This paperback workbook is a companion to **Magic Windows: Cut-Paper Art and Stories** (1999) and teaches how to create the festive banners called *banderitas* by folding and cutting tissue paper. The author stresses scissors safety and describes how to safely use a craft knife. Step-by-step instructions tell how to hold, fold, and cut the paper to create eight *papel picado* designs. *See* FINE ARTS.

Markel, Michelle. **Cornhusk, Silk, and Wishbones: A Book of Dolls from Around the World.** Boston: Houghton Mifflin, 2000. 48p. $15.00. ISBN 0-618-05487-1.

Dolls have been a part of nearly every culture throughout time. This intriguing book presents a collection of dolls from 1000 B.C. to the present, from regions in Africa, North America, South America, Europe, and Asia. They're arranged in alphabetical order according to the type of doll. An informative paragraph tells about the doll, including its origin and time period. The opposite page gives a full-color photograph of the doll arranged on a richly colored background. Cultural and historical information for each time period and region is included. This book is fascinating to read from cover to cover; it's also a pleasure to select regions or dolls of interest at random. A section on the art of doll collecting is included, along with a bibliography and a two-page map showing the origin of each doll featured in the book. This would be a wonderful book to use with students in English as a second language classes, while encouraging them to make or bring dolls from their own countries.

McDermott, Gerald. **Jabutí, the Tortoise: A Trickster Tale from the Amazon.**
Jabutí is known for his acts of kindness and flute playing and is loved by everyone but Vulture. Vulture offers to give Jabutí a lift into the heavens, but purposely drops him, breaking his shell. The other animals patch him back together, which is why the tortoise has a cracked shell. This is an excellent addition to a list of books to use when studying Latin America. *See* MYTHS, FOLKTALES, AND LEGENDS.

Merrill, Yvonne Young. **Hands-on Asia: Art Activities for All Ages.**
Merrill presents more than fifty projects reflecting folk-art traditions from Japan, China, Tibet, Mongolia, Korea, and Southeast Asia with easy-to-follow directions. This is an excellent source to use when studying Asian cultures. *See* FINE ARTS.

Musgrove, Margaret. **The Spider Weaver: A Legend of Kente Cloth.**
Two Ashanti weavers discover a new and beautiful pattern for weaving their cloth when they observe a spider making an intricate and unusual web. They return home and weave a new design known as kente cloth. The author explains the significance of kente cloth in the afterword, where there is also a pronunciation guide. The vibrant watercolor illustrations are outstanding examples of how kente cloth looks. This is an excellent source to show the importance and origin of an art form that is important to many African Americans. *See* MYTHS, FOLKTALES, AND LEGENDS.

Myers, Walter Dean. **Malcolm X: A Fire Burning Brightly.**
When gathering books on the Civil Rights Movement, be sure to add this extended picture book, which powerfully tells the story of Malcolm X, who dedicated himself to making a better life for his race during the 1950s and 1960s. Quotations from his speeches and writings abound, providing an excellent picture of his fervor. *See* BIOGRAPHIES.

Nye, Naomi Shihab, selected by. **The Space Between Our Footsteps: Poems and Paintings from the Middle East.**
This unique collection of poetry and art from twenty Middle Eastern and North African countries includes works from 130 poets. Many of our school children come from this part of the world, making this a useful tool. *See* POETRY.

Rochelle, Belinda. **Words with Wings: A Treasury of African American Poetry and Art.**
Life as an African American is portrayed in this stunning anthology that combines African American poetry with paintings by African American artists. An eloquent introduction by Rochelle explains the meaning of the book and adds to its emotional impact. *See* POETRY.

Ryan, Pam Muñoz. **Esperanza Rising.** New York: Scholastic, 2000. 262p. $15.00. ISBN 0-439-12041-1, 0-439-12042-Xpa.

When Esperanza is thirteen, her life changes from one of affluence among the Mexican upper class to one of great challenges as an immigrant worker in the San Joaquin Valley of California. After her father's murder and her uncles' betrayal, she and her mother are forced to flee Mexico and, along with thousands of others, to look for a better life in the United States. It's the Depression, and they have to compete with people from all over the country who are migrating to California in search of a better life. Esperanza knows nothing about hard labor, so she's given the easy job of sweeping. When she fails at that, she is assigned babysitting so the mothers can work in the fields. Life is very difficult; Esperanza's mother becomes ill, and what little money they save is stolen. Even with such challenges, they survive and triumph. Esperanza was Pam Ryan's grandmother, and the book is based on stories she heard as a child. This story represents tales that could be told by thousands of immigrants from around the world, making it important for our children to hear. This should be high on every student's reading list. It is the recipient of the 2002 Pura Belpré Award, which honors Latino authors and illustrators.

San Souci, Robert D. **Cendrillon: A Caribbean Cinderella.**

San Souci offers readers a wonderful picture of the Caribbean in this version of Cinderella, in which the godmother uses her magic wand to turn Cendrillon into the belle of the ball. The godmother does a makeover on herself and goes along as a chaperone. The godmother tells the story as she attends Cendrillon's wedding. Brian Pinkney's illustrations are vibrant and colorful and include details that depict the West Indies. *See* MYTHS, FOLKTALES, AND LEGENDS.

Say, Allen. **Tea with Milk.** Boston: Houghton Mifflin, 1999. 32p. $17.00. ISBN 0-395-90495-1.

Masako is growing up in San Francisco when her Japanese American parents decide to move back to their native Japan. They are homesick and tired of the language and cultural barriers. Once Masako moves to Japan, she feels those same barriers. As a teenager, she looks, dresses, and speaks differently from her peers, and she's teased for being *gaijin,* a foreigner. Her life is miserable, so when she finishes high school, she moves to Osaka, where she finds her knowledge of English is valued. She meets Joseph, a Japanese man educated in England, who understands the barriers and prejudices. They get married and decide to stay in Japan, believing a home is wherever you make it. The girl telling the story is their daughter, who says they found a way to solve the language and cultural differences. "My father called my mother May, but to everyone else she was Masako. At home they spoke English to each other and Japanese to me. Sometimes my mother wore a kimono, but she never got used to sitting on the floor for very long."

This is a marvelous book to share with immigrant students having problems with dual cultures.

Temko, Florence. **Traditional Crafts from Africa.**
This how-to book gives instructions for Senufo mud painting, Asante Adinkra stamping, Fon story pictures, Ndbele bead bracelets, Tutsi baskets, the Kigogo game, an Islamic art box and a Guro animal mask. This book celebrates the origins of many crafts still used today by Africans and those of African descent. *See* FINE ARTS.

Temko, Florence. **Traditional Crafts from the Caribbean.**
Temko offers how-to instructions for Caribbean crafts, including Jamaican woven fish, Puerto Rican *vejigante* masks, tap-tap trucks, yarn dolls, and metal cutouts. This is an excellent source to use to celebrate the talents and traditions of the people from several regions of the Caribbean. *See* FINE ARTS.

Temko, Florence. **Traditional Crafts from China.**
Temko includes directions for paper cutouts, clay figures made from dough, kites, string puppets, tangrams, a needlework purse, wheat straw pictures, and picture scrolls that showcase ancient Chinese crafts. Students can use ideas from this book to celebrate Chinese traditions. *See* FINE ARTS.

Temko, Florence. **Traditional Crafts from Japan**.
In this book, Temko presents eight traditional Japanese handicrafts handed down through the centuries. Included are *daruma* dolls, *ka-mon* (family crests), *koi nobori* (fish-shaped wind socks), *maneki neko* (welcoming cats), the origami crane, stencils for fabrics, *tanabata* festival decorations, and *den-den* (a festive toy drum). The crafts in this book can be used to celebrate present and past Japanese traditions. *See* FINE ARTS.

Temko, Florence. **Traditional Crafts from Mexico and Central America**.
This volume provides instructions on how to make Mexican and Central American handicrafts including tin ornaments, *papel picado*, Guatemalan weaving, Otomi paper figures, the Day of the Dead skeletons, a tree of life, Guatemalan worry dolls, and *Cuna molas*. The multicultural traditions showcased in this book celebrate present and past Latin American traditions. *See* FINE ARTS.

Temko, Florence. **Traditional Crafts from Native North America**.
Instructions for making Native American crafts are given for a Lakota dreamcatcher, Blackfeet beadwork, an Iroquois cornhusk doll, Seminole patchwork, Pueblo storyteller dolls, Chumash baskets, *haida* totem poles and Southwestern *cascarones*. The ideas that Temko describes are still used by tribes today, making this an excellent source to use when celebrating the traditions of Native American tribes. *See* FINE ARTS.

To Every Thing There Is a Season: Verses from Ecclesiastes.
Illustrated by Leo and Diane Dillon, sixteen full- and double-page paintings are used to present the words from Ecclesiastes I: 4 and III: 1–8, adapted from the King James Version of the Bible. Each painting represents a different culture, often from an ancient time, and is done in an artistic style that best illustrates the culture. Studying this book is like a stroll through an art gallery—a true feast for the eyes and the soul. *See* PICTURE BOOKS FOR ALL AGES.

Whelan, Gloria. **Homeless Bird.** New York: HarperCollins, 2000. 216p. $16.00. ISBN 0-06-028452-8, 0-06-028454-4, 0-06-440819-1pa.
Following ancient Hindu tradition, thirteen-year-old Koly's father arranges her marriage to a man she's never met. She is required to leave her family and travel to a distant city, cutting all ties with her parents. Upon arrival at her new home, she discovers that her sixteen-year-old husband-to-be is severely ill with tuberculosis. The money from her dowry is used to travel to the Ganges in the hope of a cure for him. He dies while there, leaving Koly to spend the remainder of her life as a widow, living with a family that doesn't want her. Her father-in-law recognizes her desire to learn and teaches her to read, but upon his death, the cruel mother-in-law abandons her in the holy city of Vrindavan. She's taken in by a widow who helps her to become independent through the use of her talented embroidery skills, allowing her to make a new life for herself. This small, beautifully written work gives the reader insight into India's customs, peoples, and daily life. It also helps the reader to understand the dilemmas that teenagers face in other cultures. The helpful glossary at the end of the book defines Hindu terms. This insightful, beautifully written tale won the *New York Times* Best Book Award in 2001.

Yin. **Coolies.** Illus. Chris Soentpiet. New York: Philomel, 2001. 40p. $17.00 ISBN 0-399-23227-3.
In an effort to keep the story of their ancestors alive, PawPaw, the grandmother, tells the story of the early Chinese immigrants who played a large part in the building of the Transcontinental Railroad. Two young brothers make their way on a dangerous voyage to San Francisco and are hired by the Central Pacific Railroad. This is the story of their dangerous, poorly paid lives as "Coolies," the derogatory term used for Chinese laborers at that time. They were given the most dangerous jobs and were paid the least, but they continued their work so money could be sent back to China. The text, told simply and frankly and without self-pity, is accompanied by outstanding watercolor paintings. The detailed, vivid illustrations provide additional information, making them perfect for extensive browsing. This is an important telling of a part of American history.

Chapter 9

Myths, Folktales, and Legends

Throughout time people have enjoyed stories in the form of myths, folktales or legends, which are often based on something that happened to someone long ago but has been embellished and enhanced so that the truth becomes fantasy. A variety of stories are included in this section, many coming from other times and other countries, but all a part of our literary culture.

Balit, Christina. **Atlantis: The Legend of a Lost City.** New York: Henry Holt, 2000. 28p. $17.00. ISBN 0-8050-6334-X.

     Poseidon, the god of the sea, travels to a rocky island where hardworking people are happy with their lives, even though they live in poverty. He falls in love with Cleito, and they marry. He is fascinated by the people and uses his powers to create a lush, productive island. Poseidon sets up the laws of peace, and he appoints his oldest son, Atlas, to be the ruler. Rule number one is that people will be peace-loving and care for one another. Happy with the success of the island, he returns to the bottom of the sea to sleep. As the years go by, the inhabitants forget peace and tranquility and begin to fight, argue, and kill. Zeus alerts Poseidon of the chaos, and in his anger Poseidon causes massive waves to wash over Atlantis, sinking it to the bottom of the sea. People have been searching for the lost city ever since. The endnote by Geoffrey Ashe, a noted historian, gives several theories about Atlantis. The story is fascinating, but the book soars because of the bright, bold, almost surrealistic paintings.

Bierhorst, John. **The People with Five Fingers: A Native Californian Creation Tale.** Illus. Robert Andrew Parker. New York: Marshall Cavendish, 2000. 32p. $16.00. ISBN 0-7614-5058-0.

This beautifully told creation myth explains why nearly every valley in California "was home to a separate Native American nation, each with different customs. Nowhere else in the Americas were so many languages spoken in so small an area." In the beginning, Coyote and all the animals carved California into the landscape it is today by forming mountains, rivers, creeks, springs, and the ocean. Once the landscape was formed, they planted all growing things in preparation for the coming of people. Lizard insisted that people be given five fingers, similar to his hand, so they could weave baskets. While the earth was being formed, the animals spoke, but once people were added, there was so much laughter and talking, the animals ran away into the woods, water, and sky, never to speak again. Coyote's plan to prepare the world for people was complete, however, with many different people "planted in every kind of place." The ancient story is told with simple text and expressive watercolor illustrations. The final page shows Coyote looking down at his work, with the Golden Gate Bridge in the background.

Casanova, Mary. **The Hunter: A Chinese Folktale.** Illus. Ed Young. New York: Atheneum Children's Books, 2000. 32p. $17.00. ISBN 0-689-82906-X.

Hai Li Bu, a young hunter from a tiny Chinese village is having trouble providing enough food for the village because of a dreadful drought. One day he saves the life of a small snake, who takes him to her father, the Dragon King. The Dragon King offers jewels and riches as a reward, but Hai Li Bu chooses to learn the language of animals so he can be a better hunter for his village. The Dragon King gives him a luminous stone, along with instructions that he will be turned to stone if he ever reveals the stone's secret. Hai Li Bu indeed becomes a gifted hunter, and the village prospers, until the day the animals tell him of an impending storm that will destroy the village. He tries to convince the villagers to flee, but they don't believe him until he reveals his secret, which turns him into stone. The storm does destroy the village, but because of the hunter's sacrifice, the people are saved. As a tribute, they erect his stone statue on the mountain top to remind them of the Hai Li Bu's great sacrifice. To help tell the story, Ed Young uses calligraphic illustrations painted on a golden brown background with a splash of pastels to highlight the stone. Each two-page spread has a red box in the lower right hand corner that contains an ancient Chinese character. The translation for each is at the beginning of the book along with notes about the tale. Both the story and the illustrations are so beautifully done, it is a must for anyone needing material on ancient China.

Coburn, Jewell Reinhart. **Angkat: The Cambodian Cinderella.** Illus. Eddie Flotte. Auburn, Calif.: Shen's Books, 1998. 32p. $17.00. ISBN 1-885008-09-0.

This Cambodian version of Cinderella includes several twists and turns that are different from the traditional version, but the basic story remains the same. A widowed fisherman marries a neighbor woman, creating instant problems because the new wife wants her daughter, rather than the fisherman's daughter, Angkat, to be the Number One daughter. A magic fish becomes Angkat's best friend, giving her the only joy she has in her dismal life. When the stepmother discovers this friendship, she kills the fish and cooks it for dinner. The Spirit of Virtue appears to Angkat and instructs her to put the bones under her sleeping mat, which results in a pair of golden slippers that eventually lead her to a prince and to marriage. The jealous family lures her away and kills her. The Spirit of Virtue appears again and transforms her into a spirit recognized by the grieving prince. She finally reappears in person, and they live happily ever after. Dr. Coburn, the author of **Jouanah: A Hmong Cinderella** (1996), discovered this Cambodian version of Cinderella among some eighteenth-century French essays while researching Khmer culture and folklore, showing us once again the universality of this story.

Compestine, Ying Chang. **The Runaway Rice Cake.** Illus. Tungwai Chau. New York: Simon & Schuster, 2001. 34p. $17.00. ISBN 0-689-82972-8.

It's Chinese New Year's Eve and the Chang family has only enough rice to make a single rice cake that they will share. But then the cake comes alive and runs through the streets with the family chasing behind. The rice cake finally collides with a starving old woman and the family allows her to eat it. When they arrive home, cold and hungry, they are rewarded for their generosity by neighbors from near and far who bring food to them. This delightful Chinese folktale is a version of "The Gingerbread Man" and a retelling of the traditional bottomless rice jar story. It also shows the customs practiced for Chinese New Year. This celebration is explained in greater detail in the back of the book along with recipes for baked and steamed *nián-gāo*. The illustrations, done in vibrant acrylic, add a whimsical touch to the story. This is an outstanding book to use in connection with Chinese New Year or the study of Chinese stories, and Chinese culture.

Demi. **The Emperor's New Clothes: A Tale Set in China.** New York: M. K. McElderry Books, 2000. 38p. $20.00. ISBN 0-689-83068-8.

This retelling of the classic Hans Christian Andersen tale, set in China, really needs to be read more than once to absorb the significance of the symbolism incorporated into the story and the drawings. It's the age-old story of the vain emperor seeking beautiful clothes who falls prey to two deceitful strangers promising to create magical clothes that "only clever people can see. Fools cannot." The Emperor falls for their story, and the rest is history. Although the story is the same, the setting depicts activities, clothing, customs, and animals of ancient China. The backgrounds often show symbols of heaven, purity, and virtue, which are explained in the author's note at the back of the book. Especially important is the paneled screen shown on the page with the hired weaver and tailor working. It displays thirty-nine symbolic characters found in Chinese art. The double-page foldout of the Emperor's parade through the countryside in his new clothes, with its multitude of people and animals running to see him, needs careful examination. Demi's signature artwork is filled with vivid colors and splashes of gold used throughout the story, including the richly colored endpapers that give the appearance of brocaded cloth.

Demi. **Kites: Magic Wishes That Fly Up to the Sky.**
Demi uses a combination of Chinese legends and down-to-earth instructions on how to construct kites to demonstrate the importance of kites in Chinese culture. *See* FINE ARTS.

Gregorowski, Christopher. **Fly, Eagle, Fly!: An African Tale.** Illus. Niki Daly. New York: M. K. McElderry, 2000. 32p. $16.00. ISBN 0-689-82398-3.
While searching for a lost calf, an African farmer finds an eagle chick. He doesn't know much about eagles, so he decides to raise it as a chicken. The eagle becomes so accustomed to behaving like a lowly chicken, it forgets how to soar. Two friends who care about his lost potential carry the eagle to a mountaintop and coax it to fly. This beautifully told Ghanian folktale uses the symbolic eagle to teach us to realize our true selves and soar to our highest potential. The watercolor illustrations aptly depict African landscapes, clothing, housing, and surroundings. The foreword by Archbishop Desmond Tutu is worth sharing again and again. He stresses "we are not bound to this earth and a humdrum existence but are made for something truly glorious: We are not mere chickens but eagles destined to soar to sublime heights."

Haddix, Margaret Peterson. **Just Ella.** New York: Simon & Schuster, 1999. 185p. $16.00. ISBN 0-689-82186-7, 0-689-83128-5pa .
CindersElla manages to win the prince's heart at a ball, which results in her being whisked to the palace to begin lessons on how to be a queen. Not only is the training tedious and boring, but she discovers that Prince Charm is boring, shallow, and against the common people. She learns that being a queen with gorgeous clothes and a fancy place to live is not all it's cracked up to be. When she tries to break the engagement, Charm throws her into prison. She manages to dig her way out and ends up in a camp for

war refugees set up by a kind young man she had met at the castle, Jed Reston. The reader is not sure if she lives happily ever after, but we do know she is able to take charge of her own life. This new twist on Cinderella is fun to use with middle school students who already know the "real" version. Haddix's use of language makes this an excellent read aloud.

Hamilton, Virginia. **The Girl Who Spun Gold.** Illus. Leo Dillon and Diane Dillon. New York: Blue Sky Press, 2000. 32p. $17.00. ISBN 0-590-47378-6.

This remarkable book combines the talents of one of our greatest storytellers with two of our greatest illustrators to give us a West Indian version of Rumpelstiltskin. Quashiba, a young spinner, is married to Big King after her mother claims she can spin regular thread into gold. After a year, Big King insists that she produce the gold, and she's locked into a room, ready to spin. A cruel-looking little creature with jagged teeth and a pointy tail appears to her and says he'll spin gold for her, but if she can't guess his name after three nights, he'll carry her away. While on a hunting trip, Big King hears the strange little man with a wooden leg chanting his name, Lit'mahn Bittyun. He relates the story to his wife, enabling her to recite the name to the little man when he arrives the third night. "Real loud noise, was Lit'mahn Bittyun going. He sounded like hot grease in a wet skillet, as all of him vanished in the dark." The acrylic illustrations are done with lavish gold borders, and gold is used wherever possible. The easygoing West Indian text makes this a great read aloud.

Hoffman, Mary. **Sun, Moon, and Stars.** Illus. Jane Ray. New York: Dutton Children's Books, 1998. 74p. $22.50. ISBN 0-525-46004-7.

When studying the heavenly bodies, it's fascinating to compare what we know now with the way past cultures from around the world explained the sun, moon, and stars. Myths and legends often explained what humans didn't know. Hoffman has collected twenty-one myths and legends from the Latvian, Aztec-Mayan, Korean, Hindu, and Australian Aboriginal cultures as well as the better-known Greek, Norse, English, and Japanese civilizations. The brightly colored illustrations combine a dreamy fantasy look with folk art that portrays the idea of myths from around the world. Gold splashes lavishly on every page. A section at the end of the book tells the origin of each myth and where the author found it. This is an excellent resource for middle school students studying the universe.

Hunt, Jonathan. **Bestiary: An Illuminated Alphabet of Medieval Beasts.**

Hunt represents each letter of the alphabet with a mythical beast from the Middle Ages, using action-filled illustrations drawn with a medieval motif. He also provides a brief explanation for each animal, and the author's notes in the back of the book add valuable information about the roots of the mythical medieval bestiaries. *See* SOCIAL STUDIES—ANCIENT AND EARLY CULTURES.

Kerstin, Chen. **Lord of the Cranes.** Illus. Jian Jiang Cheng, translated by J. Alison James. New York: North-South Books, 2000. 29p. $14.00. ISBN 0-7358-1193-8 lib. bdg.

> Tian, whose name means "heaven," lives in the clouds with the cranes. He descends to a city to test the compassion of the people, disguising himself as a beggar looking for food. It takes several days before an innkeeper, Wang, offers him food and drink. Wang does this daily for months, and Tian rewards his generosity by painting three cranes on the wall. The cranes come alive and dance, which draws huge crowds of people, making Wang very wealthy. He is indebted to Tian and promises to teach others to be kind and generous. Tian and the cranes fly back to the sky, and Wang spends the remainder of his life telling others to "share with those less fortunate." This beautiful story is based on a recurring figure found in Buddhist stories. The beautiful muted impressionistic paintings reflect the Qing dynasty from the end of the nineteenth century. Chinese characters adorn the endpapers. The moral of this tale bears repeating time and again.

Lattimore, Deborah Nourse. **Medusa.** New York: HarperCollins, 2000. 38p. $16.00. ISBN 0-06-027905-2.

> In this version of the ancient Greek myth, the sea witch gives birth to Medusa, a beautiful curly-haired maiden. Poseidon falls in love with her, but the goddess Athena, filled with jealousy and pride, turns Medusa into a gorgon—a creature with a woman's body but grotesque live snakes growing from her head. Meanwhile, an old fisherman discovers Danae and her son Perseus and gives them safe harbor on his side of the island. When Danae's evil brother, Polydectes, discovers them, he wants Danae to be his bride, but he doesn't want Perseus. So Polydectes sends Perseus out to behead Medusa, threatening that if Perseus doesn't return with the head, both Perseus and Danae will be killed. With the help of mythical creatures along the way, Perseus succeeds and returns just in time to save his mother. Polydectes looks at Medusa's head, and her evil eye turns him and his men to stone. This version of Medusa, although plenty gory and filled with action, tones down the blood, gore, and sexual aspects, making it more suitable for children. Lattimore's colored illustrations depict the action and help to explain the story.

Marshall, James. **Swine Lake.**

James Marshall and Maurice Sendak team up to create a hilarious twist on Swan Lake involving pigs and a wolf. The wolf is determined to attend a performance of Swine Lake by the Boarshoi Ballet. He plans to jump onto the stage and snag his dinner, but he becomes so entranced by the show that he leaps onto the stage and dances. The book is done in picture-book format, but the humor is suited for middle school students and up. *See* HUMOR.

McCarty, Nick. **The Iliad.**
    This fast-paced, action-packed retelling of the classic tale uses colorful, descriptive language, making this an accessible version for students. The illustrations help to describe the text and keep the story moving. *See* ENGLISH—CLASSICS.

McDermott, Gerald. **Jabutí, the Tortoise: A Trickster Tale from the Amazon.**
New York: Harcourt, 2001. 32p. $16.00. ISBN 0-15-200496-3.
    Jabutí (pronounced zha-boo-CHEE) is a flute-playing tortoise in the Amazon. Almost all the animals love him for his acts of kindness and his beautiful music. Only Vulture is jealous of Jabutí—he's constantly on the lookout for ways to harm the poor tortoise. When the King of Heaven summons Jabutí, Vulture volunteers to give him a ride but deliberately drops him, causing his shell to break into many pieces. The other animals gather him up and glue his pieces back together, which is why to this day the tortoise has a cracked and patched shell. This is a simple, clearly told tale of the Amazonian trickster accompanied by bold, vivid hot pink, geometrically drawn shapes. The author's notes at the beginning of the book give background information about Jabutí and his importance throughout Brazil. The universal trickster theme prevails: Creation comes from chaos.

Mitton, Jacqueline. **Kingdom of the Sun: A Book of the Planets.**
    The planets, the sun, and the moon are explained with up-to-date information and the Greek and Roman mythology for which the heavenly bodies are named. The information for each is told from that body's point of view, comparing modern-day information with mythology. The illustrations are outstanding, making this an informative work of art. *See* SCIENCE.

Musgrove, Margaret. **The Spider Weaver: A Legend of Kente Cloth.** Illus. Julia Cairns. New York: Blue Sky Press, 2001. 32p. $17.00. ISBN 0-590-98787-9.
    Set in seventeenth-century Ghana, two Ashanti weavers discover an exceptional spider web, which they feel would make a beautiful pattern for their cloth. Unfortunately, the web is destroyed when they attempt to take it home. Encouraged by one of their wives, the weavers seek out the spider in the forest and then watch it weave its magic. In so doing, they learn how to duplicate the intricate pattern now known as kente cloth. A detailed explanation of the significance of kente cloth is given in the afterword, followed by a useful pronunciation guide. The impressive illustrations use vivid shades of green to give the story a jungle backdrop. The bright colors used for the web can again be found in the finished cloth, showing the origins of the beautiful weavings. This is an excellent source to use when African legends and tales are needed.

Pinkney, Jerry. **Aesop's Fables.**

Sixty-one of Aesop's best and most familiar fables are retold along with Pinkney's outstanding watercolor illustrations filled with intricate detail. This volume is a must for every reader's collection. *See* ENGLISH—CLASSICS.

Rockwell, Anne. **The Boy Who Wouldn't Obey: A Mayan Legend**. New York: Greenwillow Books, 2000. 24p. $16.00. ISBN 0-688-14881-6.

The Mayan god Chac travels to earth, where he snatches a child to be his servant. This willful child refuses to obey, however, and causes Chac a great deal of misery. The boy is also miserable and gets his revenge by stealing Chac's bag of rain-making tools. This causes the worst storm ever, and Chac sends the boy back to earth. His family is happy to see him, but no one believes his tales except Monkey, the journal keeper, who saw and recorded everything. The illustrations and symbolism on each page, combined with the story that contains many important elements of the Mayan culture, make this a useful tool when studying New World cultures. The introduction gives helpful information on the Maya, and the bibliography lists other available sources.

San Souci, Robert D. **Cendrillon: A Caribbean Cinderella.** Illus. Brian Pinkney. New York: Simon & Schuster, 1998. 40p. $16.00. ISBN 0-689-80668-X.

Set in the Caribbean, this version of Cinderella is told from the godmother's point of view while she's attending Cendrillon's wedding. It includes many French Creole words and phrases, which are explained in the glossary. The godmother promises Cendrillon she'll help her attend the ball. To do this, she uses her mother's magic wand to turn breadfruit into a coach, six rodents into horses, lizards into footmen, and an opossum into the coachman. After creating a stunning Cendrillon, she turns herself into a properly dressed chaperone and goes along to the ball. The rest is history. Pinkney's colorful illustrations give the vibrant feel of the Caribbean. His use of flower borders and swirls of color give a feeling of action and movement. This is a wonderful rendition of the old story along with a delightful taste of the West Indies.

San Souci, Robert D. **Cinderella Skeleton.** Illus. David Catrow. San Diego, Calif.: Harcourt, Brace Jovanovich, 2000. 32p. $16.00. ISBN 0-15-202003-9.

Many versions of Cinderella are available, but this is the most unique and humorous. Told in rhyming verse, this Cinderella is a skeleton in a graveyard. San Souci sticks to the original story but adds a different cast of characters. The stepmother is Skreech and the stepsisters are Gistlene and Bony-Jane, all skeletons. Especially funny, if gruesome, is that when Cinderella loses her slipper at the ball, her ankle bone snaps off with it. So when the prince is looking for the correct owner, each potential princess breaks off her ankle to match bones, not just shoes. The illustrations conjure up the worst in each person, making the entire book spooky and gruesome, perfect for Halloween. The macabre tenor of the poem is summed up in the prince's tribute to Cinderella: "Cinderella Skeleton! / The rarest gem the world has seen! / Your gleaming skull and burnished bone, / Your teeth like polished kidney stones, / Your dampish silks and dankish hair, / There's nothing like you anywhere! / You make each day a Halloween!"

Singh, Rina. **Moon Tales: Myths of the Moon from Around the World.**
Throughout time, cultures from around the world have been intrigued by celestial bodies. This beautiful collection of ten mythological stories show the Chinese, Jewish, West African, Polynesian, Siberian, Canadian, Indian, English, Japanese, and Australian attempts to explain the beauty, power, and wonder of the moon. *See* SCIENCE.

Wiesner, David. **The Three Pigs.** New York: Clarion Books, 2001. 40p. $16.00. ISBN 0-618-00701-6.
In this hilarious fractured fairy tale, the three (not so little) pigs escape the wolf by disappearing through the pages of a book (folded into a paper airplane) into another world. When they meet the cat and the fiddle and the cow that jumped over the moon, the illustrations become chubby and cartoon-like with soft colors. After adventuring with those characters for a few pages, the pigs meet a dragon, which the king's oldest son is about to slay. With the help of more storybook inspiration, they are able to free the dragon and return to their original home, where the wolf is still trying to huff and puff their house down. They are able to defeat him with the help of all the fictional characters they've met along the way. Wiesner provides laughs on every page, but the reader needs to know the original stories for this book to make sense, so it's perfect to use at the middle school level. This outstanding book is the 2002 winner of the Caldecott Medal.

Chapter 10

Picture Books for All Ages

Picture books are no longer just for small children but have evolved into works of art that portray topics of interest to all ages. The selections in this section represent books in picture-book format that will please people of all ages. Many are aimed primarily at the older reader, with illustrations essential to the story being told.

Aliki, **Marianthe's Story, Painted Words** and **Marianthe's Story, Spoken Memories.**

The first story tells about a young girl moving from her native country to the United States, and the second depicts Mari's life in the new land, at her new school, and dealing with a new language. The illustrations tell the story in perfect harmony with the text. *See* MULTICULTURAL.

Baker, Jeannie. **The Hidden Forest.**

Ben and Sophie explore the underwater world off the coast of Tasmania, gaining an appreciation for the Giant Kelp forests and the creatures that live in and around it. The story is simply told, but the illustrations are spectacular. Brightly colored collages made from pressed seaweed, sponges, and sand give the effect of actually being in the water and exploring with the kids. *See* SCIENCE.

Bouchard, David. **Buddha in the Garden.** Chinese Legends series. Illus. Zhong-Yang Huang. Vancouver, British Columbia: Raincoast Books, 2001. 31p. $16.00. ISBN 1-55192-452-8.

A young gardener being raised in a Buddhist monastery is told that Buddha can be found in the garden. He only sees a starving kitten that he feeds and a small bird with a broken wing, which he befriends. On several occasions, he experiences a dream of a young woman carrying a baby. Through contemplation, he finally comes to the realization that the young woman is his mother, who left him at the monastery because she couldn't care for him. He begins to understand that Buddha will come into his life through good deeds and understanding. At the end of the story, a statue of Buddha appears in the garden next to the peony that symbolizes his mother. The statue holds the kitten and the bird in its lap. The artist includes an explanation of the story, dealing with the four symbols of Buddhist enlightenment. The bleached watercolors give a serene feeling to the text, which reflects the artist's time spent at a Buddhist monastery in preparation for illustrating this story. This is an excellent introduction to another culture and religion. Although in picture-book format, the story and concepts are more appropriate for secondary students.

Brower, David Ross, and Aleks Petrovitch. **Reading the Earth: A Story of Wildness.**

An elderly storyteller teaches three children about the history of the Earth, pointing out that human beings have been here a relatively short time. His message is simple: care for and maintain our environment. The story is presented in picture-book format but is most appropriate for older students. *See* SCIENCE.

Burleigh, Robert. **Home Run: The Story of Babe Ruth.**

The importance of the legendary Babe Ruth is told with a few well-placed words, bubble-gum baseball cards that give facts and statistics, and lifelike full-page illustrations. This effective picture book captures the amazing abilities of the Babe and the magic of baseball in a poetic manner, evoking the emotion and excitement of hitting a home run. *See* SPORTS AND GAMES.

Fleischman, Paul. **Weslandia.** Illus. Kevin Hawkes. Cambridge, Mass.: Candlewick Press, 1999. 34p. $16.00. ISBN 0-7636-0006-7.

Much to his parents' dismay, Wesley, a unique child, finds enjoyment by using his imagination, rather than by participating in conventional sports activities. It is summer vacation, and Wesley decides to plant a garden. Magic seeds produce an unusual plant with a vivid red flower. As the summer evolves, so does Wesley. He learns how to use every part of the plant—the flower, the stalk, the roots, the fruit, the bark, and the seeds—to sustain his own civilization. The plant provides him with food, drink, clothing, shelter, and even materials for recreation. He names his civilization Weslandia, and it becomes so intriguing, his classmates (who used to bully him), his nosy neighbors, and even his disinterested parents come to respect him and join in the fun. Vivid illustrations fill each page, often providing humorous details. Curious kids and neighbors peek over the fence on nearly every page, and his new language appears on the endpapers. This book can be used to discuss topics as diverse as the founding of civilizations, dealing with bullies, individuality, and gardening.

George, Jean Craighead. **Nutik, the Wolf Pup.** Illus. Ted Rand. New York: HarperCollins, 2001. 32p. $16.00. ISBN 0-06-028165-0.

Julie, from **Julie of the Wolves** (1974), **Julie** (1996), and **Julie's Wolf Pack** (1998), has a little brother, Amaroq. In this touching picture book, Julie brings home a sickly wolf pup, Nutik, for Amaroq to care for. She warns Amaroq not to fall in love with the fuzzy little creature, because his heart will break when the adult wolves come to reclaim the pup. But Amaroq and Nutik become inseparable, with Amaroq learning about wolves just as his sister Julie did. The wolf pack comes, and Julie insists that Nutik return to the wild. Amaroq sadly follows orders but is broken-hearted. After sobbing and moping, he crawls into his bearskin sleeping bag for comfort, only to find Nutik snuggled into the bottom of the bag. This simple yet beautiful story is the perfect accompaniment to the other Julie stories. The colorful, full-page illustrations are authentic and well-researched.

Guthrie, Woody. **This Land Is Your Land.**

America's favorite folk song is presented with outstanding oil paintings by Kathy Jakobsen. The lyrics and the paintings work together beautifully, making this a great picture book that will never go out of date. A tribute to Guthrie (written by Pete Seeger), a biography of Guthrie, and the score and the lyrics for the song are included. *See* FINE ARTS.

Hunt, Jonathan. **Bestiary: An Illuminated Alphabet of Medieval Beasts.**

Hunt represents each letter of the alphabet with a mythical beast from the Middle Ages, using action-filled illustrations drawn with a medieval motif. He also provides a brief explanation for each animal, and the author's notes in the back of the book add valuable information about the roots of the mythical medieval bestiaries. This colorful eye-catching picture book is aimed at older readers who can appreciate myths, legends, and the power of imagination. *See* SOCIAL STUDIES—ANCIENT AND EARLY CULTURES.

Johnston, Tony. **Desert Song.**

As the sun sets in the Sonoran desert, nocturnal animals venture out. The magical nighttime scene begins as witnessed by a bat, the first animal to emerge. The poetic text and breathtaking illustrations work together to make this a striking picture book. *See* SCIENCE.

Longfellow, Henry Wadsworth. **The Midnight Ride of Paul Revere.**

This legendary narrative poem comes alive with Christopher Bing's lavish illustrations. Extensive historical notes, maps, and documents are included which make this a masterpiece that vividly tells Revere's story. A section on the preparation of the book describes the detailed methods used to create the illustrations and text. *See* SOCIAL STUDIES—UNITED STATES.

Marshall, James. **Swine Lake.**

James Marshall and Maurice Sendak team up to create a hilarious twist on Swan Lake involving pigs and a wolf. The wolf is determined to attend a performance of Swine Lake by the Boarshoi Ballet. He plans to jump onto the stage and snag his dinner, but he becomes so entranced by the show that he leaps onto the stage and dances. The book is done in picture-book format, but the humor is suited for middle school students and up. *See* HUMOR.

Polacco, Patricia. **Thank You, Mr. Falker.** New York: Philomel, 1998. 36p. $17.00. ISBN 0-399-23166-8, 0-399-23732-1.

"The honey is sweet, and so is knowledge, but knowledge is like the bee who made the honey, it has to be chased through the pages of a book!" These were the words used in the Polacco family ritual when one of the children entered school. Trisha could hardly wait to chase knowledge through the pages of a book. Everyone in the family had read to her, and she knew the importance of reading. But when she tried to read, all the letters looked like funny squiggles, and nothing made sense to her. She became the dummy of the class, teased and taunted by everyone, making her life miserable. Finally, in the fifth grade, her teacher, Mr. Falker, realized she had a problem, and he and the reading specialist worked with Tricia after school to correct it. After four months of intense work, the letters began to make sense, and finally the knowledge flowed. In this autobiographical work, Polacco tells her painful story of learning to read, which culminates in a marvelous ending. This powerful book should be on every teacher's desk, ready to share with children with learning difficulties and their parents. It's also a worthwhile work to use with children who tease those who have learning problems.

Saltzman, David. **The Jester Has Lost His Jingle.** Afterword by Maurice Sendak. Palos Verdes Estates, Calif.: The Jester Company, 1995. 66p. $20.00. ISBN 0-9644563-0-3.

      The local jester discovers, much to his dismay, that he can no longer make people laugh. After being banished from the kingdom, he travels the world and through time, trying to determine why people can't laugh anymore. He interviews many people and discovers that they are so wrapped up in their own troubles, they've forgotten how to laugh. He finally meets a young girl in a hospital who is suffering from a tumor. The jester is able to tickle her funny bone and gets her to snicker, guffaw, chuckle, and finally laugh. Her laugher is contagious, and soon everyone around her begins to rediscover their ability to laugh. The moral of the story is simple, but the author's notes explain that the story comes from his own experiences when he learned he had a serious disease. In his afterword, Maurice Sendak, praises Saltzman for reminding us that the book brims with "promise and strength, so full of high spirits, sheer courage and humor."

Schwartz, David M. **G Is for Googol: A Math Alphabet Book.**

      This book is a perfect example of a book in picture-book format with information aimed at the secondary level. Schwartz arranges math concepts into an alphabet book that includes extensive explanations. The amusing cartoon illustrations help to explain each term, making it understandable and relevant. An extensive glossary of math terms is included. *See* MATHEMATICS.

Schwartz, David M. **Q Is for Quark: A Science Alphabet Book.**

      Every letter of the alphabet represents a science concept explained in detail with the help of cartoon-like illustrations. A glossary and index are included. This humorous, informational book is in picture-book format but is aimed at secondary students. *See* SCIENCE.

Scillian, Devin. **A Is for America: An American Alphabet.**

      Each letter of the alphabet presents topics dealing with American history, geography, and pop culture. The text, rhyming poems, sidebars, and vivid illustrations work together to give the reader a feast of Americana. *See* SOCIAL STUDIES—UNITED STATES HISTORY

Sendak, Maurice. **Where the Wild Things Are.** New York: HarperCollins, 1991. 40p. $18.00. ISBN 0-06-025493-9, 0-06-443178-9pa.

      No collection of picture books for all ages is complete without this all-time favorite. Max is sent to bed without supper because he's been behaving like a wild thing. In his dreams he travels to an island where the "real" wild things are having a wild rumpus. Children and adults love this book, first printed in 1963.

Sis, Peter. **Tibet: Through the Red Box.**
Peter Sis's father was separated from the work crews in China while film-ing a documentary on road building in the 1950s. He journeyed for two years through Tibet before finding his way back to Prague. His diary of that journey was kept in a red lacquered box, which Peter opens in this book. Unique text, il-lustrations, and stories tell the story of the journey, depicting the landscape, cul-ture, and religious life of Tibet. The story is told in picture-book format, but the interest level is for older children and adults. *See* UNIQUE PRESENTATIONS.

To Every Thing There Is a Season: Verses from Ecclesiastes. Illus. Leo Dillon and Diane Dillon. New York: Blue Sky Press, 1998. 40p. $15.00. ISBN 0-590-47887-7.
Paging through this magnificent book is akin to strolling through an art gallery. The Dillons use sixteen double-page paintings to depict phrases from the words of Ecclesiastes I: 4 and III: 1–8, adapted from the King James version of the Bible. Each painting represents a different culture: Irish, Egyptian, Japanese, Mexican, Greek, Indian, North American Indian, Ethiopian, Thai, Chinese, Russian, Australian, the Far North (from Siberia to Greenland), Middle Eastern, and the European Middle Ages. The Dillons use a variety of artistic styles in addition to their distinctive woodcuts. The purpose of the book is to "remind us that there are things in life that all peo-ple share, regardless of our diverse beliefs and cultures." The Dillons in-clude interpretive notes on each painting in the back of the book, saying which culture is portrayed, describing the type of art used, and giving the meaning of the phrase and the painting. This outstanding book should be shared and discussed with students for a better understanding of the mate-rial. A book with enduring qualities, it's a must for every library.

Turner, Ann Warren. **The Drummer Boy: Marching to the Civil War.** Illus. Mark Hess. New York: HarperCollins, 1998. 32p. $16.00. ISBN 0-06-027697-5.
Although in picture-book format, both the subject matter and the inter-est level are more appropriate for older students. The thirteen-year-old nar-rator of the book hears Lincoln speak, and he feels the call to join the forces and fight for his country. He's accepted as a drummer boy for the North and takes his assignment very seriously. After experiencing battle, however, he comes to understand the realities of war. He becomes hardened by the pain, suffering, and dying and vows to tell Mr. Lincoln that war is wrong, that he "made me go and see things no boy should ever see." The narrative is sim-ple, but combined with the full-page stunning illustrations, the message comes through loud and clear. Especially telling are the paintings at the front and the back of the story. In the beginning, he's a straw-hatted inno-cent young boy with a ready smile; the final painting portrays a sad, serious uniformed boy with a scarred face. This is recommended for use along with Gary Paulsen's **Soldier's Heart** (1998) when studying the Civil War.

Turner, Ann Warren. **Red Flower Goes West.**
A family is uprooted when the father decides to head west during the California Gold Rush. Ma takes a potted flower along, which becomes a symbol of survival. The muted illustrations and simple text give a feeling of what the difficult journey entailed. *See* SOCIAL STUDIES—UNITED STATES HISTORY.

Wiesner, David. **Sector 7.** New York: Clarion Books, 1999. 50p. $16.00. ISBN 0-395-74656-6, 0-395-74656-6.
Anyone who has ever imagined shapes and images while watching clouds will be enthralled by this visual feast. While on a class trip to the Empire State Building, a boy with artistic ability is carried away by the fog and transported to Sector 7, a station where clouds are designed, manufactured, and dispatched. The boy upsets the apple cart by designing fish and sea animals, rather than the normal cloud shapes. He returns to join his fieldtrip and on the way home sees the sky filled with unusually shaped clouds in the form of sea animals. This delightful wordless book, which won the Caldecott Medal Honor Award in 2000, takes the imagination to a new level.

Chapter 11

Poetry

Poetry has the ability to express thoughts and feelings in a way that touches and delights people of all ages. The entries listed here often tie in with curricula, but many of them can be enjoyed for the sheer pleasure of poetry and language.

Adoff, Arnold. **The Basket Counts.**
     Twenty-eight original poems give the rhythm and feel of basketball. The placement and spacing of the words on the page, the illustrations, and the text flow together to make the poems come alive. These poems are perfect for reading aloud. *See* SPORTS AND GAMES.

Alarcón, Francisco X. **Iguanas in the Snow and Other Winter Poems/ Iguanas en la Nieve y Otros Poemas de Invierno.** Illus. Maya Christina Gonzalez. San Francisco: Children's Book Press, 2001. 32p. $16.00. ISBN 0-89239-168-5.
     This collection of seventeen lively poems celebrates winter in San Francisco and Northern California from a primarily Hispanic point of view. Each poem is written in English with the Spanish version next to it. Some of the poems describe the sights and sounds of San Francisco, as in "City of Bridges," "Mission Dolores," "Dancing in the Streets" (a poem about the

cable cars), and "The Biggest San Franciscans" (about the sea lions that live at Pier 39). Some touch on Hispanic culture, such as "In My Barrio," "Ode to Buena Vista Bilingual School," "Christmas Eve" (celebrated in the Mexican tradition), and "Migrant Life in Seasons." Others celebrate the climate and weather, including "Clouds," "In Winter," "Iguanas in the Snow," "A Blank White Page," and "Giant Sequoias." The free verse poetry tells stories that children experience not only in Northern California, but throughout the world. This fun, upbeat bilingual collection of poetry, with its full-page, colorful illustrations, is a true treasure. Three other season-related bilingual books by this author and illustrator are also available: **Angels Ride Bikes and Other Fall Poems/Los Angeles Andan en Bicicleta y Otros Poemas de Otono** (1999), **From the Bellybutton of the Moon and Other Summer Poems/Del Ombligo de la Luna y Otros Poemas de Verano** (1998), and **Laughing Tomatoes and Other Spring Poems/ Jitomates Risuenos y Otros Poemas de Primavera** (1997).

Brenner, Barbara, selected by. **Voices: Poetry and Art from Around the World.** Washington, D.C.: National Geographic Society, 2000. 96p. $19.00. ISBN 0-7922-7071-1.

This collection of more than 350 poems is a combination of poetry, art, and geography rolled into one stunning work. The poems are grouped geographically from North America, South America, Europe, Africa, Asia, and Australia/Oceania. The author of each poem and his or her nationality is given. Each page has a reprint of an accompanying piece of colored artwork, labeled with the title, the artist's name, and the medium. For instance, "Apartment House" by Gerald Raftery from the United States is accompanied by Georgia O'Keeffe's "Shelton Hotel"—a perfect match. The title page for each geographic section includes a two-page color photograph representative of that part of the world along with a small globe that highlights the area. For example, a magnificent photo of Machu Picchu opens the South American section, accompanied by the phrase "Continent of mighty rivers, / lush rain forests, equatorial heat, and cold, thin mountain air— / land of countless plants and animals." A list of poetry and illustration credits, as well as indexes of the illustrations, poems, poets, and artists, complete this outstanding work. It is a must for every classroom teacher and for every secondary library.

Castillo, Ana. **My Daughter, My Son, the Eagle, the Dove: An Aztec Chant**.

Ancient Aztec chants, originally recorded in pictures, are interpreted into a tribute to sons and daughters as they go off into the world. The illustrations are glyphs depicting ancient Aztec figures that blend poetry and art in this moving work. *See* MULTICULTURAL.

Clinton, Catherine, selected by. **I, Too, Sing America: Three Centuries of African American Poetry**. Illus. Stephen Alcorn. Boston: Houghton Mifflin, 1998. 128p. $20.00. ISBN 0-395-89599-5.

Twenty-five African American poets are highlighted in this outstanding anthology, presented chronologically beginning with works by Lucy Terry and Phillis Wheatley from the 18th century through present-day poets Alice Walker and Rita Dove. The book includes biographical sketches of each poet, followed by one or two representative poems and a full-page, modernistic illustration. This combination of history, biographical sketches, poetry, and art work beautifully to illustrate the richness of the African American experience. The title is based on the poem by Langston Hughes, which prefaces the anthology.

Fleischman, Paul. **Big Talk: Poems for Four Voices.** Illus. Beppe Giacobbe. Cambridge, Mass.: Candlewick Press, 2000. 44p. $15.00. ISBN 0-7636-0636-7.

The entire class can have fun with the three poems in this volume. Fleischman divides the poems into four color strips: green, yellow, orange, and purple. To make it work, assign colors and instruct the students to read the words in their color. It's simple, fun, and effective. The first poem, "The Quiet Evenings Here," is a toe-tapping jingle about folks who enjoy staying home, rockin', strummin', hummin'. The second one, "Seventh-Grade Soap Opera," is right on the mark, talking about middle school gossip, and students will easily relate to this one. In the final piece, "Ghost's Grace," a group of ghosts watches a family eat a chicken dinner with corn on the cob and all the fixings. They salivate over the memory of how wonderful everything tastes while the mortals take it for granted. It's a mouth-watering poem guaranteed to make you hungry. These are perfect poems to stimulate student participation.

Florian, Douglas. **Insectlopedia: Poems and Paintings.** San Diego, Calif.: Harcourt Brace Jovanovich, 1998. 47p. $16.00. ISBN 0-7398-2201-2.

The world of insects can be explored through poetry in this delightful book of twenty-one poems. Each poem fits on one page with primitive-looking paintings of the insect on the opposite page. Florian presents some poems in a form representative of the insect; for example, "The Whirligig Beetles" is written in a circle. The words in "The Inchworm" inch their way up and down in a series of arcs. Who says we can't have fun with black widow spiders, weevils, and mosquitoes?

Florian, Douglas. **Lizards, Frogs, and Polliwogs: Poems and Paintings.** San Diego, Calif.: Harcourt Brace Jovanovich, 2001. 47p. $16.00. ISBN 0-15-202591-X.

Reptiles and amphibians take the spotlight in this rollicking collection of twenty-one poems. A whimsical watercolor painting of each animal accompanies each one-page poem. Humor is a part of every poem and painting, and some are arranged in an imaginative way. For example, "The Python" ("With thirty feet to squeeze your prey / Python, / you take my breath away!") is written in a circle, resembling the subject. The illustrations are watercolors painted on brown paper bags, giving the works an earthy look. The humor, wit, and information found in this collection can be enjoyed by children of all ages.

Florian, Douglas. **Mammalabilia: Poems and Paintings.** San Diego, Calif.: Harcourt Brace Jovanovich, 2000. 47p. $16.00. ISBN 0-15-202167-1.

Primitive paintings drawn on brown paper bags accompany each of the twenty-one brief, whimsical poems about mammals. Florian has fun with words as he describes animals, as in "The Aardvarks," in which he states "Aardvarks aare odd. / Aardvarks aare staark. / Aardvarks look better / By faar in the daark." An aardvark with a dismayed look on its face, hiding in a dark closet, is featured on the opposite page. Some entries are concrete poems, such as "The Lemurs," which is written in the form of a long tail, and "The Bactrian Camel," which has the words arranged in a camel's hump. Students will have fun with the wordplay, the drawings, and the information presented in this delightful book.

Greenberg, Jan, editor. **Heart to Heart: New Poems Inspired by Twentieth-Century American Art**. New York: Abrams, 2001. 80p. $20.00. ISBN 0-8109-4386-7.

Jan Greenberg, the editor of and a contributor to this anthology, invited forty-three contemporary American poets to choose a piece of twentieth-century American art and write a poem about it. The list of contributors includes well-known poets such as Angela Johnson, Bobbi Katz, X. J. Kennedy, Naomi Shihab Nye, and Jane Yolen. Artists include Alexander Calder, Christo, Grandma Moses, Alfred Stieglitz, Georgia O'Keeffe, and thirty-five others. The anthology is divided into four parts: "Stories" includes poems that tell a story about the art, "Voices" groups together poems written from the perspective of an object found in the artwork, "Impressions" transforms the visual elements of the art piece into poetic words, and "Expressions" includes poems in which the poet discusses the artist and the techniques used. Each of the four sections is explained in the introduction of the book. The artwork includes paintings that use a variety of media and methods, including photography, sculpture, and print. The poetry forms include traditional forms, free verse, and patterns. In each case, the poetry blends perfectly with the art. A useful section of biographical notes on the authors and the illustrators is included along with an index. This outstanding work should be on every library shelf and in the hands of every English and art teacher.

Harley, Avis. **Fly with Poetry: An ABC of Poetry.**
    Twenty-seven original poems serve as examples of poetic forms, each representing a letter of the alphabet. This is an excellent source to use when teaching poetic devices and a fun book of clever poetry. *See* ENGLISH—USE OF LANGUAGE.

Heller, Ruth. **A Sea Within a Sea: Secrets of the Sargasso.**
    The Sargasso Sea, off the coast of the United States in the North Atlantic, has long had the reputation of causing ships to be lost or becalmed. One by one, these mysteries are discussed and refuted by presenting the flora and fauna of the area. Written in poem form accompanied by outstanding illustrations, this is an auditory and visual feast. *See* SCIENCE.

Hopkins, Lee Bennett, selected by. **My America: A Poetry Atlas of the United States.** Illus. Stephen Alcorn. New York: Simon & Schuster, 2000. 83p. $20.00. ISBN 0-689-81247-7.
    The diversity found in the United States is captured in this anthology of poetry that divides the country into eight sections. Each section begins with a map of the states in that section, accompanied by a card (reminiscent of a baseball card) that gives statistics and facts about each state. Poems that represent the states or that section of the country follow. The majority of poems are by well-known American poets such as Carl Sandburg, Myra Cohn Livingston, Langston Hughes, David McCord, and Lee Bennett Hopkins, who compiled the work. Twenty poems were written especially for this book. Each of the fifty-one poems is accompanied by a colorful painting that appropriately describes it. An index of authors is included. This is a marvelous work that can unite literature and social studies units.

Hopkins, Lee Bennett, selected by. **Spectacular Science: A Book of Poems.**
    Fifteen poems, each presenting a different aspect of science, are included in this colorful, delightful collection. This anthology does a marvelous job of combining science and poetry to help us observe the world around us. *See* SCIENCE.

Janeczko, Paul B., selected by. **A Poke in the I: A Collection of Concrete Poems**. Illus. Chris Raschka. Cambridge, Mass.: Candlewick, 2001. 35p. $16.00. ISBN 0-7636-0661-8.
    Letters arranged in various patterns and vivid illustrations go hand in hand to create thirty lively and attractive concrete poems. A variety of clever shapes and sizes are used to describe the topic of the poem. The text of "A Seeing Poem" is arranged in the shape of a light bulb. "Tennis Anyone" causes the reader's eyes to follow the words back and forth from the left page to the right, as though watching a tennis match. The words to "Eskimo Pie" are arranged in the shape of an ice cream bar. The notes from the editor at the beginning of the book give an explanation of concrete poems and sets the stage for what's to come. The paper collage illustrations add to the fun.

Janeczko, Paul B. **That Sweet Diamond: Baseball Poems.**
Nineteen free-verse poems vividly capture the joy, beauty, and excitement of baseball. *See* SPORTS AND GAMES.

Katz, Bobbi. **A Rumpus of Rhymes: A Book of Noisy Poems.**
This noisy book consists of twenty-eight original poems that describe and display sounds. Onomatopoeia is used liberally along with fonts of different sizes, shapes, and colors, making the noisy words jump off the page. *See* ENGLISH—USE OF LANGUAGE.

Katz, Bobbi. **We the People: Poems.**
This unique work uses sixty-five poems to tell the history of the United States. Each poem tells of a person from a specific time period, some well known, others discovered by Katz during her research. The author's notes tell about her research and the many discoveries she made. This work is a treasure to be used in conjunction with U.S. history and literature. *See* SOCIAL STUDIES—UNITED STATES HISTORY.

Lewis, J. Patrick. **Freedom Like Sunlight: Praisesongs for Black Americans**. Illus. John Thompson. Mankato, Minn.: Creative Editions, 2000. 40p. $18.00. ISBN 1-56846-163-1.
Thirteen African Americans, all known for their courage and outstanding contributions, are presented through poetry and art in this outstanding work. Arthur Ashe, Harriet Tubman, Sojourner Truth, Louis Armstrong, Martin Luther King, Jr., Satchel Paige, Rosa Parks, Langston Hughes, Jesse Owens, Marian Anderson, Malcolm X, Wilma Rudolph, and Billie Holiday are featured, along with biographical notes in the appendix. The powerful poetry and the full-page paintings are poignant, making this a must for every poetry collection.

Lewis, J. Patrick. **Doodle Dandies: Poems That Take Shape.** Illus. Lisa Desimini. New York: Atheneum Children's Books, 1998. 33p. $16.00. ISBN 0-689-81075-X.
This book of concrete poems has to be seen to be believed. The letters for each poem are cleverly arranged around and between the illustrations, becoming a part of the picture. The heavy texture and dark, rich colors of the illustrations form the perfect placement for letters. "Giraffe" uses yellow letters to paint the sketch of the giraffe's long neck, a block of words to form the body, and individual letters to make each of the long legs. The words to "Winter" act as snowflakes falling through the sky. Some poems require the reader to twist and turn the book to read the words arranged at angles. Some give the reader the feeling of movement, as in "Lashondra Scores!" Each word of the poem has the letter O, painted to look like a basketball. As the poem progresses, the ball and the words arc up and into the

basket. Classroom teachers may find this unusual collection useful in presenting types of poetry, but readers may simply enjoy its playfulness, too.

Lithgow, John. **The Remarkable Farkle McBride.**
Farkle is a child prodigy who plays several musical instruments starting at the age of three. By the time he's ten, he's tired of all of them. One day the conductor becomes ill, and Farkle takes his place, satisfying him at last. Farkle's tale is told in rhyming verse and musical sounds in onomatopoeic form, making this a fun book to read out loud. *See* FINE ARTS.

Locker, Thomas. **Mountain Dance.**
This awe-inspiring book presents the geologic evolution of mountains—from their creation to their erosion—in poetic form. Each page spread has a lyrical description with an outstanding oil painting. This is an excellent example of descriptive poetry. *See* SCIENCE.

Longfellow, Henry Wadsworth. **The Midnight Ride of Paul Revere.**
This legendary narrative poem comes alive with Christopher Bing's lavish illustrations. Extensive historical notes, maps, and documents are included, making this a masterpiece that vividly tells Revere's story. *See* SOCIAL STUDIES—UNITED STATES HISTORY.

Myers, Christopher A. **Black Cat.** New York: Scholastic, 1999. 34p. $17.00. ISBN 0-590-03375-1.
A colorful descriptive picture of Harlem is displayed in this book, thanks to a confident cat that goes wherever it pleases. The story line is a free verse poem spread out with one phrase on each page. We follow the cat as it winds through cars and emergency vehicles, scales walls, chases mice and rats, rides the subway, pounds the pavement, climbs on fences, jumps through basketball hoops, and hangs out on rooftops. From the lines "black cat, black cat, / is there a place of your own? / we want to know, / where's your home? black cat answers . . . / anywhere I roam." we learn that this is a city cat, quite used to the cityscape. Photographs serve as a background for the illustrations, with heavily colored paint layered on top, giving the poem a surreal, ominous feeling. City rhythms and scenes abound in this spectacular work, which won the Coretta Scott King Award in 2000.

Nelson, Marilyn. **Carver: A Life in Poems.** Asheville, N.C.: Front Street, 2001. 103p. $17.00. ISBN 1-886910-53-7.
This book details the life of George Washington Carver (1864–1943) through a series of fifty-nine poems, beginning with his rescue from slave thieves by a white couple, the Carvers, who had owned his mother. They raised him as their own, encouraging him to think, explore, and learn—and

ultimately to become a highly respected man. Each poem depicts a particular time in Carver's life, and through these poems, we learn his inner thoughts and goals. Together they depict the cultural and political atmosphere during his lifetime and describe how Carver helped to shape history with his scientific and artistic advancements. Most of the poems are followed with a caption explaining the time and place the poem describes, often accompanied by a black-and-white photograph of Carver and the people who were influential in his life. This unusual collection of poems beautifully tells the story of an unusual man. This book won the Newbery Honor Award in 2002.

Nordine, Ken. **Colors.** Illus. Henrik Drescher. San Diego, Calif.: Harcourt, 2000. 38p. $16.00. ISBN 0-15-201584-1.

Without colors in our lives, we would be like the bored, sepia-colored math class pictured on the front endpaper. With color we come alive, just as the math class does on the back endpaper, which shows the same math class, brightly colored, having a great time. This wild and crazy collection of poems about colors began as a series of radio ads for paint. They're so creative and illustrative, Nordine went on to record them, calling it word jazz. The brightly colored, splashy illustrations, usually backed with graph paper, capitalize on this word jazz theme. Green, yellow, azure, black, lavender, orange, chartreuse, burgundy, flesh, purple, olive, and magenta are included. Each entry gives the inexact hue a personality, such as a depressed chartreuse that "wanted to quit . . . why not? Figured it would go off somewhere be by itself maybe let green or yellow take over." Purple "has class some say the highest they stand in awe of purple royally . . . loyally." Each free-wheeling verse is accompanied perfectly with the wildness of the illustrations.

Nye, Naomi Shihab, selected by. **The Space Between Our Footsteps: Poems and Paintings from the Middle East**. New York: Simon & Schuster, 1998. 144p. $20.00. ISBN 0-689-81233-7.

This unique collection of poetry and art from twenty Middle Eastern and North African countries includes works from 130 poets. As a Palestinian American writer, Nye is able to bring together this rich assortment of poems that evoke emotions and feelings from a variety of cultures. Topics include war, poverty, suffering, exile, families, feelings and emotions, and particular moments in poets' lives. Other entries play with images and language. The paintings that accompany the poems depict Middle Eastern cultures. In the introduction, the author tells about her rich background and why and how she put this anthology together. The colored map toward the back of the book shows the countries represented. The notes on the contributors is a helpful section, along with an index to poets and artists, an index to poems, and a list of illustrations and illustrators.

Prelutsky, Jack, **Awful Ogre's Awful Day.** Illus. Paul O. Zelinsky. New York: Greenwillow Books, 2001. 39p. $16.00. ISBN 0-688-07778-1, 0-688-07779-X.

A day in the life of an ogre is chronicled from the time he rises until bedtime. In the opening poem, "Awful Ogre Rises," Awful is awakened with the help of his rattlesnake, buzzard, rats, tarantula, piranha, leeches, and lizard. We then follow Awful as he grooms himself with gargoyle oil, makes a breakfast of scream of wheat, endures a storm, dances, writes a letter to his favorite fourteen-foot ogress, plays music, has lunch, entertains his great-grand nephew ogre, watches television, works in his weedy garden, eats supper at his favorite restaurant, examines his bone collection, and finally goes to bed, hugging his cactus. Each two-page illustration is filled with color, action, and humorous detail—perfectly matched to the poems. This collection of eighteen bizarre, gross, macabre, and hysterically funny poems is a sure winner.

Prelutsky, Jack. **The Gargoyle on the Roof: Poems.** Illus. Peter Sis. New York: Greenwillow Books, 1999. 39p. $16.00. ISBN 0-688-16553-2.

Every scary creature imaginable can be found in this collection of seventeen poems. Trolls, gremlins, griffins, goblins, gargoyles, vampires, werewolves, and bugaboos all show up to create scary yet humorous fun. Here's an example of Prelutsky's ability to create humor with fear from "My Sister Is a Werewolf": "My sister is a werewolf, / It's disquieting and strange. / One moonlit night I watched her / Undergo a sudden change. / Her arms and face grew hairy, / And her voice became a roar. / In some ways she looked better / Than she'd ever looked before." Sis's sinister artwork fits the poems perfectly, always adding humor to the horror. Students will love this book as much as Prelutsky's other works.

Roberts, Michael. **Mumbo Jumbo.** New York: Callaway, 2000. 60p. $25.00. ISBN 0-935112-49-9.

This is a made-to-order poetry book for older students looking for spooky, scary stuff. The oversized format with heavy cardstock pages are brimming with mystical, colorful, surreal collages that match the witty poems, one for each letter of the alphabet. Each poem features a scary topic, beginning with abracadabra, bats, and cobwebs and ending with a yeti and zombies. P is for "Pumpkin man, / pumpkin man, / Doesn't have a / dental plan. / Will he soon be that much wiser / Now he's lost his / right incisor?" The accompanying collage is filled with grinning pumpkins, sporting their toothy grins. The humor and wit of the poetry and the artwork filled with ghost, witches, and zombies makes this a book that older readers will appreciate.

Rochelle, Belinda, selected by. **Words with Wings: A Treasury of African-American Poetry and Art.** New York: HarperCollins, 2001. 48p. $17.00. ISBN 0-06-029363-2.

    Twenty contemporary poems by African American writers are paired with twentieth-century paintings by African American artists, to produce a stunning anthology that celebrates life. The combinations "explore a range of African American experiences." For example, coupling Count Cullen's poem "Incident" with *Gemini I,* by Lev T. Mills creates a powerful impact. "Women" by Alice Walker is matched with *Harriet Tubman,* painted by William H. Johnson. Other poets include Lucille Clifton, Gwendolyn Brooks, Georgia Johnson, Robert Hayden, Rita Dove, Paul Laurence Dunbar, William Stanley Braithwaite, Langston Hughes, Beauford Delaney, Ethelbert Miller, Nikki Giovanni, and Maya Angelou. Biographical sketches of the poets and artists are included in the back of the book. An eloquent introduction by Rochelle explains that the poems and paintings in this book "enable us to make our world bigger." She accomplishes her purpose in this outstanding work.

San Souci, Robert D. **Cinderella Skeleton.**

    Many versions of Cinderella are available, but this one, written in rhyme, takes place in a graveyard. Cinderella and the entire cast of characters—including the prince—are skeletons. It's macabre, gruesome, and very funny. Middle schoolers love it! *See* MYTHS, FOLKTALES, AND LEGENDS.

Siebert, Diane. **Mississippi.**

    The story of the Mississippi River is told in rhyme, along with magnificent watercolor paintings. Seldom does such a powerful and emotional book come along. This is a must for every poetry collection. *See* SCIENCE.

Smith, Charles R., Jr. **Rimshots: Basketball Pix, Rolls, and Rhythms.**

    Page design, use of italics, a variety of fonts, and the highlighting of key words all work together to give the fourteen poems about basketball energy, rhythm, and excitement. The sepia-toned photographs taken by Smith along with the exciting poems express his deep love for the game. *See* SPORTS AND GAMES.

Tang, Greg. **The Grapes of Math: Mind-Stretching Math Riddles.**

    Tang presents sixteen humorous math problems in rhyming couplets, designed to be solved using visual clues. Readers can find solutions to the problems in the back of the book. *See* MATHEMATICS.

Zahares, Wade, compiled and illustrated by. **Big, Bad and a Little Bit Scary: Poems That Bite Back!**. New York: Viking, 2001. 32p. $17.00. ISBN 0-670-03513-0.

Think of an animal that's scary, and it'll probably be found in this irreverent anthology that capitalizes on the scariness of certain animals. The front dust jacket flap has a large WARNING sign posted, giving the reader an idea of what to expect. John Gardner's poem, "Always Be Kind to Animals," appropriately introduces the collection because it warns us to "Always be kind to animals / Morning, noon and night. / For animals have feelings too, / And furthermore they bite!" From there we experience "Viper" by Eve Merriam, "Alligator" by Maxine W. Kumin, "The Panther" by Ogden Nash, "The Sparrow Hawk" by Russell Hoban, "The Shark" by Lord Alfred Douglas, "Lion" by Mary Ann Hoberman, "The Vulture" by Hilaire Belloc, "The Eel" by Robert S. Oliver, "The Porcupine" by Karla Kuskin, "Octopus" by Valerie Worth, "Strippers" by Dick King-Smith, "Bat" by D. H. Lawrence, "The Barracuda" by John Gardner, and "Hippopotamus" by William Jay Smith. The oversized illustrations in haunting tones make the poems come alive, adding to the nightmare. Readers can have all sorts of wild and wonderful fun with this overstated collection.

Chapter 12

Read Alouds

People of all ages love to be read to, but the material must be exciting and interesting enough to hold the listeners' attention. The following is a list of books that offer enjoyment to both the reader and the listener. Many may be connected with a specific curriculum, and others may be used simply for the joy of listening to and engaging in literature.

Adoff, Arnold. **The Basket Counts.**
    Twenty-eight original poems give the rhythm and feel of basketball. The placement and spacing of the words on the page, the illustrations, and the text all flow together to make the poems come alive. *See* SPORTS AND GAMES.

Avi. **Don't You Know There's a War On?**
    Nearly everyone's life is touched by World War II in 1943. Howie's father is serving in the merchant marine and hasn't been heard from for a long time. Howie feels helpless when it comes to his family situation, but he feels he can help his favorite teacher. This book is funny, sad, and touching; at the same time, it offers a picture of what it was like to be a child in the United States during the war. *See* GREATEST OF THE LATEST.

Bauer, Joan. **Hope Was Here.**

Hope and her Aunt Addie relocate often because Addie, a cook, moves from job to job with regularity. This time they move from New York to rural Wisconsin, and Hope is sure she'll wilt from culture shock. Instead, she becomes involved with local politics, Addie marries the owner of the restaurant, and everyone learns a great deal about life, love, and politics, told in a delightful humorous manner. *See* HUMOR.

Byars, Betsy. **Disappearing Acts.** A Herculeah Jones Mystery. New York: Viking, 1998. 120p. $15.00. ISBN 0-670-87735-2.

In the fourth in the Herculeah Jones series, Herculeah's sidekick, Meat, attends a comedy class, only to discover a murdered body in the restroom. Herculeah, the frizzy-haired, budding private investigator, is so busy solving the mystery of an unfinished roll of film discovered in a used camera that she leaves Meat to take center stage and solve the comedy club murder on his own. As both mysteries unfold, the whereabouts of Meat's father is discovered, giving this episode a unique twist. All four books in the Herculeah Jones series are excellent as read alouds in grades four to six because the reader is left hanging at the end of every chapter, making it urgent to find out what happens next. The characters are humorous, the plots challenging and fun.

Cooper, Susan. **King of Shadows.**

Nat Field, a member of a summer Shakespeare drama troupe, is transported back in time to become one of Shakespeare's actors. An abundance of information about Shakespeare and his times comes alive in this entertaining adventure. *See* SOCIAL STUDIES—ANCIENT AND EARLY CULTURES.

Curtis, Christopher Paul. **Bud, Not Buddy.**

Bud, a spunky ten-year-old orphan, sets out to find his father. It's the Depression era, which adds to the difficulties of his eventful yet humorous journey. Bud's adventures include sadness, danger, humor, and eventual happiness, making this an excellent read aloud. *See* GREATEST OF THE LATEST.

Haddix, Margaret Peterson. **Among the Hidden.** New York: Simon & Schuster, 1998. 153p. $16.00. ISBN 0-689-81700-2, 0-689-82475-0pa.

In this futuristic novel, overpopulation is controlled by limiting families to no more than two children. Luke is a third child, and the entire family is subject to severe punishment if he is discovered. The family hides him in the attic of their home, where he's never to be with other children or anyone outside the family. But when a new house is built near their home, Luke discovers a child's face peeking from a window. He daringly dashes to the neighboring house and meets the child, Jen, who is also a third child. She knows about many other hidden children, who communicate through the

Internet. This daring, spunky girl organizes a rally of shadow children, but Luke doesn't join. Later he learns that the children were gunned down by the Population Police. Jen's father obtains a fake identity card for Luke, and he leaves home in search of a new life. The ideas and words in this story flow well, making this an effective read aloud. The subject matter begs for discussion, and students become involved when they learn that this dilemma is already a reality in some countries at this time. The sequel, **Among the Imposters** (2001), is described in Chapter 5, GREATEST OF THE LATEST. A third work in the series, **Among the Betrayed,** 2002, continues the dilemma of population control.

Haddix, Margaret Peterson. **Just Ella.**
    In this retelling of Cinderella, Ella wins the prince's heart and is taken to the castle to begin "princess training." She finds the whole thing tedious and dreadful. Even worse, Prince Charm turns out to be shallow and boring. When she attempts to leave him, he throws her into prison. She digs her way out and goes to help out at a war refugee camp. This fractured fairy tale makes a great read aloud for those who know the original story. *See* MYTHS, FOLKTALES, AND LEGENDS.

Hamilton, Virginia. **The Girl Who Spun Gold.**
    This West Indian version of Rumpelstiltskin, retold by one of our greatest storytellers, has an easygoing lilt to the text that lends itself perfectly to being read aloud. *See* MYTHS, FOLKTALES, AND LEGENDS.

Hesse, Karen. **Witness: A Novel.**
    This unusual novel, written as a five-act play in free verse, is about the Ku Klux Klan's infiltration of a small Vermont town in 1924. Students will best understand the story if it is read aloud or presented as reader's theater. *See* UNIQUE PRESENTATIONS.

Hobbs, Will. **Down The Yukon.**
    Sixteen-year-old Jason Hawthorn and his girlfriend, Jamie, participate in the Great Race across Alaska in an attempt to win the $20,000 prize. Excitement and adventure await them around every bend of the Yukon River. *See* SCIENCE.

Johnston, Tony. **Desert Song.**
    As the sun sets in the Sonoran desert, nocturnal animals venture out. The magical nighttime scene begins as witnessed by a bat, the first animal to emerge. The poetic text and breathtaking illustrations work together to make this a striking picture book. *See* SCIENCE.

Katz, Bobbi. **A Rumpus of Rhymes: A Book of Noisy Poems.**
This noisy book consists of twenty-eight original poems that describe and display sounds. Onomatopoeia is used liberally along with fonts of different sizes, shapes and colors, making the noisy words jump off the page. These poems are most effective and fun when read out loud and possibly acted out. *See* ENGLISH—USE OF LANGUAGE.

Lithgow, John. **The Remarkable Farkle McBride.**
Farkle is a child prodigy who plays several musical instruments from the age of three. By the time he's ten, he's tired of all of them. One day the conductor becomes ill, and Farkle takes his place, satisfying him at last. Farkle's tale is told in rhyming verse and musical sounds in onomatopoeic form, making this a fun book to read out loud. *See* FINE ARTS.

McCarty, Nick. **The Iliad.**
This fast-paced, action-packed retelling of the classic tale uses colorful and descriptive language, making this an accessible version for students. The illustrations help to describe the text and keep the story moving. This version is an excellent choice to read aloud because of the action and its flowing language. *See* ENGLISH—CLASSICS.

Park, Barbara. **Skinnybones.**
Twelve-year old Alex Frankovitch's biggest dream is to be a great baseball player, but he's lousy at the game and ends up winning the Most Improved award each year—which shows him just how bad he really is. His sense of humor in dealing with his lack of athletic talent helps him to cope with everything in his life, including the school bully. The short, fast-paced chapters will have the listener laughing out loud, making this an outstanding read aloud for students in grades four through six. *See* HUMOR.

Paulsen, Gary. **Guts: The True Stories Behind Hatchet and the Brian Books.**
If you've enjoyed **Hatchet** (1987) and the other Brian books, you'll love this autobiographical work of Gary Paulsen, which gives a behind-the-scenes look at the real life experiences he used to create Brian's adventures. Read this aloud only if you can handle some blood and guts. Humor abounds, along with vividly descriptive language that will keep students glued to the story. *See* BIOGRAPHIES.

Paulsen, Gary. **Harris and Me: A Summer Remembered.**
If you're looking for a book to catch the interest of secondary students, this is the funniest book in the library. In this autobiographical tale, Paulsen relates his experiences from the summer he lived with his aunt and uncle and their two children, Glennis and Harris. Nine-year old Harris is rude and crude—a natural troublemaker filled with wild and crazy ideas. He and Paulsen team up to perform

one crazy antic after another. This fast-paced, hilarious book is sure to top the list of read-aloud favorites. *See* HUMOR.

Peck, Richard. **A Long Way from Chicago: A Novel in Stories.**
The antics of an eccentric grandmother are told by the grandson, Joe, now an adult. For seven summers he and his sister, Mary Alice, live with Grandma Dowdel, the zaniest grandmother imaginable. The entertaining and often irreverent stories are told in an easygoing manner, making this an excellent read aloud. *See* GREATEST OF THE LATEST.

Peck, Richard. **A Year Down Yonder.**
At age fifteen, Mary Alice's parents send her to stay with nonconforming Grandma Dowdel for an entire year. What she thought was a fate worse than death turns out to be an opportunity to learn that Grandma is an eccentric treasure, who teaches life's lessons in unique ways. Wit, humor, and vivid descriptions make this a terrific read aloud. *See* GREATEST OF THE LATEST.

Pinkney, Jerry. **Aesop's Fables.**
Sixty-one of Aesop's best and most familiar fables are retold accompanied by Pinkney's outstanding watercolor illustrations that are filled with intricate detail. Aesop's fables were handed down orally for hundreds of years before they were recorded into writing, so they're at their best when read aloud. Pinkney retold them with read alouds in mind. This volume is a must for every reader's collection. *See* ENGLISH—CLASSICS.

Van Draanen, Wendelin. **Flipped.**
Juli Baker has been crazy about Bryce Loski ever since second grade, when Bryce moved to Juli's street. Unfortunately, Bryce thinks she's a pain in the neck. The chapters alternate with Bryce telling his perspective of an event in one chapter and Juli telling her take on it in the one that follows. By the time they're eighth graders, they begin to see each other differently, causing them to fall for each other. The dialogue includes teenage slang and sayings, making this a great read aloud. *See* HUMOR.

Chapter 13

Science

The books listed in this section are varied. They include nonfiction works that combine science with other curricula and works of fiction involving scientific knowledge and know-how for survival. Other titles are fantasy books based on scientific facts and theories or biographies of people who have made important contributions to science. Still others celebrate through prose and poetry the beauty of the natural world and its many wonders.

Baker, Jeannie. **The Hidden Forest.** New York: Greenwillow Books, 2000. 36p. $17.00. ISBN 0-688-15761-0.

Ben's friend Sophie takes him into the undersea world off the coast of Tasmania to retrieve his lost fish trap. The story line is simple, but the depiction of the sea and all that lives in it is spectacular. Collages that consist of pressed seaweed, sponges, and sand give the reader the feeling of being in the water with Ben and Sophie. Baker vividly illustrates many varieties of kelp, along with the creatures that live in and around it. Ben is so impressed with the wonders of the "mysterious, hidden world" that he releases the catch in his fish trap, allowing it to go free in its beautiful home. The author's note gives additional information about the kelp and the habitat it creates off the coast of Tasmania.

Bang, Molly. **Nobody Particular: One Woman's Fight to Save the Bays.**

Diane Wilson, a shrimper in the bays of Texas, took on the petrochemical companies in the area to prevent them from dumping toxins into the bays. The book presents the story of her battle and also includes a second story about the freshwater ecological environment and how the intruding toxins are affecting it. This is a useful work to use when discussing the environment. *See* UNIQUE PRESENTATIONS.

Beshore, George. **Science in Ancient China.**

Many scientific advances were made in ancient China. This volume discusses the achievements made in science, medicine, astronomy, and cosmology, and discusses innovations such as rockets, the compass, water wheels, and movable type. *See* SERIES.

Beshore, George. **Science in Early Islamic Culture.**

The early Islamic culture, beginning in the 600s, was responsible for many surgical advances, medical treatises, and the development of Arabic numerals. This book describes these and other advancements and how they influence us today. *See* SERIES.

Brower, David Ross, and Aleks Petrovitch. **Reading the Earth: A Story of Wildness.** Berkeley, Calif.: Berkeley Hills Books, 2000. 49p. $16.00. ISBN 1-893163-15-6.

Brower, one of America's most prominent environmentalists, uses the picture-book format to relay the message that humanity needs to understand and protect nature. Three children gather around an elderly storyteller (Brower), who tells the story of the formation and development of the earth in terms of what happens each day of the week. Thirty seconds before midnight on Saturday, human beings are added, showing that we have been here a very short time compared with the age of the earth. Many things happen rapidly during the next few seconds, and with just three seconds left, we recognize that the planet is in danger. His question to all of us is, "What's going to happen next?" and he teaches an important lesson in just a few pages. Brower is best known as the executive director of the Sierra Club, the founder of the League of Conservation Voters, and his work with the Friends of the Earth and Earth Island. He died soon after this work was published.

Butterfield, Helen. **The Secret Life of Fishes: From Angels to Zebras on the Coral Reef.** New York: Abrams, 1999. 72p. $20.00. ISBN 0-8109-3933-9.

An astonishing amount of information about coral reefs and the life within them is packed into this alphabetically arranged book. It begins with an essay about coral reefs, describing where they're found and why they're so necessary in the ecological scheme of things, followed by an alphabetical display of fish found in the coral reefs. The capital letter of each section is drawn with a fish whose name begins with that letter swimming through it. Butterfield includes a paragraph of information about each fish, along with detailed watercolor illustrations. Nearly every letter includes several fish. For instance, H includes hawkfishes, humbugs, hamlets, halfbeaks, herring, and houndfish. The text is printed on an aquatic background that gives the reader the feeling of swimming along with the fish. A map of the world showing the locations of coral reefs and a list of the fishes, their scientific name, their size, and their habitat are included. The entire alphabet with its fishes is featured on the endpapers, adding a finishing touch to an elegant book.

Dash, Joan. **The Longitude Prize.**

In the eighteenth century, John Harrison, an uneducated village carpenter, sets out to win the prize of 20,000 pounds, offered by the British government, for devising an instrument that would determine longitude at sea. By so doing, he would save ships from being wrecked because the crew didn't know exactly where they were. After years of hard work, he succeeds in inventing the chronometer but is denied the prize because of his lack of status and education. He finally receives his due recognition—and the 20,000 pounds—only after fifty years of struggles. This book stresses the importance of math and science in Harrison's work and to the shipping industry. *See* MATHEMATICS.

Deem, James M. **Bodies from the Bog.**

We now know much more about life during the Iron Age, thanks to the two- to three-thousand-year-old bodies that were found in peat bogs of Northern Europe. The discovery of these bodies and the research methods used to analyze them is explained using both text and photos. This is a fascinating work, sure to intrigue students. *See* SOCIAL STUDIES—ANCIENT AND EARLY CULTURES.

Duffy, Trent. **The Clock.** Turning Point Inventions series. Illus. Toby Welles. New York: Atheneum Children's Books, 2000. 80p. $18.00. ISBN 0-689-82814-4.

Throughout history, humans have kept track of time using a variety of methods: observation of the heavens, sundials, hourglasses, water clocks, and calendars. The first mechanical clocks were developed during the Middle Ages, when trade increased the need for accurate time. Navigators also needed clocks to help them calculate longitude correctly. Present-day timekeeping devices include the atomic clock and computers' internal clocks. Duffy explores the influence of the clock and the impact it has on our daily lives in this well-researched, interesting book, presenting people who played a role in the development of the clock. Sketches, drawings, photographs, a large fold-out page showing clockworks throughout history, and a glossary make this an outstanding work. A companion fictional work that discusses the development of the clock and its influence on people is **The Clock** (1995) by James Lincoln Collier and Christopher Collier.

Fleischman, Paul. **Weslandia.**

Wesley develops a new civilization by using every part of his magical plant for food, clothing, shelter, and drink. His knowledge of plants and gardening are a great science tie in. This remarkable young boy also develops his own language and alphabet. *See* PICTURE BOOKS FOR ALL AGES.

Florian, Douglas. **Insectlopedia: Poems and Paintings.**

Twenty-one delightful poems give information on insects—from caterpillars to inchworms, crickets to mosquitoes. A full-page illustration opposite each poem describes the insect. Florian incorporates excellent information into each poem, making this a fun-to-use resource for studying those little critters. *See* POETRY.

Florian, Douglas. **Lizards, Frogs, and Polliwogs: Poems and Paintings.**

Amphibians and reptiles are the subject of the twenty-one humorous poems and watercolor drawings in this collection. Scientific information told in a humorous fashion makes this a fun book for a wide range of users from young children through adults. *See* POETRY.

Florian, Douglas. **Mammalabilia: Poems and Paintings.**

Florian presents twenty-one poems about animals using wordplay and various forms of poetry. Each poem is accompanied by a primitive, childlike painting of the animal, depicting the humor expressed in the poem. What a fun way to explore animals! *See* POETRY.

Gay, Kathlyn. **Science in Ancient Greece.**

This volume presents the theories and achievements of the ancient Greeks, including Ptolemy, Pythagoras, Hippocrates, and Aristotle, in astronomy, mathematics, geography, and medical science. The impact of these ancient works on modern science is discussed. *See* SERIES.

Gearhart, Sarah. **The Telephone.** Turning Point Inventions series. Illus. Toby Welles. New York: Atheneum Children's Books, 1999. 80p. $18.00. ISBN 0-689-82815-2.

Gearhart presents the history and the cultural significance of the telephone in a colorful, informative manner, tracing communication devices throughout time, as well as present and future trends and technology. The book provides information about people instrumental in the development of the telephone, especially Alexander Graham Bell. Color and black-and-white photographs and illustrations help to tell the story, along with a stunning foldout that shows how the telephone works. This is an excellent research tool.

George, Jean Craighead. **Nutik, the Wolf Pup.**

Julie, from **Julie of the Wolves** (1974), **Julie** (1996), and **Julie's Wolf Pack** (1998), brings home a sickly wolf pup for her little brother, Amaroq, to nurse back to health. Amaroq and Nutik become best friends, and Amaroq is brokenhearted when the wolf pack comes to claim their pup. The illustrations by Ted Rand depict the Arctic environment, making this simple yet touching story a perfect accompaniment for the other Julie books. *See* PICTURE BOOKS FOR ALL AGES.

Haddix, Margaret Peterson. **Turnabout.** New York: Simon & Schuster, 2000. 223p. $17.00. ISBN 0-689-82187-5, 0-689-84037-3pa.

Melly and Anny Beth are one hundred years old and living in a nursing home when they agree to participate in an experiment to reverse aging. They begin to live their lives backward, becoming younger each year. This is great for a while because they're able to rectify some mistakes they made the first time around, but in 2085, they're teenagers again, worrying about who will care for them as they become young children. They are still concerned that their real identities will be discovered, but they also know they need caregivers. When a reporter begins to track them down, they run away to Melly's childhood home, which they discover in now being occupied by Melly's great-great-great-granddaughter, A. J. Hazelwood, a reporter. The girls decide to allow A. J. to be their surrogate parent, and an unusual family is formed. This fast-paced and entertaining science fiction novel presents the reader with the serious issues from genetics and cloning to the ethical issues that surround aging, scientific experimentation, and immortality.

Harris, Jacqueline L. **Science in Ancient Rome.**

This book discusses how the ancient Romans built on other people's achievements. For example, rather than reinventing the wheel, they used previous knowledge, added to it, redefined it, and came up with new techniques and materials to improve their lives. *See* SERIES.

Harris, Robie H. **It's So Amazing!: A Book About Eggs, Sperm, Birth, Babies and Families.** Illus. Michael Emberley. Cambridge, Mass.: Candlewick Press, 1999. 81p. $22.00. ISBN 0-7636-0051-2, 0-7636-1321-5pa.

The curious bee and the shy bird found in **It's Perfectly Normal** (1996) are back to tell the story of how a baby is made, from the moment an egg and sperm join, through pregnancy and birth. The cartoon characters and dialogue balloons add a light touch to the frank, honest text dealing with reproduction, growing up, male and female body parts, reproduction, HIV and AIDS, sexual abuse, homosexuality and heterosexuality, and other related topics. Special emphasis is placed on staying safe, healthy, unafraid, and informed.

Heller, Ruth. **A Sea Within A Sea: Secrets of the Sargasso.** New York: Grosset & Dunlap, 2000. 32p. $17.00. ISBN 0-448-42417-7.

The secrets of the mysterious Sargasso Sea, found in the North Atlantic off the eastern coast of the United States, are explored and revealed in this impressive book written in rhyme form and illustrated with Heller's signature broad strokes and colors. One by one Heller presents the mysteries and explains them by describing the plants and animals that live in the Sargasso and their special adaptations, which have caused legends of lost and becalmed ships. A map of the Sargasso Sea appears at the beginning of the book, and the final page features a close-up of it, this time including the area known as the Bermuda Triangle. The catchy rhymes along with the full-page colored illustrations make this an auditory and visual feast.

Herbert, Janis. **Leonardo da Vinci for Kids: His Life and Ideas: 21 Activities.**

Leonardo da Vinci explored the world around him, including many scientific aspects. This outstanding book includes his study of human anatomy, flight, animals, botany, machines and inventions, water, and the universe. Make-it-yourself projects help students explore and create. *See* BIOGRAPHIES.

Herbert, Janis. **Lewis and Clark for Kids: Their Journey of Discovery with 21 Activities.**

This saga of the Lewis and Clark expedition includes many references to scientific discoveries recorded along the way, including plants, animals, landscape, bodies of water, and weather. The book includes related hands-on activities that explain what Lewis and Clark encountered. The science-related activities feature the use of latitude and longitude, preserving plants, making fruit leather, learning about the lunar cycle, doing a winter count, tracking animals, and learning about trail signs. *See* SOCIAL STUDIES—UNITED STATES HISTORY.

Hobbs, Will. **Down the Yukon.** New York: HarperCollins, 2001. 193p. $16.00. ISBN 0-688-17472-8, 0-06-0295450-6, 0-380-73309-9pa.

In **Jason's Gold** (1999), the three Hawthorn brothers, Jason, Ethan, and Abe are determined to make a living in Alaska during the gold rush. After many adventures, they establish a thriving sawmill business. In this sequel, sixteen-year old Jason again narrates their story of hardship and adventure. The sawmill is lost because of Ethan's gambling, and Jason is determined to buy it back. Jason's girlfriend, Jamie Dunavant, returns, and the two of them join 300 other participants in the Great Race across Alaska, which will originate in Dawson City and end in Nome, Alaska. The first team to arrive will win $20,000—more than enough to regain the sawmill. The canoe trip down the Yukon and the overland trek are the focal points of the book. The descriptions of the terrain, the flora and fauna, and the people encountered along the way are outstanding. Hobbs bases his writing on extensive research, personal experiences, and his love for the outdoors, which gives the reader accurate information as well as an exciting story. The author's notes at the end of the book separates fact from fiction by giving the sources and expanded explanations for the factual information. The map at the beginning of the book guides readers through their journey. This exciting survival adventure makes a terrific read aloud.

Hobbs, Will. **Jason's Gold.** New York: Morrow Junior Books, 1999. 221p. $16.00. ISBN 0-688-15093-4. 0-380-72914-8pa.

The Hawthorn brothers, Abe, Ethan, and Jason, the youngest, have fallen on hard times since the death of their parents, but they are determined to join the Alaskan gold rush in 1897. Jason is in New York when he hears about the rush but hurries to Seattle to meet his brothers. He misses them and has to make his own way to Dawson City. His adventures along the Dead Horse Trail and the nearly impossible Chilkoot Pass are based on the actual encounters and hardships the Klondikers of the late 1800s experienced. Against all odds, he makes it to Dawson City, meets up with his brothers, meets Jack London along the way, and is befriended by a Canadian girl, Jamie, who becomes his girlfriend. An incredible amount of information about the wilds of Alaska is packed into this book. In the author's notes at the end of the book, Hobbs explains how he came to write this tale and provides the references he used to make the book as accurate as possible. The maps at the beginning of the book are a helpful reference tool.

Hobbs, Will. **The Maze.** New York: Morrow Junior Books, 1998. 197p. $15.00. ISBN 0-688-15092-6, 0-380-72913-Xpa.

Rick Walker is a troubled teen on the run from a juvenile detention center. He ends up in a portion of Utah's Canyonlands National Park known as the Maze District, so named because of its confusing canyons. He becomes friends with a biologist, Lon Peregrino, who has devised an elaborate system to nurture six young condors bred in captivity with the goal of releasing them into the wild. Rick has a fascination with flying, and Lon teaches him to hang glide, which becomes important when two thieves intent on killing Lon and the condors enter this tranquil setting. Rick uses a dramatic hang glide rescue to help save Lon. Lon vouches for Rick, and the judge assigns Rick to Lon's care. The premise of a troubled teen helped by a caring adult is a common theme in young adult literature, but the spectacular setting, the hang gliding, and the fascinating details about condors set this book apart. The author's note provides insight into the writing of the book and the URL for the condor release program Web site.

Hoffman, Mary. **Sun, Moon, and Stars.**
Through twenty-one myths and legends from cultures around the world, Hoffman explains the heavenly bodies. She compares myths from the past with what we know now, making this an interesting work to use when studying astronomy. *See* MYTHS, FOLKTALES, AND LEGENDS.

Hopkins, Lee Bennett, selected by. **Spectacular Science: A Book of Poems.** Illus. Virginia Halstead. New York: Simon & Schuster, 1999. 37p. $17.00. ISBN 0-689-81283-3.
What is science, and why bother studying it? Answers to these questions and more can be discovered by reading the fifteen poems, by various poets, included in this gem. The first entry, "What Is Science?" by Rebecca Kai Dotlich, shows the wide range of science topics available: "What is science? / So many things. / The study of stars— / Saturn's rings. / The study of soil, / oil, and gas. / Of sea and sky, / of seed and grass." Other topics include wildlife, plants, microscopic animals, dinosaurs, magnets, rock formations, weather, and stars. The brief poems on a wide variety of subjects, along with the dramatic drawings, make this book a valuable resource.

January, Brendan. **Science in Colonial America.**
This volume in the series discusses the scientific contributions made by people in colonial America including work by Cotton Mathers on inoculation, Thomas Jefferson and John and William Bartram's study of natural history, David Rittenhouse's work in astronomy, and Ben Franklin's discoveries in electricity. *See* SERIES.

January, Brendan. **Science in the Renaissance.**
After reviewing the state of science in medieval Europe, the text goes on to discuss the changes brought about by the discoveries and observations made during the Renaissance. Topics include geometry, mathematics in art, the study of anatomy and disease in medicine, and the work of Copernicus and Galileo. *See* SERIES.

Jenkins, Steve. **The Top of the World: Climbing Mount Everest.**
A great deal of information about Mount Everest is presented in this fact-filled book describing a trek to the summit. Jenkins gives readers the history and information about the terrain, along with descriptions of the dangers of the climb—avalanches, crevasses, unstable snow layers, strong winds, extreme cold, and lack of oxygen. Outstanding cut-paper collages complement the text. *See* SPORTS AND GAMES.

Johnston, Tony. **Desert Song.** Illus. Ed Young. San Francisco: Sierra Club Books, 2000. 32p. $16.00. ISBN 0-87156-491-2.

As the searing sun sets in the Sonoran desert, nighttime magic begins. This strikingly beautiful book follows the bat as it spills from its cave and witnesses the emerging night animals—the moths, ants, weevils, beetles, and other insects, the owls, coyote, and snakes. The text is lyrical and songlike, portraying the mysticism of a desert night. The opening passage sets the stage: "Day is done. / Twilight comes. / The sun goes down / and streaks the clouds / with flame." Ed Young's full-page illustrations of pastels, collage, and textured paper vividly portray the desert's beauty. This spectacular book can be used as an example of descriptive language and artwork in addition to exploring the desert environment.

Kessler, Cristina. **Jubela.** Illus. JoEllen McAllister Stammen. New York: Simon & Schuster, 2001. 32p. $16.00. ISBN 0-689-81895-5.

Jubela, a baby rhinoceros, is orphaned after poachers shoot his mother. The inexperienced, frightened baby has trouble surviving on his own, until an older female rhino adopts him, nurses him back to health, and teaches him survival skills. Kessler, an author and photographer from Mali, based this on a true story, related by the park rangers at the Mkhaya Game Reserve in Swaziland, southern Africa. This is an appropriate story to use when discussing endangered animals and environmental concerns. A paragraph at the end of the book describes the plight of the decreasing rhino population in Africa. The pastel illustrations capture the African landscape at various times of the day and night. The portrayal of the animals of the savanna is outstanding, making this an excellent book to use when studying Africa.

Kurlansky, Mark. **The Cod's Tale.**

Kurlansky tells the history of the European and North American world in relation to the fishing and consuming of codfish from the time of the Vikings until the present. The book clearly explains the life cycle of the cod, its habitat, habits, and enemies. *See* SOCIAL STUDIES—UNITED STATES HISTORY.

Lauber, Patricia. **What You Never Knew About Tubs, Toilets & Showers.**

This history of bathing, washing, and human waste disposal could fit well within a health and hygiene unit. Students will love the humorous artwork, complete with lots of bare bottoms. *See* SOCIAL STUDIES—ANCIENT AND EARLY CULTURES.

Locker, Thomas. **Mountain Dance.** San Diego, Calif.: Silver Whistle/Harcourt, 2001. 32p. $16.00. ISBN 0-15-202622-3.

The majesty of mountains is celebrated in this beautiful book that tells the geologic evolution of mountains, beginning with volcanic eruptions and continuing with the natural forces of nature building them up or wearing them down. The text, told in free verse poetry, creates a feeling of power, movement, and grace, expressing nature's "dance" through time. The oil paintings opposite each text page match the grandeur of the mountains, are painted in rich hues, and describe each lyric. A miniature of each painting is listed in the back along with a paragraph explaining what's taking place in the painting. This beautiful work is an excellent teaching tool for a geology unit.

Mitton, Jacqueline. **Kingdom of the Sun: A Book of the Planets.** Illus. Christina Balit. Washington, D.C.: National Geographic Society, 2001. 26p. $17.00. ISBN 0-7922-7220-X.

The Greeks and Romans attempted to explain natural phenomenon through myths. This book combines modern-day knowledge about the sun, moon, and the planets with ancient mythology. Information about each planet, the sun, and the moon is told from the celestial body's point of view as a part of a two-page spread. For instance, "Venus" begins as follows: "A glittering jewel of the heavens, I blaze like a brilliant diamond. Matchless among the planets, I shine brighter than them all." The planet then goes on to tell how people throughout time have perceived it, comparing what is known now with the god for which it was named. The vivid illustrations further depict the mythological aspect, with splashes of shiny gold used as highlights. The illustrations incorporate bright shades of golds, yellows, oranges, blues, and black—the colors of the universe—making them a striking accompaniment to the text. The front endpaper depicts the relative sizes of the small planets and earth's moon, and the back endpaper shows the relative sizes of the giant planets, all done on a black background, with the sun in one corner. In the back of the book, a chart gives information about the sun, moon, and planets, along with a glossary to complete this celestial resource.

Morrison, Gordon. **Oak Tree.** Boston: Houghton Mifflin, 2000. 30p. $16.00. ISBN 0-395644-7.

At first glance this book looks like a simple telling of the life cycle of a tree, but the reader needs to carefully examine each page to absorb the detailed information that's included. The main story is a year in the life of a white oak, beginning in the spring when the sap begins to run. This story is told using normal-sized print, scientific language, and detailed pen-and-ink with watercolor drawings to explain what's happening to the tree at each stage of the year. In addition, smaller drawings of the animals that live in and around the tree and the scientific processes that are happening to the tree are described using small print and small, detailed pen-and-ink drawings. These appear toward the bottoms of the pages. This beautiful and informative book is useful as a reference book as well as for browsing.

Paulsen, Gary. **Brian's Return.** New York: Delacorte Press, 1999. 117p. $16.00. ISBN 0-385-32500-2, 0-440-41379-6pa.

After the many adventures Brian has in **Hatchet** (1987), **The River** (1991), and **Brian's Winter** (1996), he attempts to join the crowd and be a regular high school kid. However, he's having a very difficult time leaving the excitement of the wild and adjusting to pizza parlors and shopping malls. With the help of a counselor, Brian begins to realize that he needs to leave this make-believe world and get back into the outdoors. He carefully gathers all the tools and gear he'll need for survival and returns to the lakes and streams, to the wild flora and fauna—the environment that suits him the best. This is not a high adventure book but a celebration of Brian discovering who he is and where he belongs. Keen descriptions of Brian's outdoor environment and how he fits into this setting are given, demonstrating once again Paulsen's knowledge and love of this way of life. This book needs to be read after reading the previous books to understand that "when a person has once been possessed by the wild it is not possible for him to be truly normal again."

Paulsen, Gary. **Guts: The True Stories Behind Hatchet and the Brian Books.**

Gary Paulsen displays his extensive knowledge of nature in this autobiographical work that describes the incidents from his life that shaped Brian's adventures in **Hatchet** (1987) and the other Brian books. Told with humor and vividly descriptive language, this book is a true winner. *See* BIOGRAPHIES.

Redmond, Ian. **The Elephant Book: For the Elefriends Campaign.** Cambridge, Mass.: Candlewick Press, 2001. 48p. $18.00. ISBN 0-7636-1634-6.

This stunning book, updated from the 1991 edition, pays tribute to the pachyderm. The elephant is endangered because of the ivory trade, and this book is dedicated to saving the species by informing people of its wonders. Breathtaking photos of the African landscape and the elephants, along with detailed information and quotations by prominent scientists, give the reader a clear understanding of the ecological importance of the elephant. Half the royalties go to the Elefriends Project, which is working for elephant protection. Information about this project and an index are included at the back of the book. Philip Cayford, a wildlife filmmaker, says, "The elephant is a symbol of much that we aspire to ourselves—strength, dignity, wisdom, humor and close family ties. We owe it to our children and to the elephant himself, to reverse in the twenty-first century the tide of destruction that swept though Africa during the twentieth century."

Salisbury, Graham. **Lord of the Deep.**

Mikey works as a deckhand on his stepfather's charter boat in Hawaii, eager to help make money for the family and to please Bill, his stepfather. One day, a prize-winning fish is caught, but the two customers don't deserve a prize because they didn't do all the reeling in. They bribe Bill to say they did, and Mikey is involved in this moral dilemma. Excellent descriptions of Hawaii, the waters around it, and the fish in the sea are given in this fast-paced adventure. *See* GREATEST OF THE LATEST.

Schwartz, David M. **Q Is for Quark: A Science Alphabet Book.** Illus. Kim Doner. Berkeley, Calif.: Tricycle Press, 2001. 64p. $16.00. ISBN 1-58246-021-3.

Science terms from A to Z are included in this comprehensive alphabet book. Each entry includes a light-hearted two- to three-page explanation of the topic, along with cartoon drawings that illustrate the concept. The tone is light, but the explanations are extensive and thorough. The topics include atom, black hole, clone, DNA, element, fault, gravity, H2O, immune system, jet propulsion, kitchen, light, music, natural selection, occam's razor, pH, quark, rot, système international, think, universe, vortex, wow, xylem, y chromosome, and Zzzzz. An extensive glossary is included, along with an index. This book should be on every science teacher's desk.

Siebert, Diane. **Mississippi.** Illus. Greg Harlin. New York: HarperCollins, 2001. 36p. $17.00. ISBN 0-688-16446-3.

Through rhyming poetry, this powerful book tells the story of the Mississippi River from the Ice Age to the present. Each time period is captured through Siebert's nearly flawless verse along with Harlin's outstanding watercolor paintings. The reader can feel the power and majesty of the river as it rolls along through time, from the north to the south in the United States. She begins and ends with "I am the river, / Deep and strong. / I sing an old, enduring song / With rhythms wild and rhythms tame, / And Mississippi is my name." Siebert includes information about the changes and challenges—all imposed by humans—facing the river and its communities. The About the River section and the River Words glossary are helpful, as is the map of the river drawn on the endpapers. This book will leave a lasting impression on every reader.

Simon, Seymour. **Out of Sight: Pictures of Hidden Worlds.** New York: SeaStar Books, 2000. 48p. $19.00. ISBN 1-58717-011-6, 1-58717-012-4 (lib. bdg.), 1-58717-149-Xpa.

This stunning book of things not seen by the naked eye boggles the imagination and can become an "Oh, wow!" experience. A variety of instruments, including a telescope, an electron microscope, a scanning electron micrograph, an endoscope, computer-aided tomography (CAT scans), X rays, an electronic strobe, a Landsat satellite, the Hubble Space Telescope, and other technologies were used to capture these "hidden worlds." The subject of each brightly colored photograph provides a guessing game, with the text revealing what the image is and how the picture was captured.

The book is divided into four parts: "Hidden Worlds Around You," "Hidden Worlds Inside Your Body," "Hidden Worlds of Time," and "Hidden Worlds of the Earth." Some of the images captured are a spiked virus, the tiny hooks of Velcro, tooth plaque, cholesterol, the abdominal cavity of a living person, a blood cell attacking *E. coli* bacteria, a speeding bullet, the eye of a hurricane, and the Great Red Spot on the surface of Jupiter. Seymour's introduction sets the stage for this outstanding book, sure to intrigue all readers.

Singh, Rina. **Moon Tales: Myths of the Moon from Around the World.** Illus. Debbie Lush. London: Bloomsbury Children's Books, 1999. 77p. $20.00. ISBN 0-7475-4112-4.

Throughout time celestial bodies have intrigued people from around the world. This book pulls together stories that try to explain the moon, taken from Chinese, Jewish, West African, Polynesian, Siberian, Canadian, Indian, English, Japanese, and Australian traditions. Each is a moral, tale, myth, or story about the beauty, power and wonder of the moon. The brightly colored, luminous paintings, arranged in various places on the pages, depict the important elements from each story and culture, providing additional information and pleasure. This unique collection will add information and interest when studying the universe.

Spickert, Diane Nelson. **Earthsteps: A Rock's Journey Through Time.** Illus. Marianne D. Wallace. Golden, Colo.: Fulcrum Kids, 2000. 32p. $18.00. ISBN 1-55591-986-3.

During the Permian age, 250 million years ago, a rock worked loose due to freezing and expansion, rolled down a cliff, and ended up on the banks of a pond. The rock continues on a geologic journey, becoming smaller and smaller, being washed to other locations because of erosion and water movement. The story follows the geological progression of the earth, depicting the plants and animals that evolved during each time period until present day, when it is now a grain of sand. The history of the world is related in a unique manner, with the full-color illustrations doing a great deal of the telling. A geologic timescale on a two-page spread at the beginning of the book is worth careful examination. The accompanying paragraph explains how scientists determine the dating of the earth. A glossary and a bibliography are also helpful.

Stewart, Melissa. **Science in Ancient India.**

After a brief history of India, the text looks at the culture's scientific advances in the disciplines of medicine, mathematics, astronomy, and physics. There's a special emphasis on the fact that Indian scientists and philosophers studied the sciences centuries before their Western counterparts. *See* SERIES.

Wallace, Joseph. **The Camera.** Turning Point Inventions series. Illus. Toby Welles. New York: Atheneum Children's Books, 2000. 80p. $18.00. ISBN 0-689-82813-6.

Wallace examines the scientific, cultural, and historical development of photography and cameras in this attractive volume. The people instrumental in the development of the camera are discussed, as well as current and upcoming trends in photography. Pictures of some of the earliest known photographs are featured, along with full-color and black-and-white illustrations and a foldout that shows the parts of a camera and how photography works. This is an excellent book for research and for shutterbugs wanting to know more about cameras.

Wallace, Joseph. **The Lightbulb.** Turning Point Inventions series. Illus. Toby Welles. New York: Atheneum Children's Books, 1999. 80p. $18.00. ISBN 0-689-8216-0, 0-689-82816-0.

This interesting, well-written volume reveals the history and development of lighting from the earliest times through modern day. Wallace discusses the people instrumental in the development of the light bulb, especially Thomas Edison. Future trends and needs are included. Beautiful full-color illustrations and black-and-white photographs, along with a large foldout that traces the types of lighting devices and how they work, provide additional information. A glossary is included.

Wiesner, David. **Sector 7.**

While on a fieldtrip to the Empire State Building, a boy is carried away by a cloud to Sector 7, the place where clouds are designed, manufactured, and dispatched. Much to the chagrin of management, he does some redesigning and comes up with clouds like fish and other sea animals, rather than in the traditional cloud shapes. After returning to his fieldtrip group, he looks out the bus window and sees a host of animal-shaped clouds overhead. This wordless book is a fanciful way to study cloud forms. *See* PICTURE BOOKS FOR ALL AGES.

Woods, Geraldine. **Science in Ancient Egypt.**

The ancient Egyptians soared when it came to discoveries in science, mathematics, astronomy, medicine, architecture, agriculture, and technology. This volume ties their accomplishments in with today's use of these achievements. *See* SERIES.

Woods, Geraldine. **Science in the Early Americas.**

The scientific achievements of the North American tribes, along with the Inca, Aztec, and Maya cultures, are discussed in this volume. It includes advances in medicine, mathematics, engineering, and astronomy. Woods presents the theories, practices, and customs of various tribes and cultures. *See* SERIES.

Woods, Michael, and Mary B. Woods. **Ancient Machines: From Wedges to Waterwheels.**

All machines, from the earliest times to the present, are a combination of six simple machines; the lever, the wheel and axle, the inclined plane, the pulley, the wedge, and the screw. This book presents the various machines developed and used by early cultures, drawing a strong connection between ancient and modern technologies. This can be a great tie-in when studying simple machines. *See* SERIES.

Woods, Michael, and Mary B. Woods. **Ancient Medicine: From Sorcery to Surgery.**

Medical knowledge and procedures practiced during the Stone Age and in ancient Egypt, India, China, Greece, and Rome are presented in a lively manner with fascinating detail. Many of the practices presented are forerunners of procedures used today. This is a valuable resource to use when studying the human body and medical practices. *See* SERIES.

Zahares, Wade, compiled and illustrated by. **Big, Bad and a Little Bit Scary: Poems That Bite Back!**

Animal poems are usually warm and fuzzy, teaching us to love and appreciate specific animals. Not so in this collection of fifteen poems, each pointing out the scariest aspects of various animals, accompanied by overstated, oversized, scary illustrations. Scary information can be found about the viper, alligator, panther, sparrow hawk, shark, lion, vulture, eel, porcupine, octopus, piranha, bat, barracuda, and hippopotamus. This book should be used with older students who will appreciate the humor and fun in the poetry. *See* POETRY.

Chapter 14

Series

Many books written as a part of a series are available, but only a few can be included in this collection. Those listed have special significance to the middle school curricula. Also included are works of fiction, done in a series, that will especially interest secondary readers.

ANCIENT TECHNOLOGY SERIES

Each of the eight books in this outstanding series deals with a specific part of life in the ancient societies. Each title includes maps, a time line, color pictures and photographs, a glossary, a bibliography, and an index, making these books valuable for research as well as browsing. All of the books are written by the same authors, providing continuity and consistency throughout the series. Some of the information can also be found in the Science in the Past series, but this series is more detailed and inclusive.

Woods, Michael, and Mary B. Woods. **Ancient Agriculture: From Foraging to Farming.** Ancient Technology series. Minneapolis, Minn.: Runestone Press, 2000. 96p. $20.00. ISBN 0-8225-2995-5.

Food gathering and raising throughout the early societies is explored using interesting and detailed information, color photographs and reproductions, and introductory sidebars at the beginning of each chapter. The ancient civilizations discussed include those of the Stone Age, the ancient Middle East, ancient Egypt, ancient China, the ancient Americas, ancient Greece, and ancient Rome.

Woods, Michael, and Mary B. Woods. **Ancient Communication: From Grunts to Graffiti.** Ancient Technology series. Minneapolis, Minn.: Runestone Press, 2000. 88p. $20.00. ISBN 0-8225-2996-3.

Methods of communication in the ancient Middle East, India, China, Egypt, Greece, Rome, and the Americas are discussed. Painting techniques, writing systems and equipment, printing methods, and the notion of libraries are presented.

Woods, Michael, and Mary B. Woods. **Ancient Computing: From Counting to Calendars.** Ancient Technology series. Minneapolis, Minn.: Runestone Press, 2000. 88p. $20.00. ISBN 0-8225-2997-1.

The idea of computing to count, problem solve, and gather information dates back to prehistoric times and took on various forms in ancient civilizations. This book includes the use of counting, number systems, and measurement in the Stone Age, ancient Middle East, Egypt, India, China, Greece, Rome, and the ancient Americas. It makes a great tie-in with the mathematics curriculum.

Woods, Michael, and Mary B. Woods. **Ancient Construction: From Tents to Towers.** Ancient Technology series. Minneapolis, Minn.: Runestone Press, 2000. 88p. $20.00. ISBN 0-8225-2998-X.

Early buildings and how they were constructed, as well as the materials and tools used, are among the topics discussed in this information-packed work. It covers some of the earliest constructions, which were bridges, and continues to discuss other construction work done during the Stone Age, ancient Middle East, Egypt, India, China, Mesoamerica, Greece, and Rome. Various types of architecture from each society are presented with text and colored photos.

Woods, Michael, and Mary B. Woods. **Ancient Machines: From Wedges to Waterwheels.** Ancient Technology series. Minneapolis, Minn.: Runestone Press, 2000. 88p. $20.00. ISBN 0-8225-2994-7.

All machines, from the earliest times to the present, are a combination of six simple machines; the lever, the wheel and axle, the inclined plane, the pulley, the wedge, and the screw. This book presents the various machines developed and used by early cultures, drawing a strong connection between ancient and modern technologies. It is a fascinating presentation of inventions developed by each society and their importance to the world then and now.

Woods, Michael, and Mary B. Woods. **Ancient Medicine: From Sorcery to Surgery.** Ancient Technology series. Minneapolis, Minn.: Runestone Press, 2000. 88p. $20.00. ISBN 0-8225-2992-0.

Medical knowledge and procedures practiced during the Stone Age and in ancient Egypt, India, China, Greece, and Rome are presented in a lively manner with fascinating detail. Evidence shows that brain surgery was performed by doctors during the Stone Age. Huge Bengali ants were used by Hindu surgeons to suture intestinal surgery. Ancient Roman surgical instruments have been found that were better than instruments available during the Renaissance. Many of these procedures were forerunners of practices used today. This is a valuable resource to use when studying the human body and medical practices as well as ancient cultures.

Woods, Michael, and Mary B. Woods. **Ancient Transportation: From Camels to Canals.** Ancient Technology series. Minneapolis, Minn.: Runestone Press, 2000. 96p. $20.00. ISBN 0-8225-2993-9.

Transportation has always been an important factor in civilizations, a fact that is emphasized in this book presenting methods of transportation including early boats, oxen, chariots, and warships. Things associated with transportation such as maps, roads, bridges, life preservers, shipping ports, and shipping containers are included. It is believed that some technologies migrated from one culture to another, so the wheel didn't have to be reinvented many times. The text points out that knowledge of the observations, needs, and adaptations made by early cultures is still relevant to our current transportation needs.

Woods, Michael, and Mary B. Woods. **Ancient Warfare: From Clubs to Catapults.** Ancient Technology series. Minneapolis, Minn.: Runestone Press, 2000. 96p. $20.00. ISBN 0-8225-2999-8.

The authors present various weapons that were invented, developed, and used from 6000 B.C. to A.D. 476 in the Middle East, Egypt, China, Mesoamerica, Greece, Rome, and India in this attractive volume. Changes in weapons took place depending on the development of new materials. Outstanding photographs show the weaponry, armor, and military tactics described in the text.

CULTURE CRAFT SERIES

Each book in this series showcases eight crafts from a country and the cultures within it, including information on crafts in general, materials, the country's handicraft traditions, and a simple colored map. The clear, step-by-step directions also feature drawings, diagrams, and color photographs, making these books highly useful when studying cultures from around the world. Each volume includes a metric conversion chart, a short glossary, a list for further reading, and an index.

Temko, Florence. **Traditional Crafts from Africa.**

This how-to book gives instructions for Senufo mud painting, Asante Adinkra stamping, Fon story pictures, Ndbele bead bracelets, Tutsi baskets, the Kigogo game, an Islamic art box, and a Guro animal mask. *See* FINE ARTS.

Temko, Florence. **Traditional Crafts from the Caribbean.**

Temko gives how-to instructions for crafts from the Caribbean region, including Jamaican woven fish, Puerto Rican *vejigante* masks, tap-tap trucks, yarn dolls, and metal cutouts. *See* FINE ARTS.

Temko, Florence. **Traditional Crafts from China.**

Temko offers directions for paper cutouts, figures made from dough, kites, string puppets, tangrams, a needlework purse, wheat straw pictures, and picture scrolls in this volume that showcases ancient Chinese crafts. *See* FINE ARTS.

Temko, Florence. **Traditional Crafts from Japan.**

Eight traditional handicrafts handed down through the centuries are presented in this work. Included are *daruma* dolls, *ka-mon* (family crests), *koi nobori* (fish-shaped wind socks), *maneki neko* (welcoming cats), the origami crane, stencils for fabrics, *tanabata* festival decorations, and *den-den* (a festive toy drum). *See* FINE ARTS.

Temko, Florence. **Traditional Crafts from Mexico and Central America.**

In this volume, Temko provides instructions on how to make Mexican and Central American handicrafts including tin ornaments and *papel picado,* Guatemalan weaving, Otomi paper figures, Day of the Dead skeletons, a tree of life, Guatemalan worry dolls, and Cuna *molas. See* FINE ARTS.

Temko, Florence. **Traditional Crafts from Native North America.**

Temko gives instructions for making Native American crafts, including a Lakota dreamcatcher, Blackfeet beadwork, an Iroquois cornhusk doll, Seminole patchwork, Pueblo storyteller dolls, Chumash baskets, Haida totem poles, and Southwestern *cascarones. See* FINE ARTS.

THE HERCULEAH JONES SERIES

Herculeah Jones, a budding private investigator, solves mysteries in each book, with the help of her sidekick and neighbor, Meat. Herculeah's father, the town's police chief, and her mother, a private investigator, keep warning her not to get involved, but it's in her blood—she just can't leave a good mystery unsolved. These books are written on a lower reading level, making them very appropriate for grades four and up. The fast pace of the humorous mysteries make these excellent read alouds.

Byars, Betsy. **The Dark Stairs.** Herculeah Jones series. New York: Viking, 1994. 130p. $15.00. ISBN 0-670-85487-5, 0-14-036996pa.

Herculeah, while searching for a missing property owner, is locked in a dark, spooky basement. While there, she discovers a hidden staircase and finds the body of the missing homeowner. It's best to read this one first because it introduces the characters who are featured throughout the series.

Byars, Betsy. **Dead Letter.** Herculeah Jones series. New York: Viking, 1996. 146p. $15.00. ISBN 0-670-86860-4, 0-14-038138-4pa.

In the third book in the series Herculeah finds a note in the lining of a coat she purchased at the second-hand store, which indicates the previous owner has been harmed—possibly even murdered. Herculeah, with the help of Meat, solves the mystery in this cliffhanger, which incorporates danger, villains, and good doses of humor.

Byars, Betsy. **Death's Door.** Herculeah Jones series. New York: Viking, 1997. 134p. $15.00. ISBN 0-670-87423-X, 0-14-130288-7pa.

Herculeah steps up the excitement in this episode, which includes Meat's becoming the target of a hired killer and Herculeah being kidnapped by Meat's uncle. It takes a while for Herculeah and Meat to unravel this case of mistaken identity, but in the meantime they're dodging bullets and fearing for their lives.

Byars, Betsy. **Disappearing Acts.**

Meat steals the show in this episode, when he finds a dead body in the bathroom of the comedy club where he's gone to take lessons. Herculeah is involved with her own quest, but the two come together to solve the multiple mysteries presented. *See* READ ALOUDS.

Byars, Betsy. **Tarot Says Beware.** Herculeah Jones series. New York: Viking, 1995. 151p. $15.00. ISBN 0-670-85575-8, 0-14-036997-Xpa.

Herculeah discovers Madame Rosa's parrot, Tarot, outside Rosa's house, which is highly unusual. Herculeah enters the house and finds Madame Rosa's body. Meat and Herculeah manage to get to the bottom of the mystery, but only after many adventures and scrapes. As in the entire series, humor and a fast pace make these hard to put down.

THE HIGH SEAS TRILOGY

Each of the three books in this series centers around John Spencer, the son of a British ship owner during the 1800s. High adventure takes place in each book, always involving ships and sailing. The works are well researched and historically accurate, appreciated more by older readers.

Lawrence, Iain. **The Buccaneers.**

John Spencer and the crew of *The Dragon* are bound for the Caribbean. They rescue a mysterious man floating aimlessly in the sea. As the voyage continues, they encounter severe storms, illness, and cruel pirates, creating high adventure on the sea. *See* GREATEST OF THE LATEST.

Lawrence, Iain. **The Smugglers.**

John Spencer is in charge of his father's new ship, *The Dragon*. It seems jinxed from the beginning, the captain is murdered and John realizes the crew is a bunch of scalawags. The cargo is finally brought to its destination, but many adventures occur along the way. *See* GREATEST OF THE LATEST.

Lawrence, Iain. **The Wreckers.**

The *Isle of the Skye* is shipwrecked by unscrupulous townspeople who make their living looting cargo from lost ships. John Spencer, the son of the ship's owner, survives, but his life is in danger. Excitement, adventure, mystery, and intrigue abound in this page-turner. *See* GREATEST OF THE LATEST.

INFORMANIA SERIES

Each book in this series is written on hot topics of high interest, sure to be crowd pleasers. Captioned tabs divide each section, providing a good idea about the topic covered in the section. The books are assembled with a hard cover over a spiral binding, which makes it a bit fragile. The paperback versions have a regular binding. The stiff-coated, heavy stock, glossy pages give them a sturdy feel. Each entry is colorful and includes cartoons, photos, and paintings.

Jenkins, Martin. **Vampires.**

Everything you've ever wanted to know about vampires can be found in this highly attractive book, sure to attract readers. *See* UNIQUE PRESENTATIONS.

Maynard, Christopher. **Ghosts.**

Dark and eerie illustrations along with photographs, movie stills, and amusing cartoons give an entertaining look at ghosts, a favorite subject of middle grade students. This is a must for ghost lovers. *See* UNIQUE PRESENTATIONS.

Maynard, Christopher. **Sharks.**

Sharks are not really as scary and unknown as the other subjects in this series, but this book sensationalizes the accounts that will grab attention. Some serious information is given about sharks after the gross and gory material at the beginning. *See* UNIQUE PRESENTATIONS.

Mitton, Jacqueline. **Aliens.**

UFOs and aliens are always hot topics, and this book will top the list. Aliens from movie versions and supposed sightings are considered in detail. It would be wise to buy multiple copies of this one. *See* UNIQUE PRESENTATIONS.

I WAS THERE BOOK SERIES

Books in this series deal with a specific period in ancient history. Actual artifacts, their examination using modern scientific techniques, and well-researched text give excellent information about life in a given time period.

Tanaka, Shelley. **In the Time of Knights: The Real-Life Story of History's Greatest Knight.**

Readers can learn a great deal about knights and life during the time in which they lived by following the true story of William Marshall, a twelfth-century knight. He gained fame through his outstanding jousting, his battlefield performance, his participation in the Crusades, and his loyal protection of England's Prince Henry. *See* SOCIAL STUDIES—ANCIENT AND EARLY CULTURES.

Tanaka, Shelley. **Lost Temple of the Aztecs: What It Was Like When the Spaniards Invaded Mexico.**

A giant Aztec disk was discovered in 1978 when workmen were digging ditches for electrical cables under Mexico City. Expert archeologists worked for five years uncovering the Great Temple of the Aztecs, the main temple used by the Aztecs. This fantastic work uses Aztec drawings, paintings by Diego Rivera, and present-day photographs, along with works by illustrator Greg Ruhl, to tell the story of pre-Spanish Mexico. *See* SOCIAL STUDIES—ANCIENT AND EARLY CULTURES.

Tanaka, Shelley. **Secrets of the Mummies: Uncovering the Bodies of Ancient Egyptians.**

The history of mummies, the mummification process, and the techniques used to examine mummies today is presented in a colorful, informative manner. Students are fascinated by mummies, and this work provides the information they're looking for. *See* SOCIAL STUDIES—ANCIENT AND EARLY CULTURES.

THE KIN SERIES

Peter Dickinson uses four brief volumes to tell the story of six children, two hundred thousand years ago, who are separated from their band, the Moonhawk Kin, because of an invasion. The children are on a journey through Africa searching for "Good Places" that have food, water, and shelter.

They know how to use tools and fire, and they communicate with language. Interspersed with their survival tales are "Oldtale" stories, myths that help explain the world around them. Each novel can stand on its own, or the series can be used in its entirety to teach about early humans. Dickinson's **A Bone from a Dry Sea** (1992) contains much of the same material but is written at a higher reading and interest level. It's been difficult to find quality literature that effectively tells an interesting story about early *homo sapiens* that is suited for middle school readers. This series can fill that need.

Dickinson, Peter. **Mana's Story.** The Kin series. New York: Grosset & Dunlap, 1999. 152p. $15.00. ISBN 0-448-41712-X.

In this volume, the children search for food on the edge of a great marsh and fight a new enemy, whom they call the demon men.

Dickinson, Peter. **Noli's Story.** The Kin series. New York: Grosset & Dunlap, 1998. 211p. $15.00. ISBN 0-448-41710-3.

The six orphans need to find their Moonhawk Kin. Noli, who possesses powers to warn and foretell, attempts to guide the children to safety. Danger and adventure stalk them.

Dickinson, Peter. **Po's Story.** The Kin series. New York: Grosset & Dunlap, 1998. 208p. $15.00. ISBN 0-448-41711-1.

Young Po wants to prove his bravery, but he discovers he must overcome many great obstacles.

Dickinson, Peter, Dickinson, Peter. **Suth's Story.** The Kin series. New York: Grosset & Dunlap, 1998. 152p. $15.00.

The six children use their ingenuity to find food and water and to fight off wild animals in their struggle to stay alive. They are captured by the Monkey Kin and taken to a seemingly inescapable secret valley. Suth finds a way to freedom.

PASSPORT TO HISTORY SERIES

Each of the six books in this series, especially suited for the middle school social studies curriculum, takes the reader to a time period from the past, with the information arranged in a travel guide format and printed on paper made to look like parchment. The traveler is given suggestions about what cities to visit, local money matters, how to get around, local customs and manners, what to wear, what to see and do, available sports and recreation activities, where to stay, what to eat, souvenirs, health tips, and preparations necessary for the trip. Sidebars entitled "Hot Hints" give tidbits of information related to the section. Each volume includes a glossary, a time line, a pronunciation guide, a list of further readings that includes books and Internet sites, a bibliography, and an index.

Day, Nancy. **Your Travel Guide to Ancient Egypt.** Passport to History series. Minneapolis, Minn.: Runestone Press, 2001. 96p. $20.00. ISBN 0-8225-3075-9.

Imagine planning a trip to ancient Egypt. What would you need for your trip? What sites will you see? What kind of money will you be using, and what can you buy with it? All these questions and more can be answered with this book. Ancient Egypt is a vast topic, so not all aspects are covered in detail, but this is a unique way to tell about that time in history. "Preparing for the Trip" includes an activity measuring with cubits and a recipe for stew, Ful Medames.

Day, Nancy. **Your Travel Guide to Ancient Greece.** Passport to History series. Minneapolis, Minn.: Runestone Press, 2001. 96p. $20.00. ISBN 0-8225-3076-7.

Colorful photographs of the sights in Greece, along with photographs of Greek artifacts and ruins, add to the beauty and usefulness of this time travel guide that takes us back to the time from 493 B.C. to 146 B.C. A great amount of information is packed into this volume, arranged in an interesting format. To help prepare for the trip, the reader can learn how to make a mosaic and organize a mini-Olympics event using the directions given in the final section of the book.

Day, Nancy. **Your Travel Guide to Ancient Mayan Civilization.** Passport to History series. Minneapolis, Minn.: Runestone Press, 2001. 96p. $20.00. ISBN 0-8225-3076-7.

Outstanding photographs, maps, interesting sidebars, and a time line, along with lively informative text about the ancient Maya, all work together to make this a book useful for browsing as well as research. To complete the experience, directions for a Mayan recipe for tortillas and rules for the bul board game are included.

Day, Nancy. **Your Travel Guide to Civil War America.** Passport to History series. Minneapolis, Minn.: Runestone Press, 2001. 96p. $20.00 ISBN 0-8225-3078-3.

This volume gives the reader an in-depth idea of what it would have been like to live during the American Civil War period. An abundance of photographs, along with informative text, makes the time period come alive. It presents many aspects of the difficulties of life during war, and it also includes what life was like for the women at home. Clothing trends, hairstyles, and other aspects of daily life are presented with photographs, text, and quotations from men and women who lived during the time. When people visited offices or homes, they often carried calling cards called *cartes de visite*. To help make the visit more meaningful, directions for making these cards are included, as is a recipe for hardtack.

Day, Nancy. **Your Travel Guide to Colonial America.** Passport to History series. Minneapolis, Minn.: Runestone Press, 2001. 96p. $20.00. ISBN 0-8225-3079-1.

If you're considering a trip to Colonial America, this travel guide should be consulted to acquaint you with what to expect. It includes methods of travel, foods, dress, accommodations, important places to visit, and many other aspects of life at that time. Sketches and reproductions of paintings and drawings during Colonial America, along with sidebars that include quotations from people of that time and interesting tidbits of information, help to prepare the traveler. Directions for playing Nine Men's Morris and how to make a sign for your business are included.

Day, Nancy. **Your Travel Guide to Renaissance Europe.** Passport to History series. Minneapolis, Minn.: Runestone Press, 2001. 96p. $20.00. ISBN 0-8225-3080-5.

Reprints of many well-known Renaissance paintings, along with lively detailed text, tell the story of what it would be like to travel to Renaissance Europe. Details of everyday life—including politics, the social scene, slavery, manners, beliefs, clothing, hairstyles, foods, and many other topics—give an accurate picture of what to expect when traveling. The final chapter gives directions for creating a museum and painting a portrait.

THE ROYAL DIARY SERIES

Each book is written in diary form about a famous woman during her teen years. Each book is written by a well-known author of historical fiction and captures the location and the time in an interesting format. Each volume has gilded edges and is the size and shape of a diary similar to those used today. Students love these books and wait for each new addition to the series.

Gregory, Kristiana. **Cleopatra VII: Daughter of the Nile.** Royal Diary series. New York: Scholastic, 1999. 221p. $11.00. ISBN 0-590-81975-5.

Princess Cleopatra narrates her life from ages twelve to fourteen. Gregory depicts everyday Egyptian life and portrays the political intrigue of the time.

Lasky, Kathryn. **Elizabeth I, Red Rose of the House of Tudor.** Royal Diary series. New York: Scholastic, 1999. 237p. $11.00. ISBN 0-590-68484-1.

A clear picture of upper-class life in sixteenth-century England is given in this diary account of Elizabeth I from ages ten to thirteen. The young Elizabeth's writing, courtesy of Kathryn Lasky, describes her loneliness, her desperate desire for her father's attention, and family intrigue.

Lasky, Kathryn. **Marie Antoinette, Princess of Versailles.** Royal Diary series. New York: Scholastic, 2000. 236p. $11.00. ISBN 0-439-07666-8.
The life of the adolescent Marie Antoinette is depicted from the time of her betrothal to Louis Auguste, dauphin of France, when she was thirteen, to her marriage, when she must be trained to be the future queen. Her fictional diary entries offer a good picture of eighteenth-century French royalty and politics.

McKissack, Patricia. **Nzingha, Warrior Queen of Matamba.** Royal Diary series. New York: Scholastic, 2000. 136p. $11.00. ISBN 0-439-11210-9.
Nzingha, a Congo princess in the sixteenth century, breaks with tradition and refuses to be married at age thirteen. She insists on helping her father lead their people against the encroachment of the Portuguese and does her best to prevent the slave trade from affecting her people. The epilogue gives a synopsis of her life, along with woodcuts, photos, historical notes, a family tree, a pronunciation guide, and a glossary. This well-researched historical fiction gives an excellent picture of life at that time in the Congo and is an excellent addition to the series.

Meyer, Carolyn. **Anastasia, the Last Grand Duchess.** Royal Diary series. New York: Scholastic, 2000. 220p. $11.00. ISBN 0-439-12908-7.
Twelve-year-old Anastasia, the youngest daughter of the last tsar of imperial Russia, records royal life in her diary, which ends abruptly January 3, 1914—the time of the Bolshevik Revolution. Black-and-white pictures, historical notes, a family tree, information about the Russian language, a list of the characters in the book, and a calendar provide excellent background information for this time period.

Meyer, Carolyn. **Isabel: Jewel of Castilla.** Royal Diary series. New York: Scholastic, 2000. 204p. $11.00. ISBN 0-439-07805-9.
Princess Isabel of Castilla records her life as a teenager in Spain during the 1400s. This tale of romance records her struggle to marry the man of her choice, rather than one chosen for her. Meyer does a good job of describing Spanish life during the fifteenth century through Isabel's fictional diary entries. Historical notes, an annotated family tree, a small map of the Spanish states, a pronunciation guide, and a list of characters are included.

White, Ellen Emerson. **Kaiulani: The People's Princess.** Royal Diary series. New York: Scholastic, 2001. 238p. $11.00. ISBN 0-439-12909-5.
As heir to the royal Hawaiian throne, Princess Kaiulani records life in Hawaii from 1889 to 1893, at which time she is sent to boarding school in

England. She describes the political difficulties the monarchy faces because of the encroachment of American business interests. This volume offers an important piece of American history, making it especially important to young readers. The final section of the book includes historical notes, a family tree, family photos, a description of the Hawaiian language, and a glossary.

Yep, Laurence. **Lady Ch'iao Kuo: The Red Bird of the South.** Royal Diary series. New York: Scholastic, 2001. 300p. $11.00. ISBN 0-439-16483-4.
It is 531 A.D. and Lady Ch'iao Kuo is a fifteen-year-old princess of the Hsien tribe in southern China. Through her fictional diary, she describes her role as a liaison between her own tribe and the local Chinese colonists. A genealogy table and a map are included.

SCIENCE OF THE PAST SERIES

Each book in this series discusses a particular ancient culture and what scientific advances and discoveries were made within that culture. The authors present prominent scientists along with discussions on how the discoveries still influence our modern-day science. Color photographs, drawings, and reproductions are included. Each volume also includes a glossary, a bibliography, a list of Internet sites, and an index. This well-researched series has been updated from the previous series published in 1988. The books in this set offer a wealth of information for reports and projects, but they're also fascinating for browsing and are made to order for the middle school curriculum. Similar information can be found in the Ancient Technology series, which is written at a slightly higher reading and information level.

Beshore, George. **Science in Ancient China.** Science of the Past series. New York: Franklin Watts, 1998. 63p. $19.00. ISBN 0-531-11334-5.
The ancient Chinese made significant achievements in the science of medicine, astronomy, and cosmology, which Beshore describes in this work. Many innovations—from rockets, wells, and compasses to water wheels and movable type—are also attributed to them, and these continue to influence present-day life.

Beshore, George. **Science in Early Islamic Culture.** Science of the Past series. New York: Franklin Watts, 1998. 64p. $19.00. ISBN 0-531-20355-7.
This entry discusses the scientific discoveries and advances in the Islamic world beginning in the A.D. 600s, including medical and surgical advances and the development of Arabic numerals. It shows how these discoveries have influenced Western civilization into modern times.

Gay, Kathlyn. **Science in Ancient Greece.** Science of the Past series. New York: Franklin Watts, 1998. 64p. $19.00. ISBN 0-531-20357-3.

> Gay discusses the scientific discoveries of the ancient Greeks and their philosopher-scientists, such as Ptolemy, Pythagoras, Hippocrates and Aristotle. She presents ancient discoveries and their impact on modern science.

Harris, Jacqueline L. **Science in Ancient Rome.** Science of the Past series. New York: Franklin Watts, 1998. 64p. $19.00. ISBN 0-531-20354-9.

> Previous cultures discovered and experimented, and then Rome redefined and reworked the ideas to develop new techniques and ideas. This volume describes how the Romans used new themes on past discoveries to advance their lives and how these affect our lives today.

January, Brendan. **Science in Colonial America.** Science of the Past series. New York: Franklin Watts, 1999. 64p. $19.00. ISBN 0-531-11525-9.

> This volume considers the scientific contributions made by the colonial Americans, including discoveries in natural history, medicine, astronomy, and electricity. Cotton Mather's work on inoculation, Thomas Jefferson's and John and William Bartram's studies in natural history, David Rittenhouse's work in astronomy, and Ben Franklin's experiments with electricity are presented.

January, Brendan. **Science in the Renaissance.** Science of the Past series. New York: Franklin Watts, 1999. 64p. $19.00. ISBN 0-531-11526-7.

> A review of the state of science in medieval Europe is presented, followed by a discussion of the many discoveries and observations made during the Renaissance. Topics include the use of geometry, the use of mathematics in art, the study of anatomy and disease in medicine, and some of the work of Copernicus and Galileo.

Stewart, Melissa. **Science in Ancient India.** Science of the Past series. New York: Franklin Watts, 1999. 64p. $19.00. ISBN 0-531-11626-3.

> This volume describes the scientific contributions of ancient India, which include mathematics, yoga, surgery, basic chemistry and physics, and celestial observation. The author names and provides quotes from prominent scientists and mathematicians.

Woods, Geraldine. **Science in Ancient Egypt.** Science of the Past series. New York: Franklin Watts, 1998. 64p. $19.00. ISBN 0-531-20341-7.

> This fascinating volume looks at the accomplishments of the ancient Egyptians in the fields of architecture, astronomy, mathematics, medicine, engineering, agriculture, science, and technology. The final chapter, "What Ancient Egypt Gave Us," ties their developments in with the shaping of modern civilization.

Woods, Geraldine. **Science in the Early Americas.** Science of the Past series.
New York: Franklin Watts, 1999. 64p. $19.00. ISBN 0-531-11524-0.

This volume looks at the scientific contributions in medicine, mathematics, engineering, and astronomy from the indigenous cultures of North,
Central, and South America. The author describes theories, practices, and
customs from various tribes, giving information from the earliest times to
the present.

SERIES OF UNFORTUNATE EVENTS

After the death of their wealthy parents, the three Baudelaire children,
Violet, age fourteen, Klaus, twelve, and Sunny, a baby, try to make their
way in the world, but in each volume, another unfortunate event occurs to
complicate their lives. Told in a Roald Dahl fashion, Daniel Handler, a.k.a.
Lemony Snicket, uses off-the-wall, tongue-in-cheek humor to hook the
reader.

Snicket, Lemony. **The Austere Academy.** Series of Unfortunate Events, Book
5. Illus. Brett Helquist. New York: HarperCollins, 2000. 221p. $16.00. ISBN
0-06-028888-4.

In this fifth episode, the Baudelaire orphans are sent to a boarding
school, where they're tormented by others, meet two of the Quagmire trip-
lets, and are followed by the dreaded Count Olaf, who is disguised as Coach
Genghis.

Snicket, Lemony. **The Bad Beginning.** Series of Unfortunate Events, Book 1.
Illus. Brett Helquist. New York: HarperCollins, 1999. 162p. $16.00. ISBN
0-06-028312-2, 0-439-20647-2pa.

The three Baudelaire children, Violet, Klaus, and Sunny, are sent to
live with a distant relative upon the sudden death of their parents. The
guardian is only interested in their money, so the children must depend on
their own wits, their close bond with each other, and their resilient spirit for
survival.

Snicket, Lemony. **The Ersatz Elevator.** Series of Unfortunate Events, Book 6.
Illus. Brett Helquist. New York: HarperCollins, 2001. 259p. $16.00. 0-06-
028889-2.

The evil Count Olaf, the distant relative who is pursuing the
Baudelaire orphans to steal their money, shows up at the seventy-one bedroom penthouse owned by Jerome and Esmé Squalor, who want to adopt
the children. Count Olaf is again in hot pursuit, the adults are made to look
silly, and the Baudelaires continue their humorous saga of survival.

Snicket, Lemony. **The Hostile Hospital.** Series of Unfortunate Events, Book 8. Illus. Brett Helquist. New York: HarperCollins, 2001. 255p. $$10.00 ISBN 0-06-440866-3, 0-06-028891-4.

    The three Baudelaire orphans manage to escape arrest on false murder charges and end up at Heimlich Hospital, where they work in the Library of Records. While there, they uncover many new clues, getting them closer to the truth of what actually happened to their parents. Of course, evil Olaf surfaces, causing hilarity and intrigue.

Snicket, Lemony. **The Miserable Mill.** Series of Unfortunate Events, Book 4. Illus. Brett Helquist. New York: HarperCollins, 2000. 194p. $16.00. ISBN 0-06-028315-7, 0-439-27263-7pa.

    In this fourth in the series, the orphan's lives are filled with gloom and doom when they're sent to work in a lumber mill, where they're overworked and underfed. As usual, the evil Olaf is close behind, trying to steal their fortune.

Snicket, Lemony. **The Reptile Room.** Series of Unfortunate Events, Book 2. Illus. Brett Helquist. New York: HarperCollins, 1999. 190p. $16.00. ISBN 0-06-028313-0, 0-439-20648-0pa.

    In this second episode featuring the Baudelaire orphans, they are still trying to find a home while managing to stay out of Count Olaf's clutches. They actually live happily for a brief time in the home of a herpetologist before they're forced to move on.

Snicket, Lemony. **The Vile Village.** Series of Unfortunate Events, Book 7. Illus. Brett Helquist New York: HarperCollins, 2001. 256p. $16.00. ISBN 0-06-028890-6.

    While searching for a home, the three orphans are adopted by an entire village, with disastrous results. Nonetheless, they do manage to evade the evil Olaf, so the story marches on.

Snicket, Lemony. **The Wide Window.** Series of Unfortunate Events, Book 3. Illus. Brett Helquist. New York: HarperCollins, 2000. 214p. $16.00. ISBN 0-06-028314-9, 0-439-27262-9pa.

    If any bad luck or evil lurks, it will find the Baudelaire orphans. In this episode, they end up with elderly Aunt Josephine, who lives in a house built on stilts overlooking Lake Lachrymose, which is filled with killer leeches. Count Olaf disguises himself as a sailboat captain in an attempt to kill the orphans.

TURNING POINT INVENTIONS

    Each book in this series explores the historical significance of a particular invention that we often take for granted. The authors explore the world before the invention, the inventor and how the discovery was made, and how the world was changed thanks to the invention, all of which is presented with paintings, sketches, and photographs. Indexes are included.

Duffy, Trent. **The Clock.**
The history of timekeeping—in particular, of the mechanical clock, how it evolved, how it works, and its importance in the everyday lives of people throughout history—is presented in a readable, interesting format. Many drawings, photographs, and sketches plus a large foldout page showing the progression of the clock, make this a valuable research tool. *See* SCIENCE.

Gearhart, Sarah. **The Telephone.**
Gearhart offers a thorough presentation of the history and cultural significance of the telephone in a detailed yet understandable manner. The drawings, photographs, and the foldout are informative and attractive. The people important to the development of the telephone, especially Alexander Graham Bell, are discussed. *See* SCIENCE.

Wallace, Joseph. **The Camera.**
The evolution of photography and the people who were instrumental in its development are covered in this well-researched work. The illustrations and original photographs help to show the scientific and cultural development of the camera, including today's trend toward digital photography. A large color foldout describes the parts of a camera and how photography works. *See* SCIENCE.

Wallace, Joseph E. **The Lightbulb.**
This title traces the history and cultural importance of lighting from the earliest times through today's latest developments. Wallace discusses the people who helped lasso electricity for human use, especially Thomas Edison. The outstanding foldout summarizes the development of lighting. *See* SCIENCE.

THE WHOLE STORY SERIES

Viking Press is in the process of reprinting some of the best-loved classic stories in an upscale, inviting format. Each book is complete and unabridged, uses high-quality paper, and is filled with a generous amount of informative annotations and illustrations. The books in this series beg to be touched and pored over, while examining all the details. Each is a visual and literary feast.

London, Jack. **White Fang.**
London's classic tale of the half-dog, half-wolf White Fang is reprinted in the series style, featuring heavyweight paper, outstanding illustrations, and an abundance of illustrated annotations in the margins. *See* ENGLISH—CLASSICS.

Poe, Edgar Allen. **The Pit and the Pendulum and Other Stories.**
This contribution contains seven of Poe's most popular stories: "The Gold-Bug," The Oval Portrait," "The Pit and the Pendulum," The Cask of Amontillado," "Some Words with a Mummy," "The Tell-Tale Heart," and "The Murders in the Rue Morgue." *See* ENGLISH—CLASSICS.

Sewell, Anna. **Black Beauty.**
This classic story of the horse Black Beauty, which takes place in nineteenth-century England, is presented with outstanding illustrations, high-quality paper, detailed annotations, and important quotations printed in the margins. *See* ENGLISH—CLASSICS.

Other titles in the series include **The Adventures of Tom Sawyer, Around the World in Eighty Days, The Call of the Wild, A Christmas Carol, Frankenstein, Heidi, The Jungle Book, Little Women, The Picture of Dorian Gray, The Strange Case of Dr. Jekyll and Mr. Hyde,** and **Treasure Island.**

WORDS ARE CATEGORICAL

The three books in this series feature cartoon-style cats that actively demonstrate a part of speech. They're both entertaining and instructional.

Cleary, Brian P. **Hairy, Scary, Ordinary: What Is an Adjective?**
The active and comical cats act out words that explain adjectives. *See* ENGLISH—USE OF LANGUAGE.

Cleary, Brian P. **A Mink, a Fink, a Skating Rink: What Is a Noun?**
The frolicking cats provide the definition of a noun and then proceed to show it with wild and crazy situations. *See* ENGLISH—USE OF LANGUAGE.

Cleary, Brian P. **To Root, to Toot, to Parachute: What Is a Verb?**
The featured verb is printed in bright colors, and the cats, along with a fun rhyme, show the verb in action. *See* ENGLISH—USE OF LANGUAGE.

Chapter 15

Social Studies— Ancient and Early Cultures

This section covers a broad range of topics both geographically and historically. Particular emphasis is placed on the cultures of early man, ancient China, India, Japan, Europe, the Middle East, Greece, Rome, Egypt, Africa, and the early American cultures. The Middles Ages around the world and the Renaissance are also included. Many myths, legends, and folktales have been included because much can be learned about a culture based on its stories.

Aliki. **William Shakespeare & the Globe.**
    The story of Shakespeare's life is told in five acts, with each act divided into scenes. Aliki's drawings with captions depict life at that time. Maps, sketches, drawings, quotations, a list of all Shakespeare's works, a chronology of his life, a list of words and expressions he used, and a list of sites to visit make this an outstanding work. *See* BIOGRAPHIES.

Andronik, Catherine M. **Hatshepsut, His Majesty, Herself.**
This extended text picture book explains the life and times of Egypt's only female pharaoh, Hatshepsut. Out of necessity, she dressed in male clothing and even attached a gold beard to her chin. The rulers that followed Hatshepsut did their best to obliterate her from history, so new information about her is still being discovered. Illustrations in stately Egyptian style add to the Egyptian feel of the book. *See* BIOGRAPHIES.

Avi. **Midnight Magic.** New York: Scholastic, 1999. 249p. $16.00. ISBN 0-590-36035-3, 0-439-24219-3pa.
Murder, magic, intrigue, ghosts, secret passages, and conspiracies all combine to make this a story that readers can't put down. Set in medieval Italy in the fifteenth century, Mangus the magician is summoned to the king's palace to investigate the Princess Teresina's vision of a ghost. Magnus, who believes not in magic but in reason, takes his trusty young servant Fabrizio with him to solve the mystery. At the palace, they discover that the prince, Teresina's brother, has disappeared, that Teresina is about to be married to Scarponi against her will, and that the king depends on magic more than common sense. The castle's secret passages and its many dark, scary rooms give the story the perfect setting for the mysteries facing Mangus and his sidekick Fabrizio. The action is nonstop, the story line intriguing; the descriptions of the time period work together to make this a great tie-in when studying the Middle Ages.

Balit, Christina. **Atlantis: The Legend of a Lost City.**
Throughout time people have searched for the legendary lost city, Atlantis. This beautifully illustrated book retells the myth of Atlantis, how it was founded and eventually destroyed by Poseidon, the god of the sea. An endnote by British historian Geoffrey Ashe elaborates on the various theories and legends. *See* MYTHS, FOLKTALES, AND LEGENDS.

Beshore, George. **Science in Ancient China.**
Many scientific advances were made in ancient China. This volume discusses the achievements made in science, medicine, astronomy, and cosmology and discusses innovations such as rockets, wells, compasses, water wheels, and movable type. *See* SERIES.

Beshore, George. **Science in Early Islamic Culture.**
The early Islamic culture, beginning in the A.D. 600s, was responsible for early surgical advances, medical treatises, and the development of Arabic numerals. This book describes these and other advances and how they still influence us today. *See* SERIES.

Blackwood, Gary L. **Shakespeare's Scribe.** New York: Dutton Children's Books, 2000. 264p. $16.00. ISBN 0-525-46444-1, 0-14-230066-7pa.

In this sequel to **The Shakespeare Stealer** (1998) Widge is no longer using his shorthand to steal scripts, but to record what Shakespeare wants written. He also uses his "swift writing" to decipher Shakespeare's scribbles and provides scripts to the players. He becomes a part of the troupe, but their productions are slowed because of the Plague, which prevents them from taking their show on the road. As in its prequel, life in Elizabethan England is described well. Widge learns the importance of friendship, and there's ample brawling, intrigue, and excitement.

Blackwood, Gary L. **The Shakespeare Stealer.** New York: Dutton Children's Books, 1998. 216p. $16.00. ISBN 0-525-45863-8, 0-14-130595-9pa.

Blackwood offers an excellent picture of life during Shakespeare's time. In particular, the Globe Theater can be seen through the eyes of Widge, a fourteen-year-old orphan who has been taught shorthand. He's hired by a mysterious traveler, who makes him infiltrate Shakespeare's theater company to learn *Hamlet* and then orders him to record the script so it can be used by another theater company. Widge's time with the troupe is full of intrigue and adventure, but it puts him in the middle of a moral dilemma.

Bouchard, David. **Buddha in the Garden.**

An orphan boy left at the gates of a Buddhist temple is told to find Buddha in the garden. He finds only a hungry kitten, which he feeds, an injured bird, which he helps, and a wilting peony, which represents his mother. The boy reaches enlightenment through introspection and contemplation and realizes that, in this way, the real Buddha can be found. This is an excellent book to use when studying cultures and religions from around the world. *See* PICTURE BOOKS FOR ALL AGES.

Bower, Tamara. **The Shipwrecked Sailor: An Egyptian Tale with Hieroglyphs.** Melinda Hartwig, translator of hieroglyphs. New York: Atheneum Children's Books, 2000. 32p. $17.00. ISBN 0-689-83046-7.

A ship returning to Egypt is destroyed by a storm, and there is only one survivor. He is nursed back to health by the Great Serpent, who allows him to live on the Island of the Soul until an Egyptian ship takes him back to his family in Egypt. This simple story was written on a papyrus scroll around the nineteenth century B.C., during the Middle Kingdom in Egyptian history. The scroll still exists and is kept in the Hermitage Museum in Moscow. Bower retells this tale with hieroglyphs found in the original manuscript. Melinda Hartwig translates highlighted phrases into their hieroglyphic representation, drawn in bands along the top or bottom of the page. The large

colorful illustrations depict stylized Egyptian scenes based on New Kingdom tomb and temple murals. Students will enjoy decoding the story using
the hieroglyphics with the help of a detailed explanation of hieroglyphs
found in the back of the book. A map of the sailor's voyage, notes about the
story, an explanation of symbols, and further readings are also included,
making this book a useful and engaging tool when studying ancient Egypt.

Casanova, Mary. **The Hunter: A Chinese Folktale.**
    A young hunter befriends a small snake and is rewarded by the snake's
father, The Dragon King. The hunter now has the gift to communicate with animals, which helps him to bring more food to the ancient Chinese village. One
day, the animals warn him that a dangerous storm is coming that will destroy the
village. The people refuse to leave until he reveals his secret, causing him to turn
to stone. Because of his sacrifice, the villagers are saved. The story is beautiful,
and Ed Young's illustrations are outstanding. Chinese characters appear on each
two-page spread, with the translation for each featured on page one. *See*
MYTHS, FOKTALES, AND LEGENDS.

Chen, Kerstin. **Lord of the Cranes.**
    The Lord of the Cranes, Tien, goes to the city to test the people for their
generosity. He meets Wang, an innkeeper, who gives him all he needs. As a reward, Tien draws cranes on the wall that come alive and dance, which draws
large crowds of patrons and makes Wang wealthy. In return, Wang promises to
teach others to share with those less fortunate. This beautiful story, based on a recurring figure from Buddhist stories, works well with a unit on ancient China.
The artwork depicts life from the Qing dynasty at the end of the nineteenth century. *See* MYTHS, FOLKTALES, AND LEGENDS.

Compestine, Ying Chang. **The Runaway Rice Cake.**
    The Chang family wants to celebrate Chinese New Year, but they only have
enough rice to make one cake, which they decide to share. But the rice cake
comes alive and runs through the town. It is finally devoured by a starving old
woman and the family is rewarded by the neighbors, who bring a sumptuous
feast to them. This book is a combination of "The Gingerbread Man" and a retelling
of the traditional folktale of the bottomless rice jar, and it provides information
about the Chinese New Year. *See* MYTHS, FOLKTALES, AND LEGENDS.

Conover, Sarah. **Kindness: A Treasury of Buddhist Wisdom for Children
and Parents.**
    This collection of thirty-one stories and thirty-four quotations and sayings
taken from the Buddhist tradition can be used as a valuable source when studying religions of the world. Told in a soft, lyrical voice, the stories and sayings are
an excellent introduction to the diversity of religious traditions. *See* ENGLISH—
USE OF LANGUAGE.

Cooper, Susan. **King of Shadows.** New York: McElderry Books, 1999. 186p. $15.00. ISBN 0-689-82817-9, 0-689-84445-Xpa.

The past and the present come together when Nat Field, a member of a summer Shakespeare drama troupe, becomes ill and is transported back to Shakespeare's time. Nat was in *A Midsummer Night's Dream* in the summer drama troupe. When he's working at the Globe Theatre, he's actually working with Shakespeare as Puck in a production of the same play. Cooper's detailed descriptions of life during Elizabethan England are vivid, including the difficult living conditions; the sights, sounds, and smells; the food; and the fierce competition among actors and among playwrights. Shakespeare befriends Nat and acts as a father figure, which ties in with the loss of his father in the present day. This is a well-done work that works well for classes studying sixteenth-century England. It also makes an excellent read aloud.

Coulter, Laurie. **Secrets in Stone: All About Maya Hieroglyphs.** Illus. Sarah Jane English. Boston: Little, Brown, 2001. 48p. $18.00. ISBN 0-316-15883-6.

So much information about the Maya is packed into this book, it could serve as a textbook when studying early American cultures. It begins with the discovery of the Copán ruins in 1839 and the subsequent discovery and deciphering of the Mayan hieroglyphs. In addition to text, each page displays and explains a particular glyph. Inserts include information on chocolate, the calendar, counting, and Maya kings. Coulter includes a sizeable section on making and using Maya hieroglyphs, along with an explanation on the ball game *pitz,* Maya beauty tips, party giving, secret codes, and directions for a number of activities using glyphs. The endpapers include a "Glyphmaster," raised glyphs that can be rubbed onto paper to create messages. A glossary, bibliography, and index are additional features. A liberal number of photos, drawings, and artwork, along with the use of many hieroglyphs, makes this volume highly useful.

Cushman, Karen. **Matilda Bone.** New York: Clarion Books, 2000. 167p. $15.00. ISBN 0-395-88156-0, 0-440-41822-4pa.

Cushman showcases medical facilities and remedies during the fourteenth century in this thoroughly researched novel. Father Leufredus, who raised the orphan Matilda, can no longer care for her, so he takes her to "Blood and Bone Alley" in the town of Chipping Bagthorpe to serve in the house of Red Peg, the town's bonesetter. Red Peg is a no-nonsense, brusque woman who is intent on getting the job done, while her new apprentice is dreamy, somewhat spoiled, unused to physical labor, and uses her knowledge of the saints, prayer, and Latin as the answer to all of life's problems. Unfortunately, the saints don't help Matilda much when Red Peg orders her to build a fire, which she's never done before. The description of this incident and many other of Matilda's mishaps will have the reader chuckling out loud. Matilda resists learning her jobs and continues to call on the saints, hoping to be delivered from the situation. A kitchen maid introduces her to the market square and all that it has to offer, which finally makes Matilda join the world around her, rather than hang on to her feelings of superiority. It's fun to watch Matilda grow, but the main thrust of the book is the historical presentation of medical practices during the Middle Ages. The information included in the author's note at the end of the book provides additional helpful information.

Day, Nancy. **Your Travel Guide to Ancient Egypt.**

If you'd like to travel to ancient Egypt, you need to take this volume along as your guide to provide useful information on what cities to visit, the money you'll be using, the customs and manners of the people, what to wear, and which sites to see. You'll also learn about the types of recreation that are available, where to stay, and which foods you should try, as well as some important health tips. This is an excellent book for both browsing and research. *See* SERIES.

Day, Nancy. **Your Travel Guide to Ancient Greece.**

You'll find traveling in ancient Greece much easier if you use this handy guidebook. Outstanding photographs, engaging text, and interesting sidebars make this a valuable source of information on ancient Greece. *See* SERIES.

Day, Nancy. **Your Travel Guide to Ancient Mayan Civilization.**

Outstanding photographs of artifacts and present-day ruins, along with maps, drawings, a time line, sidebars, and lively text give the time traveler a good idea of what to expect from a visit to the ancient Mayan civilization. Archaeologists have provided information to make the trip as informative as possible. This is a useful work for both browsing and research. *See* SERIES.

Day, Nancy. **Your Travel Guide to Renaissance Europe.**

Paging through this book feels like a visit to an art museum because of the generous number of reproductions of important artworks produced during the Renaissance. This time travel book also includes information on daily life, politics, customs, food, health and safety, living accommodations, important sites and cities to visit, and transportation. This is an outstanding addition to the body of Renaissance literature. *See* SERIES.

Deem, James M. **Bodies from the Bog.** Boston: Houghton Mifflin, 1998. 42p. $16.00. ISBN 0-395-85784-8.

Readers can learn a great deal about the Iron Age civilization in northern Europe because of well-preserved human remains extracted from peat bogs in recent years. Color and sepia-toned historical images show how well preserved these bodies are, making them excellent tools for researchers to learn about life two to three thousand years ago. Deem describes the research and examination procedures well, and the chapter titled "The Life of a Bog" describes peat bogs and why they can preserve bodies so well. Students will love looking at the illustrative and often gruesome pictures that accompany the informative text.

Demi. **The Emperor's New Clothes: A Tale Set in China.**
This version of the classic Hans Christian Andersen tale about the vain emperor is set in ancient China. Demi uses ample doses of Chinese symbols throughout the tale, which are displayed in the illustrations. The author's note explains these symbols, their meanings, and where to look for them in the book. Add this to your list of books to use when studying ancient China. *See* MYTHS, FOLKTALES, AND LEGENDS.

Dickinson, Peter. **Mana's Story.**
While searching for food on the edge of a marsh, the six orphans encounter a new enemy, the demon men. This brief book gives excellent insight into life during prehistoric times. *See* SERIES.

Dickinson, Peter. **Noli's Story.**
Noli, one of the six orphans looking for a new home 200,000 years ago, possesses powers that help to guide the children to safety. *See* SERIES.

Dickinson, Peter. **Po's Story.**
Po is the hero in this brief entry. He overcomes many obstacles in this prehistoric setting, but in the end proves his bravery. *See* SERIES.

Dickinson, Peter. **Suth's Story.**
Suth, one of the six prehistoric orphans searching for a new home, guides the children by using ingenuity in their struggle for survival. *See* SERIES.

English, Karen. **Nadia's Hands.**
Students can study ancient Middle Eastern cultures by watching Nadia, a Pakistani American girl, as she prepares to be the flower girl in her aunt's wedding. The highlight of the preparations is the intricate traditional painting of her hands with henna paste, known as *mehndi*. The pastel-colored oil paintings beautifully illustrate this process, along with the traditional clothing worn at the wedding. *See* MULTICULTURAL.

Fleischman, Paul. **Weslandia.**
Wesley develops a new civilization by using every part of his magical plant for food, clothing, shelter, and drink. He also develops his own language and alphabet. Through his tale, the reader can see what it takes to create a civilization. *See* PICTURE BOOKS FOR ALL AGES.

Gay, Kathlyn. **Science in Ancient Greece.**
This volume presents the theories and achievements of ancient Greeks—such as Ptolemy, Pythagoras, Hippocrates, and Aristotle—in astronomy,

mathematics, geography, and medical science. The author also discusses the impact of these ancient works on modern science. *See* SERIES.

Gregory, Kristiana. **Cleopatra VII: Daughter of the Nile.**
   Princess Cleopatra narrates her life in fictional diary accounts written from ages twelve to fourteen. This work depicts everyday Egyptian life, along with political intrigue. *See* SERIES.

Hamanaka, Sheila, and Ayano Ohmi. **In Search of the Spirit: The Living National Treasures of Japan.**
   In the 1950s, Japan began a Living National Treasures program in an effort to preserve ancient crafts and techniques. Six of those National Treasures and their works are described using text, color photographs, and step-by-step descriptions of how the work is done. Kimono painting, bamboo weaving, basket weaving, puppet making, sword making, Noh theater, and pottery making are included. Much can be learned about ancient Japan from this book. *See* FINE ARTS.

Harris, Jacqueline L. **Science in Ancient Rome.**
   The ancient Romans were masters at building on other people's achievements. Rather than "reinventing the wheel," they used previous knowledge, added to it, redefined it, and came up with new techniques and materials to improve their lives. *See* SERIES.

Hunt, Jonathan. **Bestiary: An Illuminated Alphabet of Medieval Beasts.** New York: Simon & Schuster, 1998. 42p. $17.00. ISBN 0-689-81246-9.
   Twenty-six mythological beasts, one for each letter of the alphabet, are collected in this medieval alphabet book. Hunt's well-researched work explains how fanciful animals were combined with real animals to create bestiaries. Each full-page entry gives the letter, the animal representing the letter, a large illustration depicting the beast and its behavior, a small insert illustration, and a written paragraph explaining the animal's powers and peculiar habits. A helpful pronunciation guide can be found at the beginning of the book, and a map of the medieval world is featured on the endpapers. Extensive author's notes, a paragraph about the illustrations, and a bibliography describe the author's thorough research into the history, myths, and legends of bestiaries.

January, Brendan. **Science in the Renaissance.**
   After reviewing the state of science in medieval Europe, the text goes on to discuss the changes brought about by the discoveries and observations made during the Renaissance. Topics include geometry, mathematics in art, the study of anatomy and disease in medicine, and the work of Copernicus and Galileo. *See* SERIES.

Kimmel, Eric A. **Sword of the Samurai: Adventure Stories from Japan**. San Diego, Calif.: Harcourt Brace Jovanovich, 1999. 114p. $15.00. ISBN 0-15-201985-5, 0-06-442131-7pa.

Finding good literature to accompany the study of ancient Japan has been a real problem until this book was published. In this collection of eleven short stories dealing with various aspects of the samurai, Kimmel gives a good picture of the Middle Ages in Japan. In the introduction, Kimmel explains that much is known about the knights in Europe, but less is known about that time in Japan. To make the samurai more understandable, he calls them the knights of Japan's medieval period. Each story has an introduction, making it more understandable, as well as an emblematic design, resembling Japanese woodcuts. A glossary of samurai terms, source notes, and a note on Japanese names help to make this an excellent resource.

Lasky, Kathryn. **Elizabeth I, Red Rose of the House of Tudor.**

A clear picture of upper-class life in sixteenth-century England is given in this diary account of Elizabeth I from ages ten to thirteen. Lasky tells of Elizabeth's loneliness, her desperate desire for her father's attention, and family intrigue through this fictional writing. *See* SERIES.

Lattimore, Deborah Nourse. **Medusa.**

This retelling of the ancient Greek myth has plenty of action with ugly monsters and gore, but it actually downplays some of the more gruesome and sexual aspects found in some versions, making it more suitable for children. *See* MYTHS, FOLKTALES, AND LEGENDS.

Lauber, Patricia. **What You Never Knew About Tubs, Toilets & Showers.** Illus. John Manders. New York: Simon & Schuster, 2001. 32p. $16.00. ISBN 0-689-82420-3.

Much can be learned about a civilization based on its hygienic habits. Beginning with the Stone Age, Lauber traces the different attitudes involving bathing, washing, and human waste disposal. Cartoon illustrations along with dialogue balloons provide information as well as humor. The main emphasis is on bathing practices, but readers can find the history of toilets in the margins, along with comical illustrations. Early cultures such as the Indus River Valley, which had one of the world's earliest cities, piped fresh water in and sewers carried the wastewater away. The Babylonians probably invented the bathtub, which was a big pottery bowl. The Greeks and Romans prized baths, but cleanliness was out of style during the Middle Ages. In fact, the church taught that bathing was sinful because it was a pleasure of the flesh. Kids are going to love the illustration showing Louis XIV entertaining while he was on his "throne." Bathing was slow to catch on in the New World, and it took until 1851, under Millard Fillmore's presidency to have a bathtub installed in the White House. The light-hearted art works well with the informative text.

Lester, Julius. **Pharaoh's Daughter: A Novel of Ancient Egypt.** San Diego, Calif.: Silver Whistle/Harcourt, 2000. 182p. $17.00. ISBN 0-15-201826-3, 0-06-440969-4pa.

The Bible story of Moses plucked from the bulrushes and raised as an Egyptian prince is the basis for this story, but, according to the introduction, Lester "removed Moses from sacred history and sought to put him into human history." Therefore, he changes his name to Mosis and creates an involved and intricate story highlighting both the Khemetian and Habiru cultures. Mosis is forced to make the choice of which culture to follow, and Lester's well-researched facts all play a part in that decision. Lester offers an outstanding picture of the grandeur of Egypt, making this a good tie-in for units on the Ancient Egyptians. Because of its intricate story with information that is not always found in the regular curriculum, this book will appeal to proficient readers ready for a challenge.

McDermott, Gerald. **Jabutí, the Tortoise: A Trickster Tale from the Amazon.**

Jabutí is known for his acts of kindness and flute playing and is loved by everyone but Vulture. Vulture offers to give Jabutí a lift into the heavens but purposely drops him, breaking his shell. The other animals patch him back together, which is why the tortoise has a cracked shell. *See* MYTHS, FOLKTALES AND LEGENDS.

McKissack, Patricia. **Nzingha: Warrior Queen of Matamba.**

Nzingha, a Congo princess in the sixteenth century, breaks with tradition and refuses to marry at age thirteen. She insists on helping her father lead their people against the encroachment of the Portuguese and does her best to prevent the slave trade. *See* SERIES.

Meltzer, Milton. **Ten Queens: Portraits of Women of Power.**

Accurate and interesting biographies of ten queens who came to power by their own right, not because they married kings, are included in this superb collective biography. Some are well known, such as Cleopatra, Elizabeth I, Catherine the Great, Eleanor of Aquitaine, and Isabel of Spain, but some queens, including Esther, Boudicca, Zenobia, Christina of Sweden, and Maria Theresa, well be less well known to young readers. *See* BIOGRAPHIES.

Merrill, Yvonne Young. **Hands-on Asia: Art Activities for All Ages.**

Merrill presents more than fifty projects reflecting folk-art traditions from Japan, China, Tibet, Mongolia, Korea, and Southeast Asia with easy-to-follow directions. This oversized paperback book is an excellent resource to complement the middle school social studies curriculum. *See* FINE ARTS.

Meyer, Carolyn. **Isabel: Jewel of Castilla.**
Through fictional diary entries, Princess Isabel, better known to us as Queen Isabella, records her life as a teenager in Spain during the 1400s. This tale of romance records her struggle to marry the man of her choice, rather than one chosen for her. Life in fifteenth-century Spain is well detailed. *See* SERIES.

Musgrove, Margaret. **The Spider Weaver: A Legend of Kente Cloth.**
Two Ashanti weavers discover a new and beautiful pattern for weaving their cloth when they observe a spider making an intricate and unusual web. They return home and weave a new design known as kente cloth. The significance of kente cloth is discussed in the afterword, accompanied by a pronunciation guide. The vibrant watercolor illustrations are outstanding examples of how kente cloth looks. This is an excellent source of an African folktale. *See* MYTHS, FOLKTALES, AND LEGENDS.

Nye, Naomi Shihab, selected by. **The Space Between Our Footsteps: Poems and Paintings from the Middle East**.
This outstanding collection of poetry and art from twenty Middle Eastern and North African countries includes works from 130 poets. *See* POETRY.

Rockwell, Anne F. **The Boy Who Wouldn't Obey: A Mayan Legend.**
The Mayan god Chac goes down to earth to steal a child to be his servant. The unruly child refuses to obey, however, causing grief for both of them. Eventually Chac allows the boy to return home, but no one will believe his tales except Monkey, who witnessed everything and wrote it down. The illustrations show the Mayan symbolism and culture, and the introduction gives helpful background information on the Mayan culture, making this a useful source when studying New World cultures. *See* MYTHS, FOLKTALES, AND LEGENDS.

Rosen, Michael. **Shakespeare: His Work & His World.**
If the study of Shakespeare is a part of your curriculum, this book should be used to help explain his life and work, the dangers and difficulties of life at that time, and the importance of the theater. It also includes summaries of some of his plays, as well as a detailed, five-page time line of his life and works. The outstanding watercolor paintings and lively text make this an excellent book for browsing as well as research. *See* BIOGRAPHIES.

Rumford, James. **Traveling Man: The Journey of Ibn Battuta, 1325–1354**.
New York: Houghton Mifflin, 2001. 38p. $16.00. ISBN 0-618-08366-9.
When Ibn Battuta, a fourteenth-century Muslim, was twenty-one, he decided to leave his home in Morocco and travel to Mecca as a pilgrim. His

desire to see the world absorbed the next thirty years of his life, as he traveled 75,000 miles through Africa, the steppes of Asia, India, China, Turkey, and back to Morocco. Upon his return to Morocco, he told his story to a Moroccan court secretary, who wrote it down in Arabic. The original of that manuscript is now in the National Library in Paris. In Rumford's brightly illustrated book, a portion of the text on each page is written on a white road, drawn over a map showing Battuta's whereabouts. Arabic and Chinese calligraphy adorn the edges of many of the drawings, making this a feast for the eyes as well as an informative tale of life during the 1300s. A glossary of people, places, and things mentioned in the story is included along with a list of translations of the Arabic and Chinese calligraphy and a map of Battuta's travels.

Stanley, Diane. **Joan of Arc.**

Stanley tells the complicated but remarkable story of the brave Joan of Arc through detailed text and outstanding illustrations. This well-researched work tells about the Hundred Years War and portrays the difficulties of life during the fifteenth and sixteenth centuries. *See* BIOGRAPHIES.

Stanley, Diane. **Michelangelo**.

Stanley uses the extended-text picture-book format to tell Michelangelo's intriguing story. Computer-manipulated drawings of his actual work and her original watercolors work together to make this an outstanding piece of art, as well as a thorough yet easy-to-understand story. *See* FINE ARTS.

Stewart, Melissa. **Science in Ancient India.**

After giving a brief history of India, the text looks at the scientific advancements achieved by that culture in medicine, mathematics, astronomy, and physics. There's a special emphasis on the fact that Indian scientists and philosophers practiced in these areas centuries before their Western counterparts. *See* SERIES.

Tanaka, Shelly. **In the Time of Knights: The Real-Life Story of History's Greatest Knight.** I Was There Book series. Illus. Greg Ruhl. New York: Hyperion, 2000. 48p. $17.00. ISBN 0-7868-0651-6.

Tanaka describes the life and times of a knight by following the true story of William Marshall, a twelfth-century knight. He gained fame through his outstanding jousting, his battlefield performance, his participation in the Crusades, and his loyal protection of England's Prince Henry. This book includes facts about the lives and activities of knights told with the help of colorful and instructive illustrations. A bibliography and an index are included.

Tanaka, Shelley. **Lost Temple of the Aztecs: What It Was Like When the Spaniards Invaded Mexico.** I Was There Book series. Illus. Greg Ruhl. New York: Hyperion Books for Children, 1998. 48p. $17.00. ISBN 0-7868-0441-6, 0-7868-1542-6.

Aztec drawings, paintings by Diego Rivera, present-day photographs, and Ruhl's lavish paintings help to present the story of what Mexico City was like during Aztec times. In 1978, workmen digging ditches for electrical cables in Mexico City unearthed a giant disk, ten feet in diameter. Expert archeologists were called in who went on to discover the Great Temple of the Aztecs during the next five years. More than seven thousand artifacts—including masks, statues, jewelry, musical instruments, weapons, tools, shells, and many human and animal remains—were uncovered. Professor Eduardo Matos Moctezuma, a descendant of an Aztec ruler, headed the dig. Tanaka uses this newly uncovered information, along with previously known facts, to present an outstanding work. Fictional dialogue combined with fact make this an excellent tool for studying the early Americas.

Tanaka, Shelley. **Secrets of the Mummies: Uncovering the Bodies of Ancient Egyptians.** I Was There Book series. Illus. Greg Ruhl. New York: Hyperion, 1999. 48p. $17.00. ISBN 0-7868-0473-4, 0-7868-1468-3pa, 0-7868-1539-6.

This comprehensive work about mummies tells readers who (or what) were chosen to become mummies, how the mummification process worked, what items were included in tombs, how mummies have been discovered, and how and what we've learned about them. Photographs of mummies, artifacts, pyramids, and people involved in the searches and research; sketches and drawings of real and fictionalized people and places; and well-researched text make this a must for mummy research. A glossary and an index are included.

Temko, Florence. **Traditional Crafts from Africa**.

This how-to book gives instructions for Senufo mud painting, Asante Adinkra stamping, Fon story pictures, Ndbele bead bracelets, Tutsi baskets, the Kigogo game, an Islamic art box, and a Guro animal mask. This is an excellent source to use as a tie-in for units on ancient Africa. *See* FINE ARTS

Temko, Florence. **Traditional Crafts from China.**

Temko includes directions for paper cutouts, figures made of dough, kites, string puppets, tangrams, a needlework purse, wheat straw pictures, and picture scrolls in this volume showcasing ancient Chinese crafts. *See* FINE ARTS.

Temko, Florence. **Traditional Crafts From Japan.**

Temko presents eight traditional handicrafts handed down through the centuries. Included are *daruma* dolls, *ka-mon* (family crests), *koi nobori* (fish-shaped wind socks), *maneki neko* (welcoming cats), the origami crane, stencils for fabrics, *tanabata* festival decorations, and *den-den* (a festive toy drum). *See* FINE ARTS.

Temko, Florence. **Traditional Crafts from Mexico and Central America.**

This volume provides instructions on how to make Mexican and Central American handicrafts, including tin ornaments, *papel picado,* Guatemalan weaving, Otomi paper figures, Day of the Dead skeletons, a tree of life, Guatemalan worry dolls, and Cuna *molas.* This is an excellent source to use when studying the history of this part of the world and for use in Spanish classes. *See* FINE ARTS.

Thompson, Lauren. **One Riddle, One Answer.**

A Persian sultana, Aziza, devises a math riddle that only one person in the Persian kingdom is able to answer. By answering the riddle, Ahmed wins her hand in marriage and a place as an advisor in the sultan's court. The Persian setting is beautifully portrayed with acrylic paintings, and Aziza is a strong, educated woman. *See* MATHEMATICS.

Woods, Geraldine. **Science in Ancient Egypt.**

The ancient Egyptians soared when it came to discoveries in science, mathematics, astronomy, medicine, architecture, agriculture, and technology. This volume ties in their accomplishments with ongoing applications of these achievements. *See* SERIES.

Woods, Geraldine. **Science in the Early Americas.**

In this volume, Woods discusses the scientific achievements of the North American tribes, along with the Inca, Aztec, and Mayan cultures. It includes advances in medicine, mathematics, engineering, and astronomy. The theories, practices, and customs of various tribes and cultures are presented. *See* SERIES.

Woods, Michael, and Mary B. Woods. **Ancient Communication: From Grunts to Graffiti.**

This volume explores communication in early cultures. The authors present the history of writing systems, writing tools, paints, and printing methods and also show how these techniques influence communication today. *See* SERIES.

Woods, Michael, and Mary B. Woods. **Ancient Construction: From Tents to Towers.**

The authors present dwellings and other buildings and structures from prehistoric times until the end of the Roman Empire, along with methods of construction and tools and materials used. *See* SERIES.

Yep, Lawrence. **Lady Ch'iao Kuo: The Red Bird of the South.**
Lady Ch'iao Kuo, a princess from the Hsien tribe in southern China, acts as a liaison between her tribe and the local Chinese colonists. Through her fictional diary, the reader gains insight into Chinese life at that time. *See* SERIES.

Chapter 16

Social Studies— United States History

Much can be learned about the history of the United States through well-researched historical fiction that is written with great care and accuracy. History will come alive through the characters presented in these books, which span the history of the United States from the earliest settlements to the present. Nonfiction, poetry, myths and legends, biographies, art, and music are also included in this section to help tell the story of our country.

Ayers, Katherine. **Stealing South: A Story of the Underground Railroad.** New York: Delacorte Press, 2001. 201p. $15.00. ISBN 0-385-72912-X.

Will Spencer's family, from Atwater, Ohio, has helped runaway slaves for some time through the Underground Railroad. Will is now ready to strike out on his own as a peddler, driving a wagonload of goods for sale.

He is persuaded by Noah, the last runaway he helps, to use his wagon to help transport slaves from Kentucky to the North. He agrees and experiences the savagery of slavery firsthand. He becomes determined to honor his promise to Noah and in a daring move steals seven slaves that were to be taken away from their families and sold. He risks his business and his life but is ultimately successful. The story is fast paced, exciting, frightening, and historically accurate. The author's notes explain the circumstances during the 1850s after the Fugitive Slave Act, which made it more difficult for slaves to escape.

Avi. **Don't You Know There's a War On?**
Nearly everyone's life is touched by World War II in 1943. Howie's father is serving in the merchant marine and hasn't been heard from for a long time. His mother is working long hours at a factory that produces products for the war. Howie feels helpless when it comes to his family situation, but he feels he can help his favorite teacher save her job. This book is funny, sad, and touching and also gives readers a picture of what it was like to be a child in the United States during the war. *See* GREATEST OF THE LATEST.

Bierhorst, John. **The People with Five Fingers: A Native Californian Creation Tale.**
In the beginning, Coyote and all the animals busily prepare California for people. Lizard insists on giving humans five fingers for basket weaving. Upon the people's arrival, there is so much laughing and talking—all in different languages—that the animals go to the woods, waters, and sky and never speak again. This beautifully told creation myth tells a little known but lovely story. *See* MYTHS, FOLKTALES, AND LEGENDS.

Christensen, Bonnie. **Woody Guthrie: Poet of the People.**
Woodcut-like paintings and simple yet thorough text tell the story of the life of folksinger Woody Guthrie. Lines from "This Land Is Your Land" splash across every page, and the lyrics for all seven verses are printed at the end of the book, along with a chronology of Guthrie's life. Much can be learned about the history of the United States from the time of the stock market crash, the Great Depression, and the dust bowl through the 1950s. *See* BIOGRAPHIES.

Curtis, Christopher Paul. **Bud, Not Buddy.**
Bud, a spunky ten-year-old orphan, sets out to find his father. It's the Depression era, which adds to the difficulties of his eventful yet humorous journey. Much can be learned about this time period though Bud's adventures. This book was the winner of the 2000 Newbery Award. *See* GREATEST OF THE LATEST.

Day, Nancy. **Your Travel Guide to Civil War America.**
If you'd like to know what to expect if you traveled back in time to the days of the American Civil War, use this volume as your guide. It details aspects of life as a soldier, including the uniforms, food, weapons, travel, and accommodations. It also includes life of the nonmilitary people, those left behind to care for homes, farms, and businesses. Works about the Civil War seldom include information about the daily life of women, children, and others who did not do battle, making this a useful resource. *See* SERIES.

Day, Nancy. **Your Travel Guide to Colonial America.**
Sketches, drawings, maps, text, and sidebars work together to give time travelers a good idea of what to expect when they visit Colonial America. Day has gathered information about America from 1606 to 1691 from documents and artifacts and the work of historians, and archaeologists. She presents many topics, including sites and cities to visit, what money to use, what is available for purchase, and what to wear. She also offers tips on the customs and manners of the day, sports and recreation, and health. This is an excellent source for research. *See* SERIES.

Freedman, Russell. **Give Me Liberty!: The Story of the Declaration of Independence.** New York: Holiday House, 2000. 90p. $25.00. ISBN 0-8234-14448-5.
Freedman has a way of making history come alive, and he's done it again in this outstanding telling of the making of the Declaration of Independence. The first five chapters deal with the events leading up to the American Revolution, told in a lively narrative fashion. The next three chapters chronicle the actual fighting, the continued debate among the colonists, and the drafting of the document, pointing out the important part Thomas Jefferson played in the process. The final chapter discusses the significance of the document at the time it was written and its continuing influence throughout the history of our country, ending with Martin Luther King Jr. and the Civil Rights Movement. The text is filled with quotations, sayings, and songs from the era, along with drawings, sketches, and copies of paintings that depict what was happening at the time. A copy of the original Declaration of Independence is included with the full text. An interesting section on what happened to the document after it was written, where it is today, how it has been protected and cared for, and a Web site with more information is found at the end of the book, along with a chronology of events, a bibliography, and an index. This book is excellent for research, an engrossing read, and should be a part of every American history teacher's collection.

Glass, Andrew. **Mountain Men: True Grit and Tall Tales.** New York: Random House, 2001. 44p. $16.00. ISBN 0-385-32555-X, 0-385-90841-5 lib. bdg.

After the eastern states were nearly trapped out, adventurous trappers ventured west into uncharted territory to find furs and pelts. These mountain men came back with stories of wild adventures—some true, some enhanced. The biographies of legendary adventurers John Colter, Jedediah Smith, Hugh Class, Jim Bridger, Mike Fink, Kit Carson, and Jim Beckwourth are told using actual facts as well as tales told about these men. The book begins with the Louisiana Purchase in 1803 and Lewis and Clark's journey, and continues through the 1830s, when fur hats went out of fashion and the demand for pelts plummeted. Full-page color illustrations match the humor and action of the text. The final pages include information on why the era came to an end, a pictorial list of mountain man necessities (such as beaver traps, knives, and pistols), a glossary of mountain man lingo, and a bibliography. The author notes that these men were fortune hunters with little sympathy for the animals or the land, but their tales "inspired adventurous pioneers to brave the brutal odds and settle the Western wilderness."

Herbert, Janis. **Lewis and Clark for Kids: Their Journey of Discovery with 21 Activities.** Chicago: Chicago Review Press, 2000. 143p. $15.00 ISBN 1-55652-374-2pa.

Several books about Lewis and Clark have been published recently, but this is one of the most comprehensive and complete. The story is presented in a clear, concise, and thorough manner, yet it's easy to read. Side panels give additional interesting information about issues touched on in the text. Sketches, photographs, and drawings help to tell the saga. It's the supplementary items and special features that make this book so special, however. A two-page time line beginning with Jefferson's birth and ending with Clark's death and another time line of the Lewis and Clark expedition appear at the beginning of the book, along with an excellent map of the expedition. A glossary; a list of Lewis and Clark sites, organizations, and events; a list of Web sites; a bibliography; and an index appear at the end of the book. Twenty-one activities that help readers relate to Lewis and Clark are a marvelous addition. The activities include making Native American articles such as a teepee, a dance rattle, a buffalo mask, and moccasins. Other activities invite the reader to use latitude and longitude, communicate with sign language, and participate in an archaeological dig.

Hirschfelder, Arlene B. **Photo Odyssey: Solomon Carvalho's Remarkable Western Adventure, 1853–54.** New York: Clarion Books, 2000. 118p. $18.00. ISBN 0-395-89123-X.

When explorer John C. Fremont made his fifth and final expedition in 1853–1854 to find the best railroad route between the Mississippi River and the Pacific coast, he invited Solomon Carvalho, a Jewish photographer, to accompany him. This is an account of that five-month journey and the records of the amateur explorer Carvalho. The expedition encountered extreme physical hardships, including starvation, dehydration, merciless weather, and run-ins with Native Americans. The party was near death when they met up with Brigham Young and his group of Mormons, who nursed them back to health. The author used many sources for her information, but the main one is Carvalho's own diary and letters. Carvalho's three hundred daguerreotypes became Fremont's property, which he intended to use in a book about the expedition. Unfortunately, the book was never written, and no one knows what happened to the plates. There are many black-and-white pictures in the book, but only one is Carvalho's. Hirschfelder's outstanding telling of this story offers insight into the difficulties of the opening of the West.

Hoose, Phillip M. **We Were There, Too!: Young People in U.S. History.** New York: Melanie Kroupa Books/Farrar, Straus & Giroux, 2001. 264p. $26.00. ISBN 0-374-38252-2.

Young people often feel that only adults have had a hand in making history, but this book puts that notion to rest. Hoose relates U.S. history chronologically, describing the contributions of young people beginning with Columbus's first voyage and the story of Diego Bermúdez, a twelve-year-old who sailed on that journey, up to the present day with an article on fifteen-year-old Mary Fister, who works online as a "member of Nation One, a global network of young people working for social justice." Each of the 67 stories is about a young person who played an important role in events during a given historical period. Historical documents, black-and-white photographs, engravings, drawings, maps, and firsthand eyewitness quotations support the stories. Some of the names are familiar, such as John Quincy Adams, whose article describes his work as a French translator in France and Russia when he was a teenager. Most are less known, such as Caroline Pickersgill, a thirteen-year-old who was instrumental in sewing the flag flown at Fort McHenry that became the subject of Francis Scott Key's lyrics in "The Star-Spangled Banner." Each article ends with a paragraph that explains what happened to the person after he or she grew up. An amazing amount of research went into this volume. This should be a part of every American history teacher's collection and certainly in every library.

Hopkins, Lee Bennett, selected by. **My America: A Poetry Atlas of the United States.**

This collection of fifty-one poems represents seven geographic regions of the United States, plus Washington, D.C. A map for each region and fact cards for each state provide useful information. Hopkins collected the work of forty poets, and twenty poems were commissioned especially for this anthology. It is a marvelous way to combine the study of literature and U.S. history. *See* POETRY.

January, Brendan. **Science in Colonial America.**
This volume in the Science of the Past series discusses the contributions made by people in Colonial America, including work by Cotton Mathers on inoculation, Thomas Jefferson and John and William Bartram's study of natural history, David Rittenhouse's work in astronomy, and Ben Franklin's work with electricity. *See* SERIES.

Katz, Bobbi. **We the People: Poems.** Illus. Nina Crews. New York: Greenwillow Books, 2000. 102p. $16.00. ISBN 0-688-16532-X.
Each of the sixty-five poems in this collection tells the story of a person from a specific period in American history. The poems are in chronological order, beginning with "The First Americans" and working through history up to the year 2000. Katz studied diaries, journals, biographies, and letters as well as photographs and paintings to get a feel for the people and life at the time. She is a historian who expresses her passion through poetry. The author's notes at the end of the book describes how she approached her work. Full-page color illustrations depicting the time period are found at the beginning of each of the five sections.

Krull, Kathleen. **Lives of the Presidents: Fame, Shame, and What the Neighbors Thought.**
The presidents of the United States, from Washington to Clinton, are presented in a lively manner that lets us get to know them as human beings, not just as presidents. The watercolor caricatures of the men help to depict the scenery, style of dress, wives, animals, and objects that were important to them. *See* BIOGRAPHIES.

Kurlansky, Mark. **The Cod's Tale.** Illus. S. D. Schindler. New York: G. P. Putnam's Sons, 2001. 43p. $17.00. ISBN 0-399-23476-4.
The history of Europe and North America from the Vikings through the present is told through the story of the codfish, which are found in the North Atlantic. The life cycle of the fish, as well as its habitat, enemies, and characteristics, are described at the beginning of the book, followed by a discussion of the cod's influence on groups of people beginning with the Vikings. They discovered how to dry the fish, making it a food staple in their homes and also a portable food that allowed them to travel at sea for longer periods of time. The Basques learned from the Vikings and began commercial trade of cod with other European countries. The famous explorers ate cod, and the North Atlantic colonists used it for trade with the

Caribbean Islands to feed the slaves. Cod was the first frozen food developed by Clarence Birdseye. Unfortunately, however, the future of the cod is in jeopardy due to over harvesting brought about by modern ships and fishing methods. Additional tidbits of information are found in illustrated inserts that feature recipes, poems, and other interesting facts about the cod. Useful time lines run across the bottom of the pages, beginning with prehistoric times and continuing to the present. Humorous watercolor, cartoon-like illustrations give the serious information a light-hearted touch. A two-page illustration of a cod fills the front and back endpapers. Easy-to-read maps and a bibliography add to the usefulness of the book.

Lester, Julius. **From Slave Ship to Freedom Road.**
Rod Brown's twenty-two paintings depicting slavery in America are narrated by Lester, detailing the history of slavery with strong emotion surrounding this dark period in American history. *See* FINE ARTS.

Lisle, Janet Taylor. **The Art of Keeping Cool.** New York: Atheneum Children's Books, 2000. 207p. $17.00. ISBN 0-689-83787-9, 0-689-83788-7pa.
When Robert's father is sent to Europe to fight in World War II, his mother moves her little family from their farm in Ohio to Rhode Island to live with his father's parents, even though this side of the family has been totally estranged from his father. His grandfather, a doctor, rules the household; his cousin Elliott, a misfit, manages to anger the grandfather routinely. Elliott and Robert become friends, and they discover a German painter, Hoffman, who is in hiding. Elliott is also an artist, and he and Hoffman become close. As the war goes on, the townspeople heap their prejudices on Hoffman until uncontrolled fear and hatred for all Germans, causes them to burn Hoffman's paintings. As it turns out, he had fled Germany because of persecution by Hitler. This final persecution is too much, and he walks into the fire to be with his paintings. Throughout the story, Robert wonders why his father has been alienated from his parents. This mystery is finally solved as this powerful novel portrays the strong effects of the war on the home front. Don't be put off by the misleading title, which has little to do with the subject matter.

Longfellow, Henry Wadsworth. **The Midnight Ride of Paul Revere.** Engraved and painted by Christopher Bing. New York: Handprint Books, 2001. 32p. $18.00. ISBN 1-929766-13-0.
Longfellow's famous poem written in 1860, has been brought to life again in this lavishly illustrated version created by Christopher Bing. Three-fourths of each two-page spread is filled with darkly colored, shadowy illustrations that depict the sneaking, spying, and secrecy of the times. Bing drew each illustration on scratchboard with pen and ink then added watercolor after the drawings were photocopied onto watercolor paper.

On some of the pages, additional symbolic items are digitally superimposed over the paintings, making these complex artworks, explained at the end in an informative section on the book's preparation. The text is printed on the margins of the page on paper made to resemble parchment. The endpapers, printed on paper decorated to look like marble, have original looking documents and objects scattered across them, complete with bright red ribbons. The front endpaper has a copy of a document containing British General Gage's orders to his lieutenant on April 18, 1775, folded and tucked in with what looks like sealing wax. The back endpaper has a folded copy of Paul Revere's deposition of the events of April 18, signed by Revere and held together with sealing wax. A map of the ensuing British raid is found in the front and a map of Revere's ride in the back. The book is further enhanced by extensive historical notes, a bibliography, acknowledgments, and a note from Bing about why he created this outstanding piece of art. This masterpiece should be shared with students so they may appreciate its artwork, poetry, and historical significance.

Maestro, Betsy. **The New Americans: Colonial Times, 1620–1689.** The American Story series. Illus. Giulio Maestro. New York: Lothrop, Lee & Shepard, 1998. 48p. $18.00. ISBN 0-688-13448-3, 0-688-13449-1 lib. bdg.

In the early 1600s, French, English, Portuguese, Spanish, Dutch, and other European immigrants came to America in increasing numbers. Maestro begins with the arrival of the Pilgrims in 1620, then sorts out who came, where they went, the competition between the groups, what types of settlements were set up, and the increasing hostilities between the Native Americans and the newcomers. By 1689, there were more than 200,000 European settlers. The additional information section at the back of the book gives more details about the time period; a fact sheet is included about the explorations and explorers from 1634–1685. The full-color, captioned illustrations work well to further explain this time in history.

Myers, Walter Dean. **Bad Boy: A Memoir.**

Life as an African American child in Harlem during the 1940s and 1950s, before the Civil Rights Movement, is described in this autobiography of one of our most prominent authors for young adults. *See* BIOGRAPHIES.

Myers, Walter Dean. **Malcolm X: A Fire Burning Brightly.**

When gathering books on the Civil Rights Movement, be sure to add this extended picture book that powerfully tells the story of Malcolm X, who was dedicated to making a better life for his race during the 1950s and 1960s. Quotations from his speeches and writings abound, offering an excellent picture of his fervor. *See* BIOGRAPHIES.

Patent, Dorothy Hinshaw. **Homesteading: Settling America's Heartland.** Photographs by William Muñoz. New York: Walker, 1998. 32p. $17.00. ISBN 0-8027-8664-2.

For many people, the lure to move west grew intense after the Homestead Act was passed in 1862. Following the Civil War, many people were homeless, and moving on was an inviting option. The land was difficult to work, but it was free. This colorful work traces people who were involved in the settling of the land and what life was like for them. It includes the steps they followed when settling: building a home, starting a farm, planting gardens, settling into everyday life, and setting up schooling and recreation. The text tells the story well, and the color photographs are an outstanding addition to the book. The photographer used present-day museum reenactments and displays to capture life at that time.

Paulsen, Gary. **Soldier's Heart: A Novel of the Civil War.** New York: Delacorte Press, 1998. 106p. $16.00. ISBN 0-385-32498-7, 0-440-22838-7pa.

Fifteen-year-old Charlie Goddard left Minnesota in 1861, determined to help the North to victory. What begins with high enthusiasm and the best intentions soon turns to despair and disbelief as he encounters the realities of war. He fights in four major battles, witnessing more horror and bloodshed than he ever thought possible. After being severely wounded at Gettysburg, he is sent home wounded in body as well as spirit. He never recovers from "soldier's heart," which we now call shell shock or post-traumatic stress disorder. Paulsen tells Charlie's story in a matter-of-fact manner, simply relating the terrible truth of war. The author's note tells about the real Charlie Goddard, adding to the book's authenticity. This short novel is a must when studying the Civil War at the middle school level. Another book that works well in conjunction with it is **Drummer Boy** by Ann Warren Turner (1998).

Pinkney, Andrea Davis. **Let It Shine: Stories of Black Women Freedom Fighters.**

A great deal of American history is covered in this outstanding collection of biographies of ten black American women. Their courage and conviction led them to do great things, working for abolition, women's rights, and civil rights. Arranged in chronological order, some are well known, such as Harriet Tubman and Sojourner Truth, but Pinkney also tells readers about lesser-known women, such as Biddy Mason and Dorothy Irene Height. *See* BIOGRAPHIES.

Rappaport, Doreen. **No More!: Stories and Songs of Slave Resistance.** Illus. Shane W. Evans. Cambridge, Mass.: Candlewick Press, 2002. 60p. $18.00. ISBN 0-7636-0984-6.

This remarkable book includes stories, spirituals, poems, narratives, and biographies of enslaved African Americans who fought for their freedom.

The accounts, arranged in chronological order, include incidents of rebellion (some successful, some not), the Underground Railroad, education (which was forbidden), the importance of the spirituals, and a variety of other strategies that helped the slaves deal with their dreadful situation. They show "the courageous struggle waged by enslaved Africans from the time they boarded the first slave ships heading for the New World to emancipation with the ratification of the Thirteenth Amendment." The bold, dramatic, emotion-filled oil paintings depict the reality of each situation described in the text. This powerful work needs to be included on every American history list of recommended reading.

Rees, Celia. **Witch Child.** Cambridge, Mass.: Candlewick, 2000. 261p. $16.00. ISBN 0-7636-1421-1, 0-7636-1829-2pa.

Mary's grandmother, a healer in England in the 1650s, is accused of witchcraft; she is tortured and finally hanged. An anonymous wealthy woman, who turns out to be Mary's unknown mother, sends her to the New World with a group of Puritans. Mary does her best to please them and fit in, but their strict teachings and way of life are difficult for her. Mary knows how to read and write, and she also knows about using plants and remedies for healing. She knows she's different and runs the risk of being persecuted, just as her grandmother had been. She keeps a diary but hides the pages in a quilt she's making. The story, which takes place from March 1659 to October 1660, is told from these diary entries. It gives a vivid picture of the Puritan teachings, their struggles to settle in the New World, the religious zeal that dictated their lives, their attitude toward Native Americans, and the quest to rid the world of witches.

Ryan, Pam Muñoz. **Esperanza Rising.**

After her father's death and her uncles' betrayal, Esperanza and her mother join thousands of Mexican immigrants in the 1930s who go to the San Joaquin Valley in California, seeking a new life. Coming from aristocratic backgrounds, Esperanza and her mother have a great deal to learn. The work is difficult, her mother becomes severely ill with Valley Fever, and the strong competition for jobs makes life almost impossible. Even so, Esperanza is transformed and goes on to lead a successful and happy life. This powerful story is based on Ryan's grandmother and is representative of thousands who came to California in search of a better life. Children from all walks of life need exposure to this piece of literature. *See* MULTICULTURAL.

Ryan, Pam Muñoz. **Riding Freedom.**

Charlotte Parkhurst, an orphan, realizes her dream of working with horses after she disguises herself as a boy. She becomes a stagecoach driver and moves to California, where she buys and works a ranch, always maintaining her disguise. She voted in the 1868 presidential election under the name of Charles Parkhust, becoming the first woman in America to vote for a president. *See* BIOGRAPHIES.

Scillian, Devin. **A Is for America: An American Alphabet.** Illus. Pam Carroll. Chelsea, Mich.: Sleeping Bear Press, 2001. 56p. $23.00. ISBN 1-58536-015-5.
    Scillian presents a collection of American history, geography, and pop culture with the help of each letter of the alphabet. For example, "B" presents Bunker Hill through traditional text, along with a flag flying over a battlefield. The opposite page has a large illustration of the Liberty Bell, along with a rhyming poem that includes a host of "B" words: "B can be for Boston, and the Battle of Bunker Hill. / And breaking from the British who ruled here until / a band of brave believers behind a boisterous yell / brought forth a brand new nation and banged the Liberty Bell." Each two-page spread is loaded with a conglomeration of Americanisms. This is designed for informational browsing, loaded with bits and pieces of interesting facts about our history and culture.

Taylor, Mildred. **The Land.**
    This prequel to **Roll of Thunder, Hear My Cry** (1976) is set during the Civil War and Reconstruction. Paul Edward, the son of a wealthy southern landowner and his black slave, experiences racial hatred because he doesn't fit in with either black or white society. He's determined to own his own land and succeeds after years of hardship and struggle chronicled in this outstanding work. This powerful historical fiction, based on the life of Taylor's great-grandfather, depicts the attitudes of that time in the United States. It won the Coretta Scott King Award in 2002. *See* GREATEST OF THE LATEST.

Temko, Florence. **Traditional Crafts from Native North America.**
    Temko gives instructions for making Native American crafts, including a Lakota dreamcatcher, Blackfeet beadwork, an Iroquois cornhusk doll, Seminole patchwork, Pueblo storyteller dolls, Chumash baskets, Haida totem poles, and Southwestern *cascarones.* This is an excellent source to use when studying Native American tribes. *See* FINE ARTS.

Turner, Ann Warren. **The Drummer Boy: Marching to the Civil War.**
    After hearing Lincoln speak, a thirteen-year-old boy runs off to become a drummer boy for the North. The vivid illustrations plus the simple text depict the horrors, bloodshed, fear, and death that the boy encounters, causing him to go home a much sadder and wiser person. Use this with Gary Paulsen's **Soldier's Heart** (1998) for study of the Civil War. *See* PICTURE BOOKS FOR ALL AGES.

Turner, Ann Warren. **Red Flower Goes West.** Illus. Dennis Nolin. New York: Hyperion, 1999. 32p. $15.00. ISBN 0-7868-0313-4.

Sometimes more can be said in a small picture book than in an entire chapter of a textbook; this is the case with Turner's story of a family that heads west during the California Gold Rush. Ma doesn't agree with the plan, and her one form of protest is to insist on taking a geranium along, even though it will need care, tending, and precious water. Red Flower becomes a symbol of survival for the family. If the flower makes it, they will, too. The simple text and the illustrations done in soft grays and browns with a splash of red for the flower, depict the difficulties of the journey and the hazards encountered along the way. This story has been told time and again, but the symbolism and the simple telling make this version memorable and useful when studying the opening of the West.

Wells, Rosemary. **Rachel Field's 1930 Newbery Award-Winning Story Hitty, Her First Hundred Years.**

Based on the original **Hitty: Her First Hundred Years** (1930). Rosemary Wells and Susan Jeffers edited, shortened, changed some wording, and added incredible illustrations to come up with a beautiful history of what life was like in North America from 1830 to 1930. *See* ENGLISH-CLASSICS.

White, Ellen Emerson. **Kaiulani: The People's Princes**s.

Heir to the royal Hawaiian throne, Princess Kaiulani records life in Hawaii from 1889 to 1893 from her diary, written as fiction by White. Kaiulani describes the political difficulties the monarchy faces because of the encroachment of American business interests. *See* SERIES.

Wolff, Virginia Euwer. **Bat 6.**

A softball game is played each year between the sixth-grade girls from two neighboring Oregon towns in an effort to unite the communities. It has evolved, over fifty years, into a huge event with food and booths, similar to a Fourth of July celebration. In 1949, post–World War II feelings are still running high, and those emotions come to a head during the game. The story emerges as it is told by the twenty-one team members, alternating from one to the other. This is a unique way of providing historical perspective and information to readers, using softball as the backdrop. *See* SPORTS AND GAMES.

Yin. **Coolies.**

During the mid-1800s, many Chinese immigrants made their way to San Francisco and went to work building the Transcontinental Railroad. They were called Coolies, a derogatory term for Chinese workers, were given the most dangerous jobs, and were paid the least. This beautifully illustrated book gives a good picture of the part the Chinese laborers played in the building of America. *See* MULTICULTURAL.

Zindel, Paul. **The Gadget.** New York: HarperCollins, 2001. 184p. $16.00. ISBN 0-06-028255-X.

In 1944, Stephen leaves London because of the World War II bombings. He goes to the United States to live with his father, who lives in Los Alamos, New Mexico, and is working with Robert Oppenheimer on "the Gadget." Security is tight, and Stephen's father is distracted and tired from his work. Stephen becomes friends with Tilanov, whose Russian father is also involved with the research. Together they explore and gather information and realize their fathers are involved in a potential disaster. "The Gadget" turns out to be the atomic bomb, and Stephen is accidentally a witness to its first testing on July 16, 1945. Zindel's work is well researched, providing a time line of the making of the bomb, a list of the people involved with it, and a bibliography. Many moral and political issues can be discussed based on the ideas presented in this historical fiction novel. It is an excellent work that ties in with the study of World War II and the Cold War era.

Chapter 17

Sports and Games

A wide range of books about sports and games appear in this section. Some are works, such as poetry selections, that teachers can share with students as read alouds. Biographies of important sports figures and fiction involving sports are included here. The section also offers a selection of books with directions for games and activities.

Adoff, Arnold. **The Basket Counts.** Illus. Michael Weaver. New York: Simon & Schuster, 2000. 46p. $15.00. ISBN 0-689-80108-4.

Each of the twenty-eight original poems in this book makes basketball come alive through words. The wording, the spacing of the letters on the page, and the illustrations all work together to bring passion to the poetry. This isn't professional-level basketball, but ordinary kids playing in the driveway, in a local playground, a school gym, or with a hoop on the back of a bedroom door. The illustrations depict players of all shapes and sizes—girls, boys, black, white, large, small, and some using wheelchairs. The poems shine when read aloud to capture the rhythm and feel of the text.

Burleigh, Robert. **Home Run: The Story of Babe Ruth.** Illus. Mike Wimmer. 32p. $16.00. ISBN 0-8172-5764-0.

Babe Ruth's baseball life is captured in this picture book using poetic language and well-chosen words. The text is sparse, portraying emotion, while the bubble-gum baseball cards that accompany the text give facts and statistics. The vivid illustrations make the players seem alive and capable of action. Baseball fans will love to get their hands on this book.

Demi. **Kites: Magic Wishes That Fly Up to the Sky.**

Demi combines legends concerning kites with practical information on kite making, but one particularly fun idea presented here is to have kite races and competitions. Refer to this book if you need ideas for this activity. *See* FINE ARTS.

Deuker, Carl. **Night Hoops.** Boston: Houghton Mifflin, 2000. 212p. $15.00. ISBN 0-395-9736-6, 0-06-447275-2.

Life seemed much easier before Nick Abbott was in high school—and before his parent's separation. As a sophomore, he is struggling to get out of his older brother's shadow; he wants desperately to be a star basketball player, and he wants his father's support and love rather than his heavy-handedness. Deuker uses basketball as a means to tell this coming-of-age story, narrated by Nick. As Nick learns to make positive choices and think on his own, his game begins to come together. Excellent descriptions of basketball plays and moves make this an appealing book for basketball enthusiasts. Deuker offers lessons about life through the use of various subplots that have the characters making important decisions. This excellent book teaches that both basketball and life are filled with complexities and that with proper training, thought, and advice, problems can be solved.

Fleischman, Paul. **Lost!: A Story in String.** Illus. C. B. Mordan. New York: Henry Holt, 2000. 32p. $16.00. ISBN 0-8050-5583-5.

A grandmother tells her frightened granddaughter a story about a young girl who gets lost in a blizzard while looking for her dog. She survives because of her determination and knowledge of the woods. The story is simple, but what makes this book special is the use of string figures that illustrate scenes and characters in the story. The barnyard gate, dog's head, bow, whistling mouth, girl in a two-pocket dress, jay, North Star, and house are string figures that illustrate the text; step-by-step directions on how to make each figure appear at the back of the book. A section on the history of string figures, instructions on making a string loop, and a bibliography of other books about string games are included. Black-and-white ink illustrations complement the story. This is a useful book to use when playing string games, and making figures will delight children who already know how to play cat's cradle.

Janeczko, Paul B. **That Sweet Diamond: Baseball Poems.** Illus. Carole Katchen. New York: Atheneum Children's Book, 1998. 40p. 1998. ISBN 0-689-80735-X.

Close your eyes and listen to Janeczko's poems, and you'll imagine yourself at the ballpark, involved in the excitement of baseball. Each of the nineteen free-verse poems describes baseball from a different point of view, from the peanut vendor, to the batter, to the ardent fan. Some entries are humorous, such as "How to Spit," which says that "practice is the key to developing your style." Others capture the tension, as in "The Batter": "Pitcher rocks. Batter waits. Then, in the time it takes a happy heart to beat, decides." Happiness and the pure enjoyment of the game are evident throughout the book. The colorful yet dreamy pastel illustrations fully complement each poem.

Jenkins, Steve. **The Top of the World: Climbing Mount Everest.** Boston: Houghton Mifflin, 1999. 32p. $16.00. ISBN 0-395-94218-7, 0-618-19676-5.

Using stunning, detailed cut-paper collages, along with one or two paragraphs of information per page, Jenkins describes a climb to the top of Mount Everest. He begins with a map of the Himalayas, an explanation of how they were formed, how climbers get there, a brief overview of the area around Mount Everest, and some well-known people who've climbed it in the past. A two-page spread shows the necessary equipment. The trek is detailed from Kathmandu to the base camps and finally the summit. Jenkins explains the dangers of crevasses, avalanches, unstable snow layers, strong winds, extreme cold, and lack of oxygen. The final page provides additional facts about the mountain and a bibliography. This attractive, easy-to-read book is packed with excellent information about mountain climbing, and the collages make readers feel they are part of the journey.

Lankford, Mary D. **Dominoes Around the World.** New York: Morrow Junior Books, 1998. 40p. $16.00. ISBN 0-688-14052-1.

Dominoes is a common game played in many lands, and Lankford takes us to eight countries to discover the variations and history of the game around the world. A brightly colored map at the beginning of the book shows readers the location of the countries discussed. Lankford also includes a history of dominoes and an explanation of the pieces and the basic rules of play. Game-playing customs from Cuba, France, Malta, The Netherlands, Spain, Ukraine, and United States are included. Dominoes ties countries together, just as hopscotch and jacks do—the topics of Lankford's previous books, **Hopscotch Around the World** (1992) and **Jacks Around the World** (1996). Domino fans will appreciate supplemental material at the back of the book, which includes additional variations of the game, puzzles complete with answers, and a recipe for Delectable Disappearing Dominoes. A dictionary and a bibliography round out the book.

Macy, Sue, editor. **Girls Got Game: Sports Stories & Poems.** New York: Henry Holt, 2001. 152p. $16.00. ISBN 0-8050-6568-7.

Eighteen short stories and poems by twelve women authors capture girls learning to know themselves through a sport. Most of the pieces come from the authors' experiences with the sport. Virginia Euwer Wolff's love of swimming inspired her to write "Water," a story about a synchronized swimmer, tired of the endless practice, who reevaluates her reasons for competing and her desire for the sport. Jacqueline Woodson's story "Beanie" is based on the days before Title IX "when young girls didn't really have much choice about where we could go with our athletic talents." Each entry is poignant yet entertaining. The format is rather dull, with small print and no graphics, but the stories and poems are well done and should be recommended to today's young athletes.

Smith, Charles R., Jr. **Rimshots: Basketball Pix, Rolls and Rhythms**. New York: Dutton Children's Books, 1999. 31p. $16.00. ISBN 0-525-46099-3.

Charles Smith, Jr., motivated by his love for basketball, plus his photography, artistic, and writing skills, has given us fourteen poems about the game that literally bounce off the pages. The writing is quick and energetic, and the design of each page adds movement and action. Key words are highlighted in color, and the use of boldface, italics, and a variety of fonts make the words pop off the page. The words in some poems, such as "School's in Session" and "Fast Break," swirl around the page like a player dribbling down the court. Some entries are humorous, some sad, some exciting, but the final poem, "Everything I Need to Know in Life, I Learned from Basketball," is serious, filled with advice such as "Nobody is ever going to give you anything. / You must earn it," and "If you believe you are a winner, / you will become just that." The sepia-toned photographs capture basketball on the street, on a neighborhood court, and in a gymnasium, and they all reflect the photographer's passion for the game.

Smith, Charles R., Jr. **Tall Tales: Six Amazing Basketball Dreams.** New York: Dutton Children's Books, 2000. 40p. $17.00. ISBN 0-525-46172-8.

Six fantasy short stories about basketball are told creatively with the use of brightly colored print, various fonts, and with words splashed across the pages in energetic arrangements. The photographs in the background depict mostly inner-city basketball and include all sizes, genders, and abilities. Each story, told in street dialogue and rhythmic prose, stretches reality and verges on the fanciful. The page size is extra tall, making these truly "tall" tales. Basketball lovers will enjoy the action and energy.

Street, Michael. **Lucky 13: Solitaire Games for Kids.** Illus. Alan Tiegreen. New York: SeaStar, 2001. 128p. $15.00. ISBN 1-58717-013-2, 1-58717-014-0.

Who would have thought solitaire could be so fun and have so many variations? Street presents more than sixty-five versions of solitaire in a step-by-step, easy-to-follow manner. The pen-and-ink cartoon drawings add to the explanations, and the characters hold up bubbles that give additional information, hints, and strategies. The book is divided into beginning games, easy games, counting games, and advanced games, many requiring two decks of cards. This is the ultimate solitaire how-to book and will provide players with hours and hours of fun.

Wolff, Virginia Euwer. **Bat 6.** New York: Scholastic, 1998. 230p. $17.00. ISBN 0-590-89799-3, 0-590-89800-0pa.

A softball game is played each year between the sixth-grade girls from two neighboring Oregon towns in an effort to unite the communities. It has evolved over fifty years into a huge event with food and booths, similar to a Fourth of July celebration. In 1949, post–World War II feelings are still running high, and those feelings come to a head during the game when Aki, the Japanese American recently returned from an internment camp, and Shazam, a black girl whose father was killed at Pearl Harbor, play on opposing teams. Shazam is deeply troubled from the trauma of her loss, and she takes out her rage on Aki by violently attacking her during the game. The celebration that begins as the highlight of the year for these towns ends in tragedy because of unrecognized racial tensions and angry feelings remaining from the war. The story emerges as it is told by the twenty-one team members, alternating from one to the other. This is a unique way of providing historical perspective and information, using softball as the backdrop.

Chapter 18

Unique Presentations

Some works tell their story in such a unique and creative manner that they need to be highlighted and celebrated. Their uniqueness helps to make the subject matter come alive, giving the reader a better understanding of the subject presented.

Aliki. **Marianthe's Story, Painted Words** and **Marianthe's Story, Spoken Memories.**

Two stories are included in one book. The first tells about a young girl moving from her native country to the United States. Turn the book around, and the second book depicts Mari's life in the new land and school, adjusting to a new language. *See* MULTICULTURAL.

Bang, Molly. **Nobody Particular: One Woman's Fight to Save the Bays.** New York: Henry Holt, 2000. 46p. $18.00. ISBN 0-8050-5396-4.

Diane Wilson was a shrimper, like her daddy, grandpa, and great-grandpa before her, in Calhoun County, Texas. She considered herself an ordinary person, a "nobody," until she discovered it was becoming more and more difficult to catch legal-sized shrimp. She realized that the petrochemical plants in the area were dumping lethal waste into the bays, causing a dangerous change in the ecosystem. This multifaceted book tells her true story about waging war against the chemical giants. The battle caused her to lose her boat, her shimper's license, and her husband, but she is continuing her battle to keep the environment safe. This fascinating book uses comic-strip panels, which are set on a background of deep blue representing the water and its creatures, to tell Diane's story. A second story, told in hand-lettered text, tells of the ecology of the waterways and how human uses have caused harmful change. Newspaper clippings, photographs, sidebars, and speech balloons augment both stories, making this a busy and complicated work. The back endpaper gives an update on the story and tells about the ongoing work. This unusual format is used to tell about important ecological work, but the reader needs to delve into both stories with attention.

Carter, David A., and James Diaz. **The Elements of Pop-up: A Pop-up Book for Aspiring Paper Engineers.**
With more than fifty different working models explained and illustrated, this is the ultimate manual on how to make pop-ups of every kind. Carter and Diaz include an introduction, a glossary, and a list of tools and materials, along with directions for parallel folds, angle folds, wheels, and pull-tabs. A Web site is included so that users may download the die drawings listed in the book. This book is a rare find. *See* FINE ARTS.

Edelman, Marian Wright. **Stand for Children.** Illus. Adrienne Yorinks. New York: Hyperion, 1998. 32p. $17.00. ISBN 0-7868-0365-7.
Marian Wright Edelman is one of our nation's top advocates for children and the founder of the Children's Defense Fund. On June 1, 1996, more than 300,000 people attended a Stand for Children Rally in Washington, D.C. Edelman's powerful speech delivered that day is recorded in this dynamic book. As her message stresses, "It is always the right time to do right for children, who are being born and formed in mind, body, and spirit every minute as life goes on." Yorinks, a quilter, uses a wide variety of techniques to incorporate quilts and photographs in her illustrations highlighting children. This book is aimed at adults and secondary students, making this a unique and excellent tool to use with educators and child advocates.

Fleischman, Paul. **Mind's Eye.**
At age sixteen, Courtney is paralyzed after an accident and is sent to live in a nursing home. Her roommates include an Alzheimer's patient and a former teacher with fading eyesight. Written as a play, Courtney and her roommates take an imaginary trip to Italy, following a 1910 travel guide. *See* GREATEST OF THE LATEST.

Hesse, Karen. **Witness: A Novel.** New York: Scholastic, 2001. 161p. $17.00. ISBN 0-439-27199-1.

    This is the moving and powerful story of the Ku Klux Klan infiltrating a small Vermont town in 1924, told through the eyes and voices of eleven community members. The story is set as a five-act play, written in free verse and narrated by actors of various ages, colors, and creeds. The sepia-toned photographs of the characters pictured at the beginning of the book, from Walter Dean Myer's personal photograph collection, help to set the tone for the novel. Each community member brings with them their own prejudices, emotions, thoughts and feelings about the Klan entering their peaceful little town. Six-year-old Esther Hirsh, a Jewish girl with an unusual speech pattern and nine-year-old Leonora Sutter, a black girl, are targets of the Klan and the most directly affected by the events. The cast members show how townspeople relate to each other with hate, love, and caring. This unusual novel will work well as a read aloud, reader's theater, or as a play production.

Jenkins, Martin. **Vampires.** Informania series. Cambridge, Mass.: Candlewick, 1998. 92p. $16.00. ISBN 0-7636-0315-5, 0-7636-1044-5pa.

    Be prepared to buy several copies of this crowd pleaser. It gives just about all the information you'd ever want to know about vampires in a colorful, unique arrangement. The sections are divided by captioned tabs, clearly showing the five chapters: "Bram Stoker's Dracula," a graphic-novel version of the classic novel *Dracula*; "Animal Bloodsuckers," theoretical case histories of vampires; "A History of Bloodsucking"; "Vampire Movies"; semicolon and "Ready Reference." The ready reference section includes a survival guide, a vampire hunter's checklist, tips for deterring vampires, methods for disposing of vampires, a glossary, a species list, and an index. The information is written in an enjoyable, humorous manner, and middle schoolers will pore over it by the hour. It's somewhat fragile because of its camouflaged spiral binding, but the heavy stock pages give it a sturdy feel.

Knight, Margaret. **Fashion Through the Ages: From Overcoats to Petticoats.** Illus. Kim Dalziel. New York: Viking, 1998. 24p. $20.00. ISBN 0-670-86521-4.

    Twelve colorful, lift-the-flap pages depict fashion from the Roman Empire through the 1960s. Each section begins with a double-sided gatefold giving the historical background of the period, along with a map. Each two-page entry includes a man, a woman, a boy, and a girl dressed in the typical garb of the time. Each piece of clothing peels back to reveal the next layer, all the way down to the underwear. An explanation of the clothing is printed on the back of each flap. The border around each large picture is filled with smaller drawings depicting accessories, jewelry, shoes, and hairstyles. This is an excellent resource to use for research and an enjoyable book for browsing. The book is somewhat fragile, but because students enjoy it so much, they seem to take special care to keep it in good condition.

Maynard, Christopher. **Ghosts.** Informania series. Cambridge, Mass.: Candlewick, 1999. 92p. $16.00. ISBN 0-7636-0758-4, 0-7636-1114-Xpa.

Dark and eerie illustrations along with photographs, movie stills, and amusing cartoons, take an entertaining look at ghosts, a favorite subject of middle grade students. It begins with an abridged telling of Algernon Blackwood's haunting story, "The Empty House." Chapter 2, "How to Catch a Ghost," presents real cases of ghosts as recorded by a ghost hunter. "A Souvenir Guide to the National Museum of Phony Ghosts," a rated guide to movies about ghosts, and finally the "Ready Reference" section round out this light-hearted look at ghosts. The spiral binding makes it a bit fragile, but the heavy paper gives it a sturdy feel.

Maynard, Christopher. **Sharks.** Informania series. Cambridge, Mass.: Candlewick, 1997. 92p. $16.00. ISBN 0-7636-0328-7, 0-7636-1043-7pa.

Sharks are not really as scary and unknown as the other subjects in this series, but this book sensationalizes the accounts that will grab the reader's attention. It begins with "Shocking Shark Stories," accounts of human encounters with sharks using text, comics, and color photographs in a newspaper format. The second section, "Confidential Crime Files," presents solid information about specific types of sharks, set up as crime lab reports. Section three, "Database: Shark Profile," gives information about the makeup of sharks, formatted like a Web site on a computer screen. Part four, "Biology Notes: Reproduction," presents information on reproduction, written in a notebook style, and the final chapter gives random information and facts. This is a fun combination of gross and gory details, facts, and solid information about sharks. The covered spiral binding makes it a bit fragile, but the paperback edition has a regular binding.

Mitton, Jacqueline. **Aliens.** Informania series. Cambridge, Mass.: Candlewick, 1999. 92p. $16.00. ISBN 0-7636-0492-5, 0-320-16023-0pa.

UFOs and aliens are always hot topics, and this book will top the list. Chapter 1, "Fantastic UFO Sightings," is written in magazine format and presents sightings of UFOs. Section 2, "Is Alien Life Possible?," sets up the Space Cadet School with the text written in textbook fashion. Section 3, "Tips on Talking to Aliens," summarizes efforts to send and receive extraterrestrial communications, including search for extraterrestrial intelligence. Section 4 highlights various movies that involve aliens. Each movie is written as casting notes, along with many colored photos. The spiral binding adds to the uniqueness of the book, but it will make it more fragile. The paperback version has a regular binding. This wild and crazy book will attract readers like a magnet. Multiple copies are suggested.

Myers, Walter Dean. **Monster.**
A 16-year-old boy is awaiting trial for murder. He tells his riveting story in the form of a screenplay. *See* GREATEST OF THE LATEST.

Nelson, Marilyn. **Carver: A Life in Poems.**
A series of fifty-nine poems is used to tell the story of George Washington Carver (1864–1943). Each poem depicts a particular time in Carver's life or an incident that he experienced. Black-and-white photos and captions giving dates and places often accompany the poems. This is a unique method of telling the story of an unusual and inspiring man. *See* BIOGRAPHIES.

Rees, Celia. **Witch Child.**
Mary Newbury's life in the New World is told through her journal entries from 1659 to 1660. She has special powers, which she hides to prevent being branded a witch and risking persecution. Rees includes excellent information about witchcraft, along with a picture of life in Massachusetts in the 1650s. *See* SOCIAL STUDIES—UNITED STATES.

Sis, Peter. **Tibet: Through the Red Box.** New York: Farrar, Straus & Giroux, 1998. 57p. $15.00. ISBN 0-374-37552-6.
This most unusual book tells the story of Peter Sis's father, who journeyed through Tibet in the 1950s. Sis grew up in Prague during the Communist era, and his father was a filmmaker. The Communist government ordered him to make a documentary of a road construction project in China. A cave-in on the road separated him from the workers, forcing him to take an adventurous two-year journey in central Asia. Sis's father kept a diary in a red lacquered box, which is revealed as Sis unlocks the box. The story begins to unfold through the use of text, maps, drawings, symbolic illustrations, his father's writings, Tibetan tales, and brightly colored full-page illustrations. He weaves together present and past, showing the geography, culture, and religion of Tibet, while telling the story of a young boy who longs for his father's return. This creative work won the Caldecott Honor Medal in 1999.

Smith, Charles R., Jr. **Tall Tales: Six Amazing Basketball Dreams.**
Smith uses bright colors, words spread across the page, photography, rhythmic and energetic prose, and street dialogue to tell his six fantasy stories about basketball. The pages are extra tall, making these truly "tall" tales. The unique use and arrangement of words and photographs captures the energetic feel of basketball. *See* SPORTS AND GAMES.

Wolff, Virginia Euwer. **Bat 6.**
A softball game takes place each year between the sixth-grade girls from two neighboring Oregon towns in an effort to unite the communities.

It has evolved over fifty years into a huge event with food and booths, similar to a Fourth of July celebration. In 1949, post–World War II feelings are still running high, and those feelings come to a head during the game. The story emerges as it is told by the twenty-one team members, alternating from one to another. This unique method of storytelling gives multiple perspectives on the same situation. *See* SPORTS AND GAMES.

Literature Links

Many of the titles listed in this book can be used in multiple curricular areas. The following chart tells in which chapters each title will be found. An "A" denotes which chapter contains the main annotation and an "X" shows which chapters contain a brief entry.

A=Annotated Entry; X=Cross-Reference

Title	Biographies (BI)	English—Classics (ENG-CL)	English—Use of Language (ENG-USE)	Fine Arts (FI)	Greatest of the Latest (GR)	Humor (HU)	Mathematics (MA)	Multicultural (MU)	Myths, Folktales, and Legends (MFL)	Picture (PI)	Poetry (PO)	Read Alouds (RA)	Science (SC)	Series (SE)	Soc. Studies—Ancient/Early Cultures (SS-A/E)	Social Studies—United States (SS-US)	Sports and Games (SG)	Unique Presentations (UP)
A Is for America: An American Alphabet										X						A		
Aesop's Fables		A							X			X						
Alice In Wonderland		A																
Alida's Song					A													
Aliens													X					A
Almost Starring Skinnybones						A												
Among the Hidden												A						
Among the Imposters			A															
Anastasia, the Last Grand Duchess															A			
Ancient Agriculture: From Foraging to Farming															A			
Ancient Communication: From Grunts to Graffiti															A	X		
Ancient Computing: From Counting to Calendars							X								A			

189

	(BI)	(ENG-CL)	(ENG-USE)	(FI)	(GR)	(HU)	(MA)	(MU)	(MFL)	(PI)	(PO)	(RA)	(SC)	(SE)	(SS-A/E)	(SS-US)	(SG)	(UP)
Ancient Construction: From Tents to Towers													A	X				
Ancient Machines: From Wedges to Waterwheels												X	A					
Ancient Medicine: From Sorcery to Surgery												X	A					
Ancient Transportation: From Camels to Canals													A					
Ancient Warfare: From Clubs to Catapults													A					
Angkat: The Cambodian Cinderella								X	A									
Art of Keeping Cool, The					X										A			
Atlantis: The Legend of a Lost City									A						X			
Austere Academy, The						X							A					
Author Talk: Conversations With Judy Blume, et al.	A																	
Awful Ogre's Awful Day						X					A							
Bad Beginning, The						X					A							
Bad Boy: A Memoir	A															X		
Basket Counts, The											X	X					A	
Bat 6																X	A	X
Because of Winn-Dixie					A													
Bestiary: An Illuminated Alphabet of Medieval Beasts								X	X						A			
Big, Bad and a Little Bit Scary: Poems That Bite Back!											A	X						
Big Numbers: And Pictures That Show Just How Big They Are!							A											
Big Talk: Poems for Four Voices											A							
Black Beauty		A												X				
Black Cat			X								A							
Black Mirror					A													

	(BI)	(ENG-CL)	(ENG-USE)	(FI)	(GR)	(HU)	(MA)	(MU)	(MFL)	(PI)	(PO)	(RA)	(SC)	(SE)	(SS-A/E)	(SS-US)	(SG)	(UP)
Blues Singers: Ten Who Rocked the World, The	X		A															
Bodies from the Bog													X	A				
Boy Who Wouldn't Obey: A Mayan Legend, The								A							X			
Breaking Through	X				X		A											
Brian's Return					X								A					
Brilliant Streak: The Making of Mark Twain, A	A																	
Buccaneers, The					A									X				
Bud, Not Buddy					A						X					X		
Buddha in the Garden										A				X				
Bug Off!: A Swarm On Insect Words			A															
Camera, The													A	X				
Can You Count to a Googol?						A												
Carver: A Life in Poems	X										A							X
Caught by the Sea: A Life in Boats	A																	
Cendrillon: A Caribbean Cinderella								X	A									
Cinderella Skeleton					X			A		X								
Circuit: Stories from the Life of a Migrant Child, The	X				X		A											
Cleopatra VII: Daughter of the Nile													A	X				
Clock, The						X							A	X				
Cod's Tale, The													X			A		
Colors				X							A							
Coolies							A									X		
Cornhusk, Silk, and Wishbones: A Book of Dolls from Around the World				X			A											
Dancing in Cadillac Light					A													
Dark Stairs, The														A				

	(BI)	(ENG-CL)	(ENG-USE)	(FI)	(GR)	(HU)	(MA)	(MU)	(MFL)	(PI)	(PO)	(RA)	(SC)	(SE)	(SS-A/E)	(SS-US)	(SG)	(UP)
Dave At Night					A													
Dead Letter														A				
Death's Door														A				
Desert Song									X		X	A						
Disappearing Acts												A		A				
Dominoes Around the World								X									A	
Don't You Know There's a War On?					A							X			X			
Doodle Dandies: Poems That Take Shape		X							A									
Down the Yukon					X							X	A					
Drummer Boy: Marching to the Civil War, The									A						X			
Earthsteps: A Rock's Journey Through Time												A						
Eat Your Words: A Fascinating Look at the Language of Food		A																
Elements of Pop-up: A Pop-up Book for Aspiring Paper Engineers, The			A															X
Elephant Book: For the Elefriends Campaign, The												A						
Elizabeth I, Red Rose of the House of Tudor														A	X			
Elvis Lives!: And Other Anagrams		A																
Emperor's New Clothes: A Tale Set in China, The							X	A							X			
Ersatz Elevator, The					X									A				
Esperanza Rising							A								X			
Fabrics of Fairytales: Stories Spun from Far and Wide, The			X				A											

	(BI)	(ENG-CL)	(ENG-USE)	(FI)	(GR)	(HU)	(MA)	(MU)	(MFL)	(PI)	(PO)	(RA)	(SC)	(SE)	(SS-A/E)	(SS-US)	(SG)	(UP)
Fairy Tale Catalog: Everything You Need to Make a Fairy Tale, The		A																
Fashion Through the Ages: From Overcoats to Petticoats			X															A
Flipped						A						X						
Fly with Poetry: An ABC of Poetry		A							X									
Fly, Eagle, Fly!: An African Tale								X	A									
Frank O. Gehry: Outside In	A		X															
Freedom Like Sunlight: Praise-songs for Black Americans	X						X				A							
From Slave Ship to Freedom Road			A													X		
G Is for Googol: A Math Alphabet Book							A		X									
Gadget, The				X												A		
Gandhi	A																	
Gargoyle on the Roof: Poems, The						X					A							
Gathering Blue					A													
Ghosts														X				A
Girl Who Spun Gold, The		~						A				X						
Girls Got Game: Sports Stories & Poems																	A	
Give Me Liberty!: The Story of the Declaration of Independence																A		
Grapes of Math: Mind-Stretching Math Riddles, The							A		X									
Guts: The True Stories Behind Hatchet and the Brian Books	A					X						X	X					
Hairy, Scary, Ordinary: What Is an Adjective			A											X				
Handel, Who Knew What He Liked	A			X														

	(BI)	(ENG-CL)	(ENG-USE)	(FI)	(GR)	(HU)	(MA)	(MU)	(MFL)	(PI)	(PO)	(RA)	(SC)	(SE)	(SS-A/E)	(SS-US)	(SG)	(UP)
Hands-on Asia: Art Activities for All Ages			A					X							X			
Harris And Me: A Summer Remembered						A						X						
Hatshepsut, His Majesty, Herself	A														X			
Heart to Heart: New Poems Inspired by Twentieth-Century American Art			X							A								
Heaven Eyes					A													
Here Come the Brides							A											
Hidden Forest, The										X			A					
History of Counting, The						A												
Home Run: The Story of Babe Ruth	X									X							A	
Homeless Bird					X		A											
Homesteading: Settling America's Heartland																A		
Hope Was Here					X	A						X						
Hostile Hospital, The						X							A					
How Tall, How Short, How Far Away							A											
Hunter, The								X	A						X			
I, Too, Sing America								X			A							
If You Hopped Like a Frog							A											
Iguanas in the Snow and Other Winter Poems								X		A								
Illiad, The		A						X			X							
In Search of the Spirit: The Living National Treasures of Japan	X		A												X			
In the Time of Knights: The Real-Life Story of History's Greatest Knight															X	A		
Insectlopedia												A	X					
Isabel: Jewel of Castilla														A	X			

	(BI)	(ENG-CL)	(ENG-USE)	(FI)	(GR)	(HU)	(MA)	(MU)	(MFL)	(PI)	(PO)	(RA)	(SC)	(SE)	(SS-A/E)	(SS-US)	(SG)	(UP)
It's So Amazing: A Book About Eggs, Sperm, Birth, Babies and Families													A					
Jabutí, the Tortoise: A Trickster Tale From the Amazon							X	A							X			
Jason's Gold					X								A					
Jester Has Lost His Jingle, The									A									
Joan of Arc	A														X			
Journey of English, The		A																
Jubela													A					
Just Ella									A		X							
Kaiulani: The People's Princess														A		X		
Kids Around the World Celebrate!: The Best Feasts and Festivals from Many Lands					X			A										
Kindness: A Treasury of Buddhist Wisdom		A													X			
King of Shadows					X						X				A			
Kingdom of the Sun: A Book of the Planets									X			A						
Kites: Magic Wishes That Fly Up to the Sky					A				X								X	
Lady Ch'iao Kuo: The Red Bird of the South														A	X			
Land, The					A										X			
Leonardo da Vinci for Kids: His Life and Ideas: 21 Activities	A				X								X					
Leonardo's Horse	X				A													
Let It Shine: Stories of Black Women Freedom Fighters	A														X			
Lewis and Clark for Kids: Their Journey of Discovery with 21 Activities					X								X		A			
Lightbulb, The												A	X					
Lives of Extraordinary Women: Rulers, Rebels (and What the Neighbors Thought)	A																	

	(BI)	(ENG-CL)	(ENG-USE)	(FI)	(GR)	(HU)	(MA)	(MU)	(MFL)	(PI)	(PO)	(RA)	(SC)	(SE)	(SS-A/E)	(SS-US)	(SG)	(UP)
Lives of the Presidents: Fame, Shame, and What the Neighbors Thought	A															X		
Lizards, Frogs and Polliwogs: Poems and Paintings											A		X					
Long Way from Chicago, A					A	X						X						
Longitude Prize, The	X					A							X					
Lord of the Cranes							X	A						X				
Lord of the Deep					A								X					
Lord of the Nutcracker Men					A													
Lost! A Story in String																	A	
Lost Temple of the Aztecs: What It Was Like When the Spaniards Invaded Mexico													X	A				
Lucky 13: Solitaire Games for Kids																	A	
Magic Windows: Cut-Paper Art and Stories		X					A											
Making Magic Windows: Creating Papel Picado/Cut-Paper Art		A					X											
Malcom X: A Fire Burning Brightly	A						X									X		
Mammalabilia											A		X					
Mana's Story														A	X			
Marianthe's Story						A	X											X
Marie Antoinette, Princess of Versailles													X					
Matilda Bone				X									A					
Maze, The				X								A						
Medusa								A					X					
Michelangelo	X		A										X					
Midnight Magic				X									A					
Midnight Ride of Ppaul Revere, The									X	X				A				
Mind's Eye					A													X

	(BI)	(ENG-CL)	(ENG-USE)	(FI)	(GR)	(HU)	(MA)	(MU)	(MFL)	(PI)	(PO)	(RA)	(SC)	(SE)	(SS-A/E)	(SS-US)	(SG)	(UP)
Mink, a Fink, a Skating Rink: What Is a Noun, A		A												X				
Miserable Mill, The						X							A					
Mississippi											X		A					
Moon Tales: Myths of the Moon from Around the World									X				A					
Monster					A													X
Mountain Dance											X		A					
Mountain Men: True Grit and Tall Tales	X														A			
Mumbo Jumbo											A							
My America: A Poetry Atlas of the United States											A				X			
My Daughter, My Son, the Eagle, the Dove				X				A			X							
My Louisiana Sky					A													
Nadia's Hands								A							X			
New Americans: Colonial Times, 1620–1689, The															A			
Night Hoops																	A	
No More!: Stories and Songs of Slave Resistance															A			
Nobody Particular: One Woman's Fight to Save the Bays													X					A
Noli's Story													X	A				
Nutik, the Wolf Pup										A			X					
Nzingha, Warrior Queen of Matamba													A	X				
Oak Tree													A					
On Beyond a Million							A											
On Time: From Seasons to Split Seconds							A											
One Riddle, One Answer							A								X			
Out of Sight: Pictures of Hidden Worlds													A					
People with Five Fingers: A Native Californian Creation Tale, The								X	A						X			

	(BI)	(ENG-CL)	(ENG-USE)	(FI)	(GR)	(HU)	(MA)	(MU)	(MFL)	(PI)	(PO)	(RA)	(SC)	(SE)	(SS-A/E)	(SS-US)	(SG)	(UP)
Peter Pan	A																	
Pharaoh's Daughter: A Novel of Ancient Egypt														A				
Photo Odyssey: Solomon Carvalho's Remarkable Western Adventure, 1853–54															A			
The Pit and the Pendulum and Other Stories	A													X				
Po's Story														A	X			
Poke in the I, A			X							A								
Q Is for Quark: A Sciencew Alphabet Book								X				A						
Quotations for Kids			A															
Rachel Field's 1930 Newbery Award-Winning Story Hitty, Her First Hundred Years	A															X		
Reading the Earth								X				A						
Red Flower Goes West								X							A			
Remarkable Farkle McBride, The			A								X	X						
Reptile Room, The					X									A				
Riding Freedom	A															X		
Rimshots: Basketball Pix, Rolls & Rhythms											X						A	
Ruby Holler					A													
Rumpus of Rhymes: A Book of Noisy Poems, A			A								X	X						
Runaway Rice Cake, The							X	A							X			
Sailor Returns, A					A													
Science in Ancient China													X	A	X			
Science in Ancient Egypt													X	A	X			
Science in Ancient Greece													X	A	X			
Science in Ancient India													X	A	X			
Science in Ancient Rome													X	A	X			
Science in Colonial America													X	A		X		
Science in Early Islamic Culture													X	A	X			
Science in the Early Americas													X	A	X			

	(BI)	(ENG-CL)	(ENG-USE)	(FI)	(GR)	(HU)	(MA)	(MU)	(MFL)	(PI)	(PO)	(RA)	(SC)	(SE)	(SS-A/E)	(SS-US)	(SG)	(UP)
Science in the Renaissance													X	A	X			
Sea Within a Sea: Secrets of the Sargasso, A											X		A					
Secret Life of Fishes: From Angels to Zebras on the Coral Reef, The			X										A					
Secrets In Stone: All About Maya Hieroglyphs														A				
Secrets of the Mummies: Uncovering the Bodies of Ancient Egyptians													X	A				
Sector 7										A			X					
Shakespeare Stealer, The					X									A				
Shakespeare: His Work and His World	A	X	X											X				
Shakespeare's Scribe					X									A				
Sharks														X				A
Shipwrecked Sailor: An Egyptian Tale with Hieroglyphs, The														A				
Silent to the Bone					A													
Sir Cumference and the Dragon of Pi: A Math Adventure						A												
Sir Cumference and the First Round Table						A												
Sir Cumference and the Great Knight of Angleland						A												
Sit on a Potato Pan, Otis!: More Palindromes			A															
Skinnybones						A			X									
Smugglers, The					A									X				
Soldier's Heart: A Novel of the Civil War					X										A			
Space Between Our Footsteps: Poems and Paintings from the Middle East, The							X		A				X					

	(BI)	(ENG-CL)	(ENG-USE)	(FI)	(GR)	(HU)	(MA)	(MU)	(MFL)	(PI)	(PO)	(RA)	(SC)	(SE)	(SS-A/E)	(SS-US)	(SG)	(UP)
Spectacular Science: A Book of Poems											X		A					
Spider Weaver: A Legend of Kente Cloth, The								X	A						X			
Stand for Children																		A
Stealing South: A Story of the Underground Railroad															A			
Story of Clocks and Calendars: Marking a Millennium, The							A											
Story of the Incredible Orchestra: An Introduction to Musical Instruments and the Symphony Orchestra, The		A																
Sun, Moon, and Stars								A					X					
Suth's Story															A	X		
Swine Lake					A			X	X									
Sword of the Samurai: Adventure Stories From Japan															A			
Take Me out of the Bathtub and Other Silly Dilly Songs		X			A													
Tall Tales: Six Amazing Basketball Dreams																	A	X
Tarot Says Beware													A					
Tea with Milk							A											
Telephone, The													A	X				
Ten Queens: Portraits of Women of Power	A													X				
Thank You, Mr. Falker										A								
That Sweet Diamond: Baseball Poems								X									A	
They Saw the Future: Oracles, Psychics, Scientists, Great Thinkers and Pretty Good Guessers	A																	
This Land Is Your Land					A					X								
Three Pigs, The					X			A										

	(BI)	(ENG-CL)	(ENG-USE)	(FI)	(GR)	(HU)	(MA)	(MU)	(MFL)	(PI)	(PO)	(RA)	(SC)	(SE)	(SS-A/E)	(SS-US)	(SG)	(UP)
Tibet: Through the Red Box										X								A
Tiger Rising, The					A													
To Every Thing There Is a Season: Verses from Ecclesiastes			X					X	A									
To Root, to Toot, to Parachute: What Is a Verb		A												X				
Top of the World: Climbing Mt. Everest, The													X				A	
Traditional Crafts from Africa			A					X						X	X			
Traditional Crafts from the Caribbean			A					X						X				
Traditional Crafts from China			A					X						X	X			
Traditional Crafts from Japan			A					X						X	X			
Traditional Crafts from Mexico and Central America			A					X						X	X			
Traditional Crafts from Native North America			A					X						X		X		
Traveling Man: The Journey of Ibn Battuta, 1325–1354														A				
Turnabout					X							A						
Vampires														X				A
Vile Village, The						X						A						
Voices: Poetry and Art from Around the World			X					X		A								
Warlord's Puzzle, The							A											
We the People: Poems											X				A			
We Were There, Too!: Young People in U.S. History	X														A			
Weslandia									A				X		X			
What You Never Knew About Tubs, Toilets & Showers													X		A			
When Zachary Beaver Came to Town					A													
Where the Wild Things Are										A								
White Fang		A												X				

	(BI)	(ENG-CL)	(ENG-USE)	(FI)	(GR)	(HU)	(MA)	(MU)	(MFL)	(PI)	(PO)	(RA)	(SC)	(SE)	(SS-A/E)	(SS-US)	(SG)	(UP)
Who Ordered the Jumbo Shrimp?: And Other Oxymorons			A															
Wide Window, The					X									A				
William Shakespeare & the Globe	A		X												X			
William Shakespeare's Romeo and Juliet		A																
Wisdom of Narnia, The			A															
Witch Child					X										A			X
Witness: A Novel					X							X						A
Woody Guthrie: Poet of the People	A		X												X			
Words with Wings: A Treasury of African-American Poetry and Art			X					X	A									
World of Words: An ABC of Quotations, A		A																
Wreckers, The					A									X				
Year Down Yonder, A					A	X						X						
Your Travel Guide to Ancient Egypt														A	X			
Your Travel Guide to Ancient Greece														A	X			
Your Travel Guide to Ancient Mayan Civilization														A	X			
Your Travel Guide to Civil War America														A		X		
Your Travel Guide to Colonial America														A		X		
Your Travel Guide to Renaissance Europe														A	X			

Index

A Is for America: An American Alphabet, 91, 173

Adler, David A., 57

Adoff, Arnold, 95, 107, 177

Adventures of Tom Sawyer, The, 145

Aesop's Fables, 14, 84, 111

Agee, Jon, 17, 18

Alarcón, Francisco X., 65, 95

Alice in Wonderland, 14

Alida's Song, 47

Aliens, 135, 186

Aliki, 1, 25, 66, 87, 147, 183

Almond, David, 37

Almost Starring Skinnybones, 52

Among the Betrayed, 109

Among the Hidden, 41, 108

Among the Impostors, 41, 109

Anastasia, the Last Grand Duchess, 139

Ancient Agriculture: From Foraging to Farming, 129

Ancient Communication: From Grunts to Graffiti, 130, 160

Ancient Computing: From Counting to Calendars, 63, 130

Ancient Construction: From Tents to Towers, 130, 160

Ancient Machines: From Wedges to Waterwheels, 127, 130

Ancient Medicine: From Sorcery to Surgery, 127, 131

Ancient Transportation: From Camels to Canals, 131

Ancient Warfare: From Clubs to Catapults, 131

Anderson, Matthew T., 2, 25

Andronik, Catherine M., 2, 148

Angels Ride Bikes and Other Fall Poems/Los Angeles Andan en Bicicleta y Otros Poemas de Otono, 96

Angkat: The Cambodian Cinderella, 68, 79

Antics, 21

Around the World in Eighty Days, 145

Art of Keeping Cool, The, 46, 169

Atlantis: The Legend of a Lost City, 77, 148

Austere Academy, The, 54, 142

Author Talk: Conversations with Judy Blume . . . et al., 7

Avi, 38, 107, 148, 164

Awful Ogre's Awful Day, 54, 103

Ayers, Katherine, 163

Bad Beginning, The, 54, 142

Bad Boy: A Memoir, 8, 170

Baker, Jeannie, 87, 113

Balit, Christina, 77, 148

Bang, Molly, 114, 183

Barrie, J. M., 13

Basket Counts, The, 95, 107, 177

Bat 6, 174, 181, 187

Batt, Tanya Robyn, 26, 66

Bauer, Joan, 38, 51, 108

Because of Winn-Dixie, 40

Beshore, George, 114, 140, 148

Bestiary: An Illuminated Alphabet of Medieval Beasts, 81, 89, 154

Bierhorst, John, 66, 78, 164

Big, Bad and a Little Bit Scary: Poems That Bite Back!, 105, 127

Big Numbers: And Pictures That Show Just How Big They Are!, 60
Big Talk: Poems for Four Voices, 97
Black Beauty, 15, 145
Black Cat, 32, 101
Black Mirror, 50
Blackwood, Gary L., 38, 39, 149
Blues Singers: Ten Who Rocked the World, The, 7, 30
Bodies from the Bog, 115, 152
Bone from a Dry Sea, 136
Bouchard, David, 88, 149
Bower, Tamara, 149
Boy Who Wouldn't Obey: A Mayan Legend, The, 84, 157
Breaking Through, 5, 43, 69
Brenner, Barbara, 26, 67, 96
Brian's Return, 47, 123
Brian's Winter, 47, 123
Brilliant Streak: The Making of Mark Twain, A, 6
Brook, Donna, 18
Brower, David Ross, and Aleks Petrovitch, 88, 114
Buccaneers, The, 44, 134
Bud, Not Buddy, 39, 108, 164
Buddha in the Garden, 88, 149
Bug Off!: A Swarm on Insect Words, 21
Burleigh, Robert, 2, 88, 178
Butterfield, Helen, 18, 114
Byars, Betsy, 108, 133

Call of the Wild, The, 145
Camera, The, 126, 144
Can You Count to a Googol?, 63
Carroll, Lewis, 14
Carter, David A., and James Diaz, 26, 184
Carver: A Life in Poems, 9, 101, 187
Casanova, Mary, 67, 78, 150
Castillo, Ana, 26, 67, 96
Caught by the Sea: A Life in Boats, 9

Cendrillon: A Caribbean Cinderella, 73, 84
Chen, Kerstin, 67, 150
Christensen, Bonnie, 3, 26, 164
Christmas Carol, A, 145
Cinderella Skeleton, 54, 84, 104
Circuit: Stories from the Life of a Migrant Child, The, 5, 43, 69, 70
Cleary, Brian P., 18, 19, 145
Cleopatra VII: Daughter of the Nile, 138, 154
Clinton, Catherine, 68, 96
Clock, The, 58, 115, 144
Coburn, Jewell Reinhart, 68, 79
Cod's Tale, The, 121, 168
Collier, James Lincoln, and Christopher Collier, 115
Colors, 32, 102
Compestine, Ying Chang, 68, 79, 150
Conover, Sarah, 19, 150
Cookcamp, The, 47
Coolies, 75, 174
Cooper, Susan, 39, 108, 151
Cornhusk, Silk, and Wishbones: A Book of Dolls from Around the World, 31, 71
Coulter, Laurie, 151
Coville, Bruce, 14
Creech, Sharon, 39
Curtis, Christopher Paul, 39, 108, 164
Cushman, Karen, 40, 151

Dancing in Cadillac Light, 42
Dark Stairs, The, 133
Dash, Joan, 3, 58, 115
Dave at Night, 45
Day, Nancy, 137–138, 152, 165
Dead Letter, 133
Death's Door, 133
Deem, James M., 115, 152

Demi, 3, 27, 68, 79, 80, 153, 178
Desert Song, 90, 109, 121
Deuker, Carl, 178
DiCamillo, Kate, 40
Dickinson, Peter, 136, 153
Disappearing Acts, 108, 133
Dominoes Around the World, 70, 179
Don't You Know There's a War On?, 38, 107, 164
Doodle Dandies: Poems That Take Shape, 22, 100
Down the Yukon, 42, 109, 118
Drummer Boy: Marching to the Civil War, The, 92, 173
Duffy, Trent, 58, 115, 144

Earthsteps: A Rock's Journey Through Time, 125
Eat Your Words: A Fascinating Look at the Language of Food, 20
Edelman, Marian Wright, 184
Elements of Pop-up: A Pop-up Book for Aspiring Paper Engineers, 26, 184
Elephant Book: For the Elefriends Campaign, The, 123
Elizabeth I, Red Rose of the House of Tudor, 138, 155
Elvis Lives!: And Other Anagrams, 17
Emperor's New Clothes: A Tale Set in China, The 68, 79, 153
English, Karen, 68, 153
Ersatz Elevator, The, 54, 142
Esperanza Rising, 73, 172

Fabrics of Fairytales: Stories Spun from Far and Wide, 26, 66
Fairy Tale Catalog: Everything You Need to Make a Fairy Tale, 20
Fashion Through the Ages: From Overcoats to Petticoats, 29, 185

Fleischman, Paul, 41, 88, 97, 116, 153, 178, 184
Flipped, 54, 111
Florian, Douglas, 97, 98, 116
Fly, Eagle, Fly!: An African Tale, 69, 80
Fly with Poetry: An ABC of Poetry, 20, 99
Foltz, Charlotte, 20
Frank O. Gehry: Outside In, 4, 28
Frankenstein, 145
Freedman, Russell, 165
Freedom Like Sunlight: Praisesongs for Black Americans, 7, 70, 100
Fritz, Jean, 3, 27
From Slave Ship to Freedom Road, 30, 169
From the Bellybutton of the Moon and Other Summer Poems/Del Ombligo de la Luna y Otros Poemas de Verano, 96

G Is for Googol: A Math Alphabet Book, 61
Gadget, The, 50, 175
Gandhi, 3
Gardner, Sally, 20
Gargoyle on the Roof: Poems, The 54, 103
Gathering Blue, 46
Gay, Kathlyn, 116, 141, 153
Gearhart, Sarah, 116, 144
George, Jean Craighead, 89, 117
Ghosts, 134, 186
Girl Who Spun Gold, The, 81, 109
Girls Got Game: Sports Stories & Poems, 180
Give Me Liberty!: The Story of the Declaration of Independence, 165
Glass, Andrew, 4, 166

Go Hang a Salami! I'm a Lasagna Hog!, 17

Grapes of Math: Mind-Stretching Math Riddles, The, 61, 104

Greenberg, Jan, 27, 98

Greenberg, Jan, and Sandra Jordan, 4, 28

Gregorowski, Christopher, 69, 80

Gregory, Kristiana, 138, 154

Guthrie, Woody, 28, 89

Guts: The True Stories Behind Hatchet and the Brian Books, 9, 53, 110, 123

Haddix, Margaret Peterson, 41, 80, 108, 109, 117

Hairy, Scary, Ordinary: What Is an Adjective?, 18, 145

Hamanaka, Sheila, and Ayano Ohmi, 4, 28, 154

Hamilton, Virginia, 81, 109

Handel, Who Knew What He Liked, 2, 25

Hands-on Asia: Art Activities for All Ages, 31, 72, 156

Harley, Avis, 20, 99

Harris, Jacqueline L., 117, 141, 154

Harris, Robie H., 117

Harris and Me: A Summer Remembered, 53, 110

Hatchet, 9, 47, 53, 110, 123

Hatshepsut, His Majesty, Herself, 2, 148

Heart to Heart: New Poems Inspired by Twentieth-Century American Art, 27, 98

Heaven Eyes, 37

Heidi, 145

Heller, Ruth, 99, 118

Hepworth, Cathi, 21

Herbert, Janis, 4, 28, 29, 118, 167

Here Come the Brides, 69

Hesse, Karen, 41, 109, 185

Hidden Forest, The, 87, 113

Hirschfelder, Arlene B., 167

History of Counting, The, 60

Hitty: Her First Hundred Years, 15, 174

Hobbs, Will, 42, 109, 118, 119

Hoffman, Mary, 81, 120

Holt, Kimberly Willis, 42, 43

Home Run: The Story of Babe Ruth, 2, 88, 178

Homeless Bird, 50, 75

Homesteading: Settling America's Heartland, 171

Hoose, Phillip M., 5, 166

Hope Was Here, 38, 51, 108

Hopkins, Lee Bennett, 99, 120, 167

Hopscotch Around the World, 179

Hostile Hospital, The, 54, 143

How Tall, How Short, How Far-away, 57

Hunt, Jonathan, 81, 89, 154

Hunter: A Chinese Folktale, The, 67, 78, 150

I, Too, Sing America: Three Centuries of African American Poetry, 68, 97

If You Hopped Like a Frog, 62

Iguanas in the Snow and Other Winter Poems/Iguanas en la Nieve y Otros Poemas de Invierno, 65, 95

Iliad, The, 14, 83, 110

In Search of the Spirit: The Living National Treasures of Japan, 4, 28, 154

In the Time of Knights: The Real-Life Story of History's Greatest Knight, 135, 158

Insectlopedia: Poems and Paintings, 97, 116

Isabel: Jewel of Castilla, 139, 157

It's Perfectly Normal, 117

It's So Amazing! A Book About Eggs, Sperm, Birth, Babies and Families, 117

Jabutí, the Tortoise: A Trickster Tale from the Amazon, 71, 83, 156
Jacks Around the World, 179
Jackson, Ellen B., 69
Janeczko, Paul B., 21, 99, 100, 179
January, Brendan, 120, 141, 154, 168
Jason's Gold, 42, 118, 119
Jenkins, Martin, 134, 185
Jenkins, Steve, 120, 179
Jester Has Lost His Jingle, The, 91
Jiménez, Francisco, 5, 43, 69, 70
Joan of Arc, 10, 158
Johnston, Tony, 90, 109, 121
Jones, Lynda, 29, 70
Jouanah: A Hmong Cinderella, 79
Journey of English, The, 18
Jubela, 121
Julie, 89, 117
Julie of the Wolves, 89, 117
Julie's Wolf Pack, 89, 117
Jungle Book, The, 145
Just Ella, 80, 109

Kaiulani: The People's Princess, 139, 174
Katz, Alan, 29, 52
Katz, Bobbi, 21, 100, 110, 168
Kerstin, Chen, 82
Kessler, Cristina, 121
Kids Around the World Celebrate!: The Best Feasts and Festivals from Many Lands, 29, 70
Kimmel, Eric A., 155
Kindness: A Treasury of Buddhist Wisdom for Children and Parents, 19, 150
King of Shadows, 39, 108, 151

Kingdom of the Sun: A Book of the Planets, 83, 122
Kites: Magic Wishes That Fly up to the Sky, 27, 80, 178
Knight, Margaret, 29, 185
Konisgsburg, E. L., 43
Koscielniak, Bruce, 29
Krull, Kathleen, 5, 6, 168
Kurlansky, Mark, 121, 168

Lady Ch'iao Kuo: The Red Bird of the South, 140, 161
Land, The, 49, 173
Lankford, Mary D., 70, 179
Lasky, Kathryn, 6, 138–139, 155
Lattimore, Deborah Nourse, 82, 155
Lauber, Patricia, 121, 155
Laughing Tomatoes and Other Spring Poems/Jitomates Risuenos y Otros Poemas de Primavera, 96
Lawrence, Iain, 44–45, 134
Leonardo da Vinci for Kids: His Life and Ideas: 21 Activities, 4, 28, 118
Leonardo's Horse, 3, 27
Lester, Julius, 7, 30, 156, 169
Let It Shine: Stories of Black Women Freedom Fighters, 10, 171
Levine, Gail Carson, 45
Lewis, C. S., 22
Lewis, J. Patrick, 22, 100
Lewis, Patrick J., 7, 70
Lewis and Clark for Kids: Their Journey of Discovery with 21 Activities, 29, 118, 167
Lightbulb, The, 126, 144
Lisle, Janet Taylor, 46, 169
Lithgow, John, 31, 101, 110
Little Women, 145
Lives of Extraordinary Women: Rulers, Rebels (and What the Neighbors Thought), 5

Lives of the Presidents: Fame, Shame and What the Neighbors Thought, 6, 168

Lizards, Frogs, and Polliwogs: Poems and Paintings, 97, 116

Locker, Thomas, 101, 121

Lomas Garza, Carmen, 31, 71

London, Jack, 14, 144

Long Way from Chicago: A Novel in Stories, A, 47, 48, 53, 111

Longfellow, Henry Wadsworth, 90, 101, 169

Longitude Prize, The, 3, 58, 115

Lord of the Cranes, 67, 82, 150

Lord of the Deep, 48, 123

Lord of the Nutcracker Men, 44

Lost!: A Story in String, 178

Lost Temple of the Aztecs: What It Was Like When the Spaniards Invaded Mexico, 135, 159

Lowry, Lois, 46

Lucky 13: Solitaire Games for Kids, 181

Macy, Sue, 180

Maestro, Betsy, 58, 170

Magic Windows: Cut-Paper Art and Stories, 31, 71

Making Magic Windows: Creating Papel Picado, Cut-Paper Art, 31, 71

Malcolm X: A Fire Burning Brightly, 8, 72, 170

Mammalabilia: Poems and Paintings, 98, 116

Mana's Story, 136, 153

Marcus, Leonard S., 7

Marianthe's Story, One, Painted Words, Marianthe's Story, Two, Spoken Memories, 66, 87, 183

Marie Antoinette, Princess of Versailles, 139

Markel, Michelle, 31, 71

Marshall, James, 52, 82, 90

Matilda Bone, 40, 151

Maynard, Christopher, 134, 186

Maze, The, 42, 119

McCarty, Nick, 14, 83, 110

McDermott, Gerald, 71, 83, 156

McKissack, Patricia, 139, 156

Medusa, 82

Meltzer, Milton, 8, 156

Merrill, Yvonne Y., 31, 72, 156

Meyer, Carolyn, 139, 157

Mi Hija, Mi Hijo, El Aguila, La Paloma: Un Canto Azteca, 67

Michelangelo, 10, 32, 158

Midnight Magic, 38, 148

Midnight Ride of Paul Revere, The, 90, 101, 169

Mind's Eye, 41, 184

Mink, a Fink, a Skating Rink: What Is a Noun?, 19, 145

Miserable Mill, The, 54, 143

Mississippi, 104, 124

Mitton, Jacqueline, 83, 122, 135, 186

Monster, 46, 187

Moon Tales: Myths of the Moon from Around the World, 85, 125

Morrison, Gordon, 122

Mountain Dance, 101, 121

Mountain Men: True Grit and Tall Tales, 4, 166

Mumbo Jumbo, 103

Musgrove, Margaret, 72, 83, 157

My America: A Poetry Atlas of the United States, 99, 167

My Daughter, My Son, the Eagle, the Dove: An Aztec Chant, 26, 67, 96

My Louisiana Sky, 42

Myers, Christopher A., 32, 72, 101

Myers, Walter Dean, 8, 46, 170, 187

Nadia's Hands, 68, 153
Nelson, Marilyn, 9, 101, 187
Neuschwander, Cindy, 59
New Americans: Colonial Times,
    1620–1689, The, 170
Night Hoops, 178
No More!: Stories and Songs of
    Slave Resistance, 171
Nobody Particular: One Woman's
    Fight to Save the Bays, 114,
    183
Noli's Story, 136, 153
Nordine, Ken, 32, 102
Nutik, the Wolf Pup, 89, 117
Nye, Naomi Shihab, 72, 102, 157
Nzingha, Warrior Queen of
    Matamba, 139, 156

Oak Tree, 122
On Beyond a Million: An Amazing
    Math Journey, 62
On Time: From Seasons to Split
    Seconds, 61
One Riddle, One Answer, 62, 160
Out of Sight: Pictures of Hidden
    Worlds, 124

Packard, Edward, 60
Park, Barbara, 52, 53, 110
Patent, Dorothy Hinshaw, 171
Paulsen, Gary, 9, 47, 53, 92, 110,
    123, 171, 173
Peck, Richard, 47–48, 53, 111
People with Five Fingers: A Native
    Californian Creation Tale, 66,
    78, 164
Peter Pan, 13
Pharaoh's Daughter: A Novel of
    Ancient Egypt, 156
Photo Odyssey: Solomon Carvalho's
    Remarkable Western
    Adventure, 167
Picture of Dorian Gray, The, 145

Pilegard, Virginia Walton, 60
Pinkney, Andrea Davis, 10, 171
Pinkney, Jerry, 14, 84, 111
Pit and the Pendulum and Other
    Stories, The, 15, 145
Poe, Edgar Allen, 15, 145
Poke in the I: A Collection of
    Concrete Poems, A, 21, 99
Polacco, Patricia, 90
Po's Story, 136, 153
Prelutsky, Jack, 54, 101

Q is for Quark, 91, 124
Quotations for Kids, 22

Rachel Field's 1930 Newbery
    Award-Winning Story Hitty,
    Her First Hundred Years, 15,
    174
Rappaport, Doreen, 171
Reading the Earth: A Story of Wild-
    ness, 88, 114
Red Flower Goes West, 93, 174
Redmond, Ian, 123
Rees, Celia, 48, 172, 187
Remarkable Farkle McBride, The,
    31, 101, 110
Reptile Room, The, 54, 143
Riding Freedom, 10, 172
Rimshots: Basketball Pix, Rolls, and
    Rhythms, 104, 180
River, The, 47, 123
Roberts, Michael, 103
Rochell, Belinda, 32, 72, 104
Rockwell, Anne, 84, 157
Roll of Thunder, Hear My Cry, 49, 173
Rosen, Michael, 10, 22, 32, 157
Ruby Holler, 39
Rumford, James, 157
Rumpus of Rhymes: A Book of Noisy
    Poems, 21, 100, 110
Runaway Rice Cake, The, 68, 79, 150
Ryan, Pam Muñoz, 10, 73, 172

Sailor Returns, A, 49

Salisbury, Graham, 48, 123

Saltzman, David, 91

San Souci, Robert D., 54, 73, 84, 104

Say, Allen, 73

Schmandt-Besserat, Denise, 60

Schwartz, David M., 61, 62, 91, 124

Science in Ancient China, 114, 140, 148

Science in Ancient Egypt, 126, 141, 160

Science in Ancient Greece, 116, 141, 153

Science in Ancient India, 125, 141, 158

Science in Ancient Rome, 117, 141, 154

Science in Colonial America, 120, 141, 168

Science in Early Islamic Culture, 114, 140, 148

Science in the Renaissance, 120, 141, 154

Science of the Early Americans, 126, 142, 160

Scillian, Devin, 91, 173

Sea Within a Sea: Secrets of the Sargasso, A, 99, 118

Secret Life of Fishes: From Angels to Zebras on the Coral Reef, The 18, 114

Secrets in Stone: All About Maya Hieroglyphs, 151

Secrets of the Mummies: Uncovering the Bodies of Ancient Egyptians, 135, 159

Sector 7, 93, 126

Sendak, Maurice, 91

Senn, J. A., 22

Sewell, Anna, 15, 145

Shakespeare: His Work & His World, 10, 22, 32, 157

Shakespeare Stealer, The, 38, 39, 149

Shakespeare's Scribe, 38, 149

Sharks, 134, 186

Shipwrecked Sailor: An Egyptian Tale with Hieroglyphs, The 149

Siebert, Diane, 104, 124

Silent to the Bone, 43

Simon, Seymour, 124

Singh, Rina, 85, 125

Sir Cumference and the Dragon of Pi: A Math Adventure, 59

Sir Cumference and the First Round Table: A Math Adventure, 59

Sir Cumference and the Great Knight of Angleland: A Math Adventure, 59

Sis, Peter, 92, 187

Sit on a Potato Pan, Otis!: More Palindromes, 17

Skinnybones, 52, 53, 110

Skurzynski, Gloria, 61

Smith, Charles R., Jr., 104, 180, 187

Smugglers, The, 44, 134

Snicket, Lemony, 54, 142–143

So Many Dynamos!, 17

Soldier's Heart: A Novel of the Civil War, 47, 92, 171, 173

Space Between Our Footsteps: Poems and Paintings from the Middle East, 72, 102, 157

Spectacular Science: A Book of Poems, 99, 120

Spickert, Diane Nelson, 125

Spider Weaver: A Legend of Kente Cloth, The, 72, 83, 157

Stand for Children, 184

Stanley, Diane, 10, 32, 158

Stealing South: A Story of the Underground Railroad, 163

Stewart, Melissa, 125, 141, 158

Story of Clocks and Calendars: Making a Millennium, The, 58

Story of the Incredible Orchestra: An Introduction to Musical Instruments and the Symphony Orchestra, 29

Strange Case of Dr. Jekyll and Mr. Hyde, The, 145

Street, Michael, 181

Sun, Moon, and Stars, 81, 120

Suth's Story, 136, 153

Swine Lake, 52, 82, 90

Sword of the Samurai: Adventure Stories from Japan, 155

Take Me Out of the Bathtub and Other Silly Dilly Songs, 29, 52

Tall Tales: Six Amazing Basketball Dreams, 180, 187

Tanaka, Shelley, 135, 158, 159

Tang, Greg, 61, 104

Tarot Says Beware, 133

Taylor, Mildred D., 49, 173

Taylor, Theodore, 49

Tea with Milk, 73

Telephone, The, 116, 144

Temko, Florence, 33–35, 74, 132, 159–160, 173

Ten Queens: Portraits of Women of Power, 8, 156

Thank You, Mr. Falkner, 90

That Sweet Diamond: Baseball Poems, 100, 179

They Saw the Future: Oracles, Psychics, Scientists, Great Thinkers and Pretty Good Guessers, 6

This Land Is Your Land, 28, 89

Thompson, Lauren, 62, 160

Three Pigs, The, 55, 85

Tibet: Through the Red Box, 92, 187

Tiger Rising, The, 40

To Every Thing There Is a Season: Verses from Ecclesiastes, 33, 75, 92

To Root, to Toot, to Parachute: What Is a Verb?, 19, 145

Tobias, Tobi, 23

Top of the World: Climbing Mount Everest, The, 120, 179

Traditional Crafts from Africa, 33, 74, 132, 159

Traditional Crafts from the Caribbean, 33, 74, 132

Traditional Crafts from China, 34, 74, 132, 159

Traditional Crafts from Japan, 34, 74, 132, 159

Traditional Crafts from Mexico and Central America, 34, 74, 132, 160

Traditional Crafts from Native North America, 34, 74, 132, 173

Traveling Man: The Journey of Ibn Battuta, 1325–1354, 157

Treasure Island, 145

Turnabout, 41, 117

Turner, Ann Warren, 92, 93, 173–174

Vampires, 134, 185

Van Draanen, Wendelin, 54, 111

Vile Village, The, 54, 143

Voices: Poetry and Art from Around the World, 26, 67, 96

Wallace, Joseph, 126, 144

Warlord's Puzzle, The, 60

We the People: Poems, 100, 168

We Were There, Too!: Young People in U.S. History, 5, 166

Wells, Robert E., 63

Wells, Rosemary, 15, 174

Werlin, Nancy, 50

Weslandia, 88, 116, 153

What You Never Knew About Tubs, Toilets & Showers, 121, 155

Whelan, Gloria, 50, 75

When Zachary Beaver Came to Town, 43

Where the Wild Things Are, 91

White, Ellen Emerson, 139, 174

White Fang, 14, 144

Who Ordered the Jumbo Shrimp? And Other Oxymorons, 18

Wide Window, The, 54, 143

Wiesner, David, 55, 85, 93, 126

William Shakespeare & the Globe, 1, 25, 147

William Shakespeare's Romeo and Juliet, 14

Wisdom of Narnia, The, 22

Witch Child, 48, 172, 187

Witness: A Novel, 41, 109, 185

Wolff, Virginia Euwer, 174, 181, 187

Woods, Geraldine, 126, 141, 142, 160

Woods, Michael, and Mary B. Woods, 63, 127, 129–131, 160

Woody Guthrie: Poet of the People, 3, 26, 164

Words with Wings: A Treasury of African-American Poetry and Art, 32, 72, 104

World of Words: An ABC of Quotations, 23

Wreckers, The, 45, 134

Year Down Yonder, A, 48, 53, 111

Yep, Laurence, 140, 161

Yin, 75, 174

Your Travel Guide to Ancient Egypt, 137, 152

Your Travel Guide to Ancient Greece, 137, 152

Your Travel Guide to Ancient Mayan Civilization, 137, 152

Your Travel Guide to Civil War America, 137, 165

Your Travel Guide to Colonial America, 138, 165

Your Travel Guide to Renaissance Europe, 138, 152

Zahares, Wade, 105, 127

Zindel, Paul, 50, 175

DATE DUE			